Mario Lanza

Mario Lanza

SINGING TO THE GODS

DEREK MANNERING

UNIVERSITY PRESS OF MISSISSIPPI / JACKSON

www.upress.state.ms.us

The University Press of Mississippi is a member of the
Association of American University Presses.

Frontis: Studio portrait (Michelle Short Collection)

Copyright © 2005 by Derek Mannering

Manufactured in the United States of America

First American edition 2005

British edition 2001, published by Robert Hale

Library of Congress Cataloging-in-Publication Data

Mannering, Derek, 1948–
Mario Lanza : singing to the gods / Derek Mannering.— 1st American ed.
    p. cm. — (American made music series)
    Includes bibliographical references (p.), discography (p.),
filmography (p.), and index.
    ISBN 1-57806-741-3 (cloth : alk. paper)
    1. Lanza, Mario, 1921–1959. 2. Tenors (Singers)—United States—
Biography. I. Title. II. Series.
ML420.L24M362   2005
782.1′092—dc22   2004023805

British Library Cataloging-in-Publication Data available

Dedicated in loving memory to my parents,
Thomas and Mary Mannering,
to Kate, for her kindness of heart and gentle spirit,
and to Jonathan, my son, who fills my life
with the best of everything.

CONTENTS

FOREWORD

After reading *Singing to the Gods*, I was touched by a certain melancholy, reliving my father's life and his career. It evoked emotions that are bittersweet. Questions of why and what might have been. We will never fully understand the complexities of my father, Mario Lanza, his meteoric rise to fame and the demons that plagued him throughout his career, but Derek Mannering's fair and objective biography of my father's life ensures his musical legacy will live on.

My mother and father had a deep love for each other, and I will always cherish my memories of them. As his daughter I knew him to be a loving, kind, and generous father. His children always came first. My sister, Colleen, and I would be so excited when we were at a recording session or on a movie set. Our favorite time with him was at night when he would tell wonderful bedtime stories and sing us to sleep. He was bigger than life and a lot of fun, too.

Through his recordings and his movies, my father gave the world an amazing and beautiful legacy of unparalleled music, which even today thrills and influences people from all walks of life. I don't believe you can truly judge a person unless you have walked in his shoes. In the end it is the public who has spoken. They have perpetuated his music and his memory for more than four decades after his death.

Over the years my family has had to live with the ever-growing and grossly exaggerated tales of his behavior. During and after his life he was betrayed by people he trusted and hounded by the press, always looking for a negative angle. What I most appreciate about this book is the fact that my father's life is depicted without judgment. The biography is admirable, straightforward, and without exaggeration or melodrama, and the author's research and knowledge of my father's music and career is most impressive.

Anyone who wants to know about the life and times of Mario Lanza need go no further than this book.

Ellisa Lanza Bregman
Los Angeles 2005

ACKNOWLEDGMENTS

The level of commitment and support shown to me by Mario Lanza's daughter, Ellisa, friends, colleagues, and admirers while I was researching this book has been extraordinary. Ellisa Lanza Bregman's eloquent and moving foreword enhances this work beyond measure, and my debt of gratitude to Ellisa's Uncle T, the wonderful Terry Robinson, is beyond measure. Sincere thanks also go to Terry's lovely wife, Silvia, who opened her home and her heart to me during my many visits to Los Angeles.

Special thanks also to Elaine Murphy and the gracious Carol Russell, whose constructive and enthusiastic support of my earliest writing efforts undoubtedly prepared me for this latest work. My good friend John Rice from Wexford, Ireland, must also be singled out here for his exceptional kindness and unwavering support throughout this project. Warmest appreciation also goes to the rest of the Irish Lanza team: Christy and Marie Smith, Geraldine McCann, Grosvenor and Gill Swift, and Marian Rice, along with a fond remembrance of another dear friend who has since passed on, Phyllis Savage.

The British Mario Lanza Society, the flagship of Lanza organizations, also provided sterling support at every level, and I am especially grateful to the wonderful Pam Latham, who toiled tirelessly to deal with all my requests, and to Ron Stilwell, whose legerdemain in the darkroom ensured that a few rare and previously damaged photographs made their way into this volume. Thanks too to the gentle Bill Earl, chairman of the British Mario Lanza Foundation, who was always there with a kind word, and to his delightful wife, Judith, who provided me with critical information on Mario Lanza's stay at the Park Sanitarium in Walchensee, Bavaria. A special thanks also to Elsie Sword (née Kiss), Joan Marsden (née Kesingland), and Molly Howard for sharing their wonderful stories of time spent with Mario Lanza in 1958. Susan and Helmut Klee, devoted Lanza supporters from Germany, were equally unfailing in their efforts to assist me with my research. No source shed more light on the singer's final years than the remarkable letters contained in the Lanza files at the John Coast Agency in London, copies of which were generously provided to me a number of years ago by Frank Powis.

Closer to home, I am deeply indebted to Alan Burns, whose knowledge and insight into Mario Lanza's career knows no measure. Thanks also to the delightful Leila Edwards for her fascinating account of her time spent coaching Mario Lanza. I am equally grateful to John Durso, who provided me with a steady stream of articles, anecdotes, and clippings relating to Lanza's formative years in Philadelphia. Eddie Durso, John's dad and Mario Lanza's closest boyhood friend, was always on call to answer any questions. John was also instrumental in introducing me to another childhood pal, Phil Sciscione, who generously walked the extra mile to provide me with previously unrecorded information about Freddy Cocozza's adventures from those halcyon days in South Philly.

Maynard Bertolet, valued friend and a former president of the Mario Lanza Institute in Philadelphia, provided informed, insightful and steadfast support at every turn, and a fond acknowledgment also goes to Maynard's darling wife, Jeannine. I am also indebted to Reverend Mother Dolores Hart, who took time to share special memories of her Uncle Mario, to Shirley Borregaard and Gladys Kincaid, Betty Lanza's sisters, and to Philip and Dorothy Solomon for conveying their fond recollections of time spent with Mario Lanza in Europe.

My thanks also to Roland Bessette whose exhaustive research into Mario Lanza's contractual affairs provided a fascinating and invaluable glimpse into the tenor's extraordinary business dealings, and to Giovanni Franchitti and Giancarlo Stopponi for relating details of Mario Lanza's final days at the Valle Giulia Clinic in Rome.

From the world of grand opera, my thanks to Licia Albanese, Renée Fleming, Richard Leech, and his wife, Laurie Higgins, and Karen Kriendler Nelson. And a very special salute to a great Chicago actor, Lawrence McCauley, whose encyclopedic knowledge of all things opera proved invaluable to me in my research. Information on Mario Lanza's early career was generously provided by Barbara Perkel and Bridget Carr at Tanglewood, Kelly Pepper of the New Orleans Opera Association, and Tracie Williams at Columbia Artists Management, Inc.

The task of selecting the many photographs featured throughout this book was made all the more easy by the outstanding support shown to me by Terry Robinson, the lovely Michelle Short, my good friend Buddy Mantia, Stephen Cutler, Maynard F. Bertolet, Ron and Wendy Stilwell, Fred J. Desjarlais, Al Teitelbaum (and through that association the splendid Jeff Rense), Ray Holfeld, Todd Wells, and the indispensable John Rice. For their tireless help in providing me with invaluable information on Lanza's recording and film career, heartfelt thanks goes to Daniel Guss at BMG/RCA and to George Feltenstein at Turner Entertainment in Hollywood. My sincere gratitude also goes Carolyn Whitaker, literary agent extraordinaire, whose steady hand and sound advice guided me through this venture from the very outset. And my friend and fellow author David Weaver must also be singled out here for bringing this work to the attention of the University Press of Mississippi.

Many others gave generously of their time, knowledge, and friendship as well, including Tom Balfe, Ralph Blumenthal, Vincent Boyle, Armando Cesari, Joe Curreri, Dan Franklin, Vincent and Antoinette De Fini, Joseph Di Fiore, Edna Falloon, Katherine Gardner, Andrew Karzas, Alan Kayes, Cees Kouwenberg, Bernard Lozea, Barbara Knight, Stephen Pattinson, Joan Ritti, Jim Thompson, George Thomson, Heidi Vergien, and Tony White.

Mention must also be made of some dear Lanza friends who helped with my earlier research and who have since passed on. Two gentle souls, Vito Torelli and Pauline Franklin, are deeply missed by me, and sad farewells were also paid to Hilda Lanza, Arnold Lanza, Joe Siciliano, Nicholas Petrella, and a number of other fine people closely associated with Mario Lanza's legacy. Death also paid untimely visits to the tenor's daughter, Colleen, and his youngest son, Marc, accounts of which are detailed in this book.

A writer's style is shaped and colored by the unforgettable people he or she meets along the way, and I cannot bring these acknowledgements to a close without special mention of Sharon Schindler and Tracy Airey, both of whom played an integral part in the thinking I brought to this work.

Finally, the task of completing this book on time would not have been possible without the support, enthusiasm, and ongoing encouragement of two members of my family, Kate and Jonathan. Both are singled out in this book's dedication but the level of gratitude owed by me to these two cannot be overstated.

All of the wonderful people listed above have helped me in one way or another to complete this biography. All have my deepest appreciation and thanks.

Derek Mannering
Chicago 2005

INTRODUCTION

It is a testament to Mario Lanza's enduring appeal that even today, over four decades after his untimely passing in a Rome clinic at age thirty-eight, the magnitude of his contribution to popular music is still hotly debated.

To his followers—and they are legion in number—Lanza personified the romantic ideal of a tenor, the logical successor to the great Enrico Caruso. His critics, however, took a more jaundiced view. The Lanza voice may have been a force of nature but given that the tenor had appeared only twice on the professional opera stage—as Pinkerton in two performances of *Madama Butterfly* for the New Orleans Opera House Association in 1948—a lot more operatic quality time was called for before Mario Lanza was ready to be crowned Caruso's successor.

Lanza's lifelong association with the Italian tenor owed much to his dazzling 1951 tribute to his idol, *The Great Caruso*. The groundbreaking film shattered box-office records everywhere and influenced an entire generation of future opera stars. José Carreras, Plácido Domingo, Luciano Pavarotti, Richard Leech, Roberto Alagna, and scores of others answered the call, all of them responding to one man's larger-than-life persona and golden voice.

The Great Caruso made Mario Lanza a star, but the film also created operatic expectations from him that he was unwilling to fulfill. Despite repeated encouragement from his peers, Lanza declined to return to the classical stage, choosing instead to focus his talents on more lucrative areas of the entertainment industry. That decision ensured him fame and considerable fortune, but it also denied him the legitimacy of being recognized as one of the twentieth century's greatest opera singers, something that was well within his grasp.

Blessed with the sort of singing voice that immediately called for superlatives, Mario Lanza was a superstar before that word was even coined. For a time, everything he touched turned to gold. His recordings for RCA Victor sold as fast as the record stores could stock them, and on one memorable occasion concertgoers literally crashed through a plate glass window in an attempt to touch their idol. Lanza's appeal was further enhanced by his effortless ability to cater to all musical tastes. Operatic arias, popular tunes of the day, Neapolitan favorites, operettas, sacred songs, and standards from the Great American Songbook: Lanza sang them all and sang them better than anyone had a right to expect. To this today he is still seen as the crossover artist supreme.

Lanza's time in the spotlight also coincided with a sea change in other popular art forms. With *A Streetcar Named Desire* and *On the Waterfront*, Brando brought a whole new concept of raw, improvisational acting to a medium that had looked to Gable and Bogart for tough-guy realism on the big screen. And from dirt-poor beginnings in Tupelo, Mississippi, a shy young kid named Elvis Aaron Presley was about to change the face of popular music forever. In his own inimitable way, Mario Lanza played an important part in that creative revolution. After Lanza, no popular tenor would ever be looked at in quite the same way again.

Like all young gods who fly too high too soon, the fall to earth for Mario Lanza when it came was spectacular. Following a dispute with MGM over filming of *The Student Prince*, Lanza walked off the set, sending his life into a free-fall from which it never fully recovered. At the time of his death he was still the most famous tenor in the world, still maintaining that he would return to the opera house. But years of overindulgence and rich living had taken a terrible toll on his health, and by that fateful day in October 1959 there was simply no turning back.

But legends live on. If Brando took acting to previously untapped levels and Elvis practically invented rock "n" roll, Lanza's contribution was to remind music lovers everywhere that grand opera was exciting and accessible and fun, not just something to be enjoyed by the privileged few. The people up there in the movie galleries may not have been patrons of the Met, but they were still listening, still thrilling to the glorious sounds pouring forth from that impossibly handsome young man who, like all true originals, enjoyed breaking the rules.

That sense of spirited rebellion is well captured in a brief but telling scene from *The Great Caruso*. After a string of roaring successes throughout Europe, the Italian tenor has received an unexpectedly luke-warm reception from the patrons of New York's Metropolitan Opera House; an audience totally unprepared for the visceral, sexual quality of a young upstart from the back streets of Naples. In an effort to win the respect of the house, the singer is implored hold back a little, to "take his hands out of his pockets" before strolling on stage. But the celluloid Caruso will have none of it; his character is cold and hungry and he will keep his hands is his pockets whether the audience likes it or not.

In the end, that sense of bravado, that need to challenge the system, said a lot more about Lanza than it did about the man he portrayed so unforgettably on the screen. For Mario Lanza, the enduring image remains one of stand-alone accomplishment, a young man who taught the world how to sing, hands in his pockets, forever defying the conventions.

Mario Lanza

Freddy Cocozza was born to sing. Born to be a tenor. Born to create a great and joyous outpouring of beautiful sound that would touch the hearts and souls of music lovers everywhere. With impeccable timing, he chose a significant year in the music calendar to make his entrance into the world.

It was a time for tenors. In addition to Freddy, the roster of future greats born in 1921 included Franco Corelli and Giuseppe Di Stefano, both of whom would carve out rich and acclaimed careers on the opera stage. The world of Giacomo Puccini and his contemporaries would also play a key part in shaping Freddy Cocozza's own remarkable journey, but the most significant impact on his calling was made by another singer, an artist whose extraordinary life was drawing to a close just as Freddy's was about to begin.

In December 1920, a month before Freddy's birth, Enrico Caruso, the grandest operatic tenor of them all, had been taken ill during a performance of *L'Elisir d'Amore* at the Brooklyn Academy of Music in New York. The omens had been there in his dressing room beforehand, but Caruso, ever the fatalist, had insisted on carrying on with the performance, one, sadly, he would never complete. In the audience that evening Dorothy Caruso had watched in despair as her husband began to cough blood on stage, hemorrhaging discreetly into a handkerchief in between singing. It was a theatrically gruesome moment that would be replayed, with some liberties, thirty years later when the great Caruso's life was brought to the silver screen.

The troubled performance in New York that night marked the beginning of the end for the Italian tenor. After singing the aria "Quanto è bella," Caruso was unable to continue and the curtain was quickly brought down. As his friend, the impresario Gatti-Casazza recalled,

"At that very moment I had a fleeting premonition that Caruso was lost."[1]

Caruso would sing again, briefly, but his time was running out. On 28 May 1921 the tenor and his family set sail from New York for Italy on the liner *Presidente Wilson*. Upon arrival in Naples, the Caruso entourage took a boat across the bay to Sorrento, where they rented a floor at the Hotel Vittorio. It was there, a little over two months later in the early morning hours of 2 August 1921 that the great Italian tenor died. He was forty-eight.

The death of a great artist is always an occasion for universal grief. The death of the man seen even today as the greatest tenor of them all sent shock waves across the world. Caruso had been one of the first important artists to lend his stature to the then-fledgling recording industry, a commitment, moreover, that helped in no small part to ensure his own imperishable legacy. His passionate rendition of "Vesti la giubba" became the first recording in history to sell more than one million copies, and it seemed that just about everyone who had a record player had a recording by Caruso.

The Lanza family in South Philadelphia certainly had an abundance of them, and the sound of the Italian tenor and his contemporaries filled the small home at 636 Christian Street. Salvatore Lanza, the family patriarch, had immigrated to America in 1902 from the town of Tocco da Casauria in the Abruzzi region of Italy. An astute, hard-working, and frugal businessman, Salvatore initially found work by selling vegetables from a horse and cart along Philadelphia's Main Line. He eventually established a more permanent outlet for his wares at a small, two-story building on Christian Street, in a working class area known at the time as "Little Italy." Elisena Lanza, or Ellisa as she came to be known, followed her husband to America aboard the liner *Trave* a year later with their eleven-month-old daughter Maria, arriving at Ellis Island on 5 May 1903. The family's cramped conditions at Christian Street grew even more crowded over the years as the number of Lanza children expanded to eight: Maria, Lucia, Giulia, Agnes, Hilda, Arnold, Anna, and Roberto. The house still stands to this day, though Salvatore's general store that fronted it is long gone.

As the children grew older, Salvatore saw to it that each took turns helping in the store. Maria, the eldest, had a light and pleasant soprano voice and at one time had courted dreams of a career in the opera house.

But Salvatore would have none of it, openly warning of the pitfalls that awaited a young woman seeking a career on the classical stage. Maria instead confined her singing to the family parlor, but dreams of La Scala and the Metropolitan Opera House were never far from her thoughts.

The turning point in Maria's life, and the life of the entire Lanza family, came on a summer's day in 1919, when a handsome young man in military uniform strolled into the store. Antonio Cocozza had stopped in for the less-than-romantic purpose of buying salami, but all thoughts of food disappeared when he saw the attractive seventeen-year-old girl standing behind the counter. For her part, Maria was struck by his gallant deportment, though she was also quick to notice his badly injured right arm.

Like Maria, Antonio Cocozza had traveled to the United States from Italy. He was born in 1894 in the small town of Collemacchia near Filignano, in the Molise region. In 1905, Tony, his parents, three sisters, and a brother set sail for America aboard the *Lombardi*, arriving at Ellis Island on 1 June. Tony brought with him a deep passion for sports and opera, and it was ironic and appropriate that one of the first jobs he found was varnishing cabinets for the Victor Talking Machine Company, the very one that had recorded the great Caruso. The Victor Company would eventually become better known as RCA Victor and would one day reap vast fortunes from its exclusive recording contract with Tony's only child.

Tony Cocozza was a keen cyclist who had competed in six-day bicycling events and at Madison Square Garden. All that changed following his call up to the armed services in 1918. With the world at war, he was soon sailing overseas again, this time as a soldier with the 37th Division, 145th Infantry. For his courage under fire at the battle of the Meuse Argonne forest in France, Tony was awarded a Purple Heart, but the price he paid for his gallantry was considerable. Soon after capturing a German prisoner, he was seriously wounded by a notorious dum-dum, or split-head bullet, which completely shattered his lower right arm. He also fell victim to mustard gas poisoning, which some felt added to his nervous reluctance in later years to travel. Following his discharge with a disability benefit from the Veterans Association, Tony returned to the United States and an uncertain future.

This, then, was the young man who made such an immediate impact on Maria Lanza in her father's store that day in 1919. If Tony was self-conscious of his injured arm, Maria made it clear that it didn't matter to her in the slightest. Indeed, the very opposite was true: Tony Cocozza was seen by Maria and her family as the hero that he was, and a courtship between the two young people was soon under way. Shortly after Maria's eighteenth birthday they were married, and Tony joined his new bride in the already overcrowded conditions at Christian Street. (In later years Maria often claimed that she was sixteen when she married Tony, but a Philadelphia Census recorded in 1920, soon after the two had exchanged vows, states that she was eighteen at the time.)

It was in the cramped quarters at Christian Street the following year that the entire family learned of the passing of their beloved Caruso, but by then a happy event had graced the Lanza-Cocozza household. On the last day of January 1921, in an upstairs bedroom at 636 Christian Street in the early hours of the morning, Tony and Maria Cocozza welcomed their son Alfred Arnold into the world. Freddy would be their only child, idolized to distraction by his adoring parents for the remainder of his life.

The boy was baptized at the nearby church of St. Mary Magdalen de Pazzi on Montrose Street, which had the distinction of being Philadelphia's first Catholic Church. To many, far greater significance was to be found in the name of the celebrant that day: Father Caruso. It was an irony that would provide much fodder for the media in the golden career that lay ahead for Freddy Cocozza.

When the child was eleven months old he suffered a convulsion while he was teething, which left him with partial vision his left eye, though the impairment never affected him in later years. Freddy was an energetic, forceful young boy with a willful and headstrong attitude all of his own, one that tested the patience of his grandfather more times than Salvatore Lanza would care to admit. Salvatore was a stern taskmaster but even he held a soft spot for the boy. Many youthful infractions were overlooked and forgiven in those formative years.

A cornerstone of both families' heritage was their collection of operatic recordings, not just by Caruso but also Pertile, Ruffo, Gigli, and the great voices of their day. Money was often tight in the Lanza-Cocozza household, but the musical legacy of the great Italian masters brought sustenance to all, particularly Freddy. The boy also developed a passionate love of horses, filling scrapbooks with their photos and dreaming of having one of his own someday.

A turning point in Freddy Cocozza's young life came in 1928, when he was seven. One evening, alone in an upstairs room at 636 Christian Street, the boy turned on the family's beloved Victrola and listened enthralled to the great Caruso's immortal rendition of Pagliacci's lament. "Vesti la giubba," which eventually became Freddy's own self-described "lucky aria," was reportedly played by the young child twenty-seven times at a single sitting that night. Caruso was his musical god, and even his opera-loving family was struck by the child's devotion to the great singer.

In 1930 space to breathe and grow was found at last when the Cocozza's and their nine-year-old son took their leave of the small house at Christian Street. The family moved to nearby 2040 Mercy Street, a two-story, red brick house with six small rooms and a bath. To Freddy, free from the constraints of Christian Street and his grandfather's constant admonitions, it was like traveling to another world.

He grew up in South Philadelphia, attending St. Mary Magdalen de Pazzi School on Seventh and Montrose and later Edgar Allan Poe Elementary School. From the outset it was clear to Maria that her beloved son would never become an academic. In September 1932, Freddy was enrolled at Edwin H. Vare Junior High School at Twenty-fourth and Jackson Street, where he met Eddie Durso, who would become one of his closest childhood friends. Their first encounter took place in the high school gym. Durso remembers Freddy as a chunky boy, very much into sports and making people laugh. Sixty years later Eddie would recall those days with Freddy in a loving memoir, *My Memories of Mario Lanza*: "Before [he] became the 'King of the High C's,' he was Freddy, the 'King of Fun.'"[2]

In *The Pilot*, Vare Junior School's graduation booklet of June 1935, students were invited to list their choice of future occupation. Freddy Cocozza's was "another Columbo," a reference to the late Bing Crosby–like crooner Russ Columbo. The streets of South Philadelphia were far too rough in those days for a fourteen-year-old to be caught professing a love of opera. Columbo wasn't Caruso, but Durso knew whom his friend was referring to.

After Vare, Durso and Freddy moved to the nearby South Philadelphia High School for Boys. Joe Curreri, who would play a key part in honoring Freddy's legacy in later years, became another part of the team. It was at South Philly that Freddy—or "Al Coke," as he liked to be called—developed a keen interest in boxing and weight lifting; that, and a tendency to hit the occasional loud musical note in the school halls. Durso didn't pay too much attention to the vocalizing, though his friend did have an amusing talent for imitating the popular singers of the day. Freddy and Durso spent a lot of time at the News Boy's Gym at Thirteenth and Shunk Street and Al Coke soon became known as a fearless opponent in the amateur ring. Freddy also worked out at the South Philadelphia Boys Club at Thirteenth and Moimamensing Avenue, where another close friend, Phil Sciscione, taught him how to lift weights.

One of the more colorful stories from Freddy Cocozza's childhood took place when he was six years old. According to a lurid account he later gave to Eddie Durso, Freddy witnessed the shooting of his Uncle Vincent "Scabby" Cocozza in front of a restaurant at 824 South Eighth Street. Just before six o'clock on the evening of 30 May 1927, Freddy, who was standing nearby, watched as a speeding car drove past the building. Shots were fired from the vehicle and in an instant "Scabby" Cocozza and another man lay dying on the sidewalk. In graphic detail Freddy told Durso how he ran across the street and stood staring at the two men lying motionless in their own blood. The shooting made front-page news in the *Philadelphia Inquirer* the following day, where it was revealed that Cocozza had not been the intended victim. The perpetrators, who had been quickly captured, had been aiming to kill a local gangster named Anthony "Muski" Zanghi. The incident, not surprisingly, made a deep impression on Freddy, who kept a photograph of Uncle "Scabby" in his bedroom at Mercy Street.

It was at Mercy Street in the summer of 1937 that Freddy Cocozza first discovered he could really sing. As popular legend tells it, the sixteen-year-old was listening yet again to his beloved Caruso recording of "Vesti la giubba." As the golden tones pored forth from the Victrola, another younger voice filled the room, a clear, vibrant, and surprisingly powerful voice that beckoned Tony Cocozza from another part of the house. The singer was Freddy, and his father was simply amazed at what he had just heard.

No one at the time had the slightest inkling of the incredible triumphs that were to come, but Maria and Tony were impressed enough to arrange for their son to audition for a local voice teacher, Antonio Scarduzzo. Scarduzzo, a baritone, agreed that the boy had a powerful voice but he warned of the dangers of pushing the instrument too soon.

Instead, Freddy was directed toward language studies. Then, when the voice had settled, singing lessons could begin in earnest. In particular Scarduzzo encouraged the boy to study solfeggio, the sight-reading of music, but this relatively uncomplicated practice was one that Freddy Cocozza never quite mastered. Constantine Callinicos, his accompanist and conductor in later years, speculated on the reasons behind this shortcoming: "He had a kind of aversion regarding the theoretical side of music and mostly learning solfeggio, which is not such a difficult thing. Somehow he must have fallen into the hands of somebody who drove him to hate solfeggio, which he knew would help him in learning scores . . . in every facet of his work."[3]

The Cocozza's engaged a language teacher, Mario Pellizon, who worked with Freddy on French, German, and Italian (Maria taking care of the Neapolitan dialect), and Giovanni De Sabato, who tutored the boy twice a week in the dreaded solfeggio. Invariably, though, when the studies became too tedious Freddy would turn to the family's record collection for inspiration. Freddy Cocozza never openly imitated any singer but he looked to their recordings constantly for hints in phrasing and vocal technique.

Freddy and Eddie Durso would also pay occasional visits to Philadelphia's famed Victor's Café, which had an extensive collection of operatic recordings. For the price of a good meal, the two would sit and listen to the best voices in the world in surroundings that have changed little to this day. Many of the old records are still there, augmented now by those of the young boy from Christian Street whose celebrity photograph is given pride of place in the establishment.

As Salvatore Lanza's business expanded, he invested in a summer home in Wildwood, New Jersey. The house on Rio Grande Avenue became a welcome retreat from the hot South Philadelphia streets for Freddy and his friends. In addition to Durso, regular visitors to the shore included boyhood friends Phil Sciscione, Joe Siciliano, Gus DiPrimo, and the Graziano twins. Siciliano, who in later years would act as the curator of a museum named in his friend's honor, recalled a typical moment from those halcyon summer days in New Jersey: "Freddy got a summer job there, driving a trolley car. We used to wait at a certain corner and we could hear when his car was coming five blocks away, because we could hear him singing . . . "O Sole Mio" or something . . . and lo and behold, we'd all get on the trolley car for nothing, like he owned the transportation company or something."[4]

Meanwhile, the Cocozzas had begun the serious task of looking for a voice teacher for their son. Salvatore, ever the pragmatist, expressed doubts at the notion of his grandson pursuing a career on the classical stage, but Maria this time stood her ground. The need for formal study became even more important after Freddy made an unexpected exit from Southern High, following an altercation there with a teacher. In his defense Freddy claimed that his superior had made an ethnic slur against his Italian heritage, but his excuse was not enough and the boy was compelled to finish out his high school year at Lincoln Preparatory Academy.

The Cocozzas eventually found the voice coach they were looking when Maria's sister Agnes, a school teacher, recommended Irene Williams, a soprano who had sung with Nelson Eddy and who boasted an impressive résumé of her own. Ms. Williams had sung with the New York, Chicago, Los Angeles, and San Francisco symphonies, and she was quick to realize the exceptional potential in her young protégé. To help pay for the studies, Maria, a talented seamstress, took up extra work at the local Quartermasters Depot, a sacrifice that would not be forgotten by her son in later years: "My mother, when she did not have to go to work, realized that at that time I needed all these lessons so badly to lay the foundation for a career in the future. She went and worked in the Quartermasters Depot in South Philadelphia, which made uniforms for the American soldiers. She worked very hard. She used to get up at 5 o'clock in the morning and be at work by 6—imagine that!—and come home at 6 in the evening. Long, long hours!"[5]

Freddy Cocozza reported for work with Irene Williams fired with enthusiasm and a determination to do whatever was asked of him. Not surprisingly, he soon tired of the dull regimen of vocal studies—all he really wanted to do was sing—but Irene Williams pushed him relentlessly, never ceasing to marvel at the magnificent sound that emanated from the boy's throat. It was a glorious voice, free and clear, with a dazzling and seemingly effortless top, remarkable in one so young. In all, he studied with Irene Williams for just under two years, and their time together produced impressive if unfinished results.

By this time too, Freddy had started to play around with a name change. Proud though he was of "Cocozza" it was not a name he could visualize in lights: something else was needed, something more dramatic, more exciting. In a copy of his high school book from that period, his penciled ruminations fill the pages: Alfredo Cocozza, Fred Lanza, Tony Cocozza, Anthony Cocozza, until finally, in the very last column of the very last page: Mario Lanza. He could hardly have chosen a better name, "Lanza," in particular, conjuring up a sense of Mediterranean expansiveness that would come to symbolize his passionate style of singing in later years. Maria, naturally, was thrilled at her son's choice of the masculine version of her name. Tony, sensing he was outnumbered, raised no real objections.

Williams also saw to it that her pupil appeared in recital at a number of Philadelphia society homes; while everyone noticed the lack of deportment, the sound produced by the young tenor never failed to thrill. It was through one of those recitals that Mario Lanza came to make his first student recordings. Lanza had made a deep impression on a wealthy society hostess from Manhattan who he called "the Countess." In the fall of 1940, she invited the young tenor and a friend to visit her in New York for ten days, all expenses paid. In return for a few well-chosen appearances at her private soirees, Mario Lanza would live like a king. She also would see to it that he was exposed to the type of people and the right sort of classical environment to help him with his future career.

Lanza could hardly believe his good fortune. He left for New York in December with Phil Sciscione, whose parents had recently bought him a new Pontiac. Lanza didn't have a driver's license, but that didn't stop him from finishing the journey behind the wheel as the car roared into Manhattan. True to her word, the Countess had arranged for room and board for both of them at one of the city's upmarket hotels. It was the first real taste of the sweet life the tenor would come to know so well. A few brief society recitals followed and Lanza worked hard to match his personal charm to the magnificence of the voice. For the most part he succeeded. The Countess responded in kind with lavish trips about town, one of which took Lanza and Sciscione to the Metropolitan Opera on 12 December for a production of *Il Trovatore* with tenor Jussi Björling. Nicola Moscona, with whom Lanza would sing in later years, was also in the cast. The Countess also arranged for the two men to meet the star of the show before the performance. Although Sciscione was overcome by the surroundings, Lanza seemed to take it all in his stride.

We saw [soprano] Rosa Ponselle, who was visiting the theatre, talking to someone on stage, and Freddy waved to her like they were best friends.

She had no idea who he was but that didn't seem to bother him at all. Then we went back stage and met Björling—real nice guy, good looking, big chest—but we were surprised to see he had been drinking . . . surprised because he was going on that night. But he sang great later on— just gorgeous—until he tried for the C note on "Di quella pira." It didn't work and he cracked on it—sounded terrible. So he stopped the orchestra—stopped the whole show and made them repeat the music. He nailed it perfectly on the second try. Fantastic![6]

To Lanza, that was what great singing was all about. The ability to screw up, stay in control, then blow your audience away with a fabulous, fearless second shot at that unforgiving C. Of course, as he freely demonstrated to Sciscione afterward, *he* never had any problems with that killer note.

Shortly before he was due to return to Philadelphia, the Countess made arrangements for her young visitor to make a couple of test recordings. There would be no orchestra, of course—just the voice and piano—but it would be professionally captured on disc at a downtown studio, something he could take back with him to play for Irene Williams and his family. As Sciscione remembered it, the occasion also offered a glimpse of the infamous Lanza temperament that would manifest itself so dramatically in later years: "The Countess had booked the studio for 11 o'clock but the guy before us [tenor James Melton] was still using it and we had to wait. After an hour Freddy was ready to take him on—'I'll fight him with fists or voice,' he told me. Luckily, Melton finished right then and Freddy got to make his recording, but he was real mad—didn't like being kept waiting."[7] James Melton, a well-regarded lyric tenor in the 1930s and 1940s, befriended Lanza in later years, though it is doubtful that he was ever reminded of his young friend's hot-tempered bravado in the studio that morning in 1940.

In a touching gesture to his parents, the young tenor recorded three songs for them on the occasion of their twentieth wedding anniversary. Following a brief spoken introduction he began, not surprisingly, with a spirited rendition of "Vesti la giubba," followed by "Ch'ella mi creda" from *La Fanciulla del West*—the only occasion in his life that he would record Puccini's lovely aria. A full-voiced "Sorrento" brought the session to a powerful close. Heard today the performances highlight all the vocal naiveté of a young student, but there is no denying the immediacy of the singing. Freddy Cocozza's natural God-given talent can be heard in every note. Another session dedicated to his father included a one-time-only recording by the young singer of the popular Neapolitan song "Pecchè?"

In December 1940, Earl Denny, a popular Philadelphia bandleader, invited Lanza to sing at Christmas morning mass at St. Mary Magdalen de Pazzi Church. The piece chosen for him was the Bach-Gounod "Ave Maria," and the young singer's impassioned vocal that morning reportedly moved many parishioners to tears. It was that sort of voice.

Lanza's work with Irene Williams progressed in leaps and bounds in the months that followed, and by the spring of 1942 he was accomplished enough to sing a demanding program of arias and duets on stage. On 1 April 1942 he appeared at a pops concert at the Sam Wanamaker store in Philadelphia, where he sang "Cielo e mar" and "Someday" from *The Vagabond King* under the orchestral direction of Emanuel Balaban. Soprano Carolyn Long joined Lanza for three duets: "O soave fanciulla," "Wanting You" and "Will You Remember?" William K. Huff, director of Philadelphia Forum Concerts and a friend of Williams was in the audience for the performance and was deeply impressed, "I did not believe there was anything like [his voice] in this country. He will replace Caruso."[8]

By now, too, the need for more advanced vocal studies had become critical. Maria Cocozza's sacrifice at the Quartermaster Depot notwithstanding, the family did not have the financial means for serious, full-time coaching for their son. A scholarship to a prestigious school of music was the ideal, and Irene Williams turned to Huff for help. The opportunity to advance the tenor's career presented itself sooner than anyone expected. Conductor Serge Koussevitzky and the Boston Symphony Orchestra were due in town for a series of concerts at the Philadelphia Academy of Music at Broad and Locust Streets. Huff felt that if Koussevitzky could be persuaded to hear Lanza sing, important career doors might be opened.

Two years earlier Koussevitzky had inaugurated the Berkshire Music Center at Tanglewood, in northwestern Massachusetts, which provided a unique and unparalleled educational program for talented young musicians. Located on the Tappan family estate a mile and a half southwest of the center of Lenox, a village in the Berkshire Mountains, Tanglewood was the summer home to Koussevitzky and the Boston

Symphony Orchestra. For six weeks, July through August, the chosen few would come and work with some of the finest instructors and musicians in the land. Aaron Copland and Paul Hindemith taught. Lukas Foss and Leonard Bernstein practiced their craft as they worked with the students, and the surrounding environment was one of idyllic beauty. Bernstein, Koussevitzky's protégé at the time, described it as "A green fertile wooded mountain of youth and joy."[9]

Just about everyone agreed it was the perfect place to launch Mario Lanza's operatic career. All that remained was the not insignificant matter of persuading Koussevitzky to hear him sing. The sequence of events that followed might have been scripted for a motion picture. In fact, it provided fodder for a key sequence in Lanza's first film six years later.

The Red Cross at that time had turned the basement of the Philadelphia Academy of Music into a canteen and entertainment center for servicemen on leave. Lanza's publicity machine would later claim that the tenor was helping to move a piano into the recreation room when he spontaneously burst into song outside the conductor's dressing room. Koussevitzky—startled by the golden sounds emanating from the hall—reportedly rushed from his room, scholarship in hand, and embraced the young tenor. Not surprisingly, only part of the story was true.

As Lanza himself later told it, Koussevitzky had finished an afternoon rehearsal and was resting in his dressing room prior to the evening performance. Huff immediately sprang into action. Irene Williams, in the middle of a voice lesson, was quickly summoned to Rush Street to partner her pupil on piano, which Huff had conveniently set up near the conductor's room. On cue, Lanza then broke into a full-voiced rendition of a certain well-known aria: "Mr. Huff told me 'Now you start to sing' . . . so I started what I called my 'lucky' aria, 'Vesti la giubba'. . . . Just when I finished, Koussevitzky put both arms around me, kissed me in true Russian style, and said 'You will come and live with me in the Berkshires.' I realized at that moment that something terrific was happening in my life, in my career."[10]

Some indication of the impact Lanza made on Koussevitzky that day is to be found in a letter the tenor received shortly afterward from William Judd, of New York's prestigious talent agency Columbia Concerts, Inc. (later Columbia Artists Management, Inc., or CAMI):

"I understand from my father, George Judd of Boston, that you have recently sung an audition, which pleased Dr. Koussevitzky very much. If you would care to give an informal audition for Columbia Concerts sometime in the near future, we would be very glad indeed to hear you. Columbia Concerts is always anxious to hear worthwhile new talent with a view to expanding the list of artists under its management."[11]

Lanza sang for Judd and Arthur Judson of Columbia Concerts later that summer, though four more years would pass before the agency signed him to their exclusive roster of artists. The voice was every bit as spectacular as Koussevitzky had claimed, but Judson knew that there was still much work to be done before the tenor was ready for the professional stage.

On 5 April 1942, Lanza appeared at an Easter Sunday concert at Vernon Room, Haddon Hall in Atlantic City, New Jersey. Anthony Coletti conducted the Chalfonte–Haddon Hall Orchestra, and the tenor was partnered by Josepha Chekova, soprano, and Stuart Ross, piano. Full of confidence following his acceptance to Tanglewood, the young tenor thrilled his audience with a choice Handel aria, "Ombra mai fu" as well as "Lamento di Federico," "Ch'ella mi creda," and "Come un bel di di maggio." Ms. Chekova joined him for duets from *Tosca* and *Cavalleria Rusticana*.

Confirmation of Lanza's scholarship to the Berkshire Music Center came in a letter dated 4 June 1942 from Margaret Grant, the center's executive secretary. "In view of your qualifications and recommendations," it read, "the Koussevitzky Music Foundation, Inc., through funds provided by Miss Alice Clapp, grants you a scholarship to cover your tuition for the school term, from July 5 to August 16, amount to $120.00."

Tony and Maria were ecstatic, Irene Williams even more so. Now, she believed, Lanza would get the career launch his talent so richly warranted. She even took the time to see him off at the train station. Just before he departed, she had him sign a contract guaranteeing her five percent of any singing income he received over $5000 a year, and ten percent if that sum exceeded $7500. It was merely a safeguard, she maintained, aimed at protecting her protégé from unscrupulous talent agents who might be out to defraud him. Lanza, for his part, would probably have signed away his entire career at that time. His outgoing nature led him to trust almost everyone he came in contact with and, like many other impulsive gestures he would make in the years to come, the contract with Irene Williams was something he would later come to regret.

Ironically, the Berkshire Music Festival came close to being cancelled that year. With the United States now in the war, the Boston Symphony withdrew from the summer festival. Koussevitzky, tenacious and defiant to the end, refused to give ground and instead promoted the student orchestra to festival status. Leonard Bernstein was promptly named as Koussevitzky's assistant, and the 1942 festival with the young Mario Lanza on the student roster was soon underway.

CHAPTER TWO

Caruso Redivivus!

Much has been made in the intervening years of Lanza's problems with tutorials at Tanglewood. By all accounts he was not the most disciplined of students. Boris Goldovsky, the Russian-born conductor and music director of Opera Workshop at the Berkshires, worked with the tenor on a number of in-house projects and complained to Koussevitzky that the singer put more effort into chasing women than he did his work. Still, like Irene Williams before him, Goldovsky forgave a multitude of sins once Lanza began to sing, and stories were soon filtering out of Tanglewood of a great Caruso-like voice on the campus.

In his memoir *My Road to Opera,* Goldovsky recalled Koussevitzky listening in as Lanza and a young South American lyric soprano named Irma Gonzalez ran through an excerpt from Act III of *La Bohème.* At the close, Koussevitzky, deeply moved at the impassioned singing, was heard to exclaim "Caruso redivivus!" (Caruso reborn!). Problems with solfeggio notwithstanding, Mario Lanza was clearly making an impression.

During his time at Tanglewood, Lanza stayed with the Reverend J. Herbert Owen at the Church on the Hill in the suburb of Lenox. In later years, when the Lanza career was in full flight, media accounts of his escapades—some real, some imagined—regularly referred to him as an *enfant terrible.* To Herbert Owen, though, he was nothing less than an angel. In a letter to the Cocozza's in August 1942, the Reverend Owen observed:

After having Mario in our home for 6 weeks we feel as though we could call you, his parents, our friends. It was a great pleasure to have him among our summer family. For a boy his size I do not yet understand how he could be so quiet. He and John Fiasca shared a room directly over our room and we never heard them.

You have much to be proud of because of your son. It is a great gift you have given him in voice, for it his inheritance from you and God.

The letter also contained an interesting aside about an unexpected visitor from Philadelphia: "I am sorry that Miss Williams felt when she came here that she 'owned' him and must dictate to him."[1] With that signed contract very much in mind, Irene Williams was determined to keep a close watch on her young pupil's progress.

The opera department at Tanglewood, under the direction of Metropolitan stage director Herbert Graf, was justifiably proud of the results they achieved with their students. Graf would accept nothing less than the very best from everyone. The orchestral and operatic productions at Koussevitzky's festival that year more than lived up to expectations. So too, in the end, did Mario Lanza.

Though Leonard Bernstein reportedly took turns coaching him, the ultimate responsibility for Lanza's vocal development rested with Goldovsky. Koussevitzky had encouraged the Russian to prepare Lanza for the tenor role in a planned performance of Beethoven's Ninth Symphony, but in the end Lanza was assigned to work on the role of Fenton, for an English-language production of Otto Nicolai's comic opera *The Merry Wives of Windsor*. It was a smart decision, one that produced happy results for all concerned.

Lanza's graduation performance at Tanglewood took place on the evening of 7 August 1942. The production was repeated six days later on 13 August with a slightly different cast. Even at that young age, Lanza looked every inch the star, resplendent in colorful uniform and rakish hat, eager to thrill the audience with his powerful voice. Koussevitzky's faith in his young Caruso was more than borne out the following morning by a review from noted music critic Noel Straus that appeared in the *New York Times*: "Honors went to the Fenton of the cast, 21-year-old Mario Lanza, an extremely talented, if as yet not completely routined student, whose natural voice has few equals among tenors of the day in quality, warmth and power."[2] The critique in the *New York Post*, though slightly more reserved, did make one good observation: "Another outstanding member of the cast was a young tenor, Mario Lanza, in the part of Fenton. If Lanza's natural abilities are developed in the proper direction, he will own a splendid voice. At present he needs more fundamental training and rudiments of style. Yet even now, he offers good musicality and diction."[3]

Mario Lanza did have an innate sense of musicality that helped him over many a technical hurdle, and his diction, especially in his later, more developed years, was second to none. Lanza often reminisced about his time at Tanglewood, describing it as "the most glorious period of my life."

After his heady experience in the Berkshires, life was far too exciting for the young tenor to return to Philadelphia. A violinist at the festival, struck like so many before him by the superb voice, arranged for Lanza to audition for Michael De Pace, a seasoned concert promoter with offices on the eighteenth floor of the RKO Building in New York. Once again the voice worked its magic, and De Pace, enthralled, accepted Lanza on the spot. De Pace also promoted Giovanni Martinelli, Nino Martini, and Robert Weede, an outstanding young baritone who was carving quite a reputation for himself at the Metropolitan Opera. Lanza, in his own unique way, would eclipse them all, though not in the manner any of them foresaw at that time.

In the months that followed, Lanza spent much of his time being coached by Weede. The two became close friends. Under Robert Weede's patient teaching, the tenor's vocal technique continued to improve dramatically. Weede gave generously of his time and his talent, and his contribution to Lanza's early training has been much undervalued.

Lanza's voice was also committed to disc on at least two occasions that year, the first when he, Weede, and soprano Lois MacMahon recorded a number of excerpts from Puccini's *La Bohème*. Accompanied by Weede's girlfriend, Dora Reinhardt, on piano, the trio produced spirited if unpolished readings. It has been speculated that Weede arranged for the recording to show his young charge where he needed to improve his singing. Lanza entertained dreams of an audition for the Metropolitan Opera House, but even he knew that there was still much work to be done on the voice before that approach could be made. Lanza was also briefly captured on record poking fun at one of De Pace's more celebrated clients, Giovanni Martinelli. A clever mimic when he chose to be, Lanza can be heard imitating Martinelli singing "M'appari." The tribute, while good-natured at heart, was clearly never intended for outside ears.

It was during his time with Michael De Pace that Lanza first met Maria Margelli. Margelli, older than Lanza by some nineteen years, was immediately smitten by the man as well as the voice and offered to do what she could to help further his career. It has been suggested that the two embarked on a brief affair, but no evidence has ever surfaced to support the theory. Indeed, in a letter to De Pace in 1944 she wrote: "I have been like a mother to him."[4] The truth, nevertheless, did not prevent one supposed illegitimate son of Mario Lanza from claiming her as his mother some forty years later, after she had passed on. The claimant, who coincidentally happened to be a tenor, even managed to secure a profile in *People* magazine on the strength of his dubious assertion. It remains an allegation that not only sullied Lanza's name but Maria's, too. By all accounts she was a gentle soul whose memory deserved a better eulogy.

By December 1942, the ever-generous Weede was busy prepping his friend for a planned concert tour. Lanza, his voice growing stronger and more secure by the day, felt that nothing could stop him now. He was so lost in that rarified environment that he had paid little attention to the turmoil in Europe that was currently reshaping the world. An urgent phone call from his mother in Philadelphia quickly brought him back to reality.

A telegram had arrived at Mercy Street addressed to Alfred Cocozza, which the family found surprising as by now almost all correspondence was being sent to Mario Lanza. The reason for the formality soon became clear as an increasingly distraught Maria read the message to her son over the phone. The telegram was from Local Board No. 75 in Philadelphia instructing Alfred Arnold Cocozza to report for duty as a private in the United States Army. In an instant everything had changed. No concert tour. No more studies to shape and perfect the voice. No paid appearances on radio and—most tragically of all—no audition for the Met. Everything was on hold.

De Pace did what he could to seek a stay of duty. In a letter to the local board dated 16 December 1942, he wrote: "Mr. Giovanni Martinelli, noted tenor of the Metropolitan, has heard Mr. Lanza and has taken a great interest in him. He has urged Mr. Lanza to study certain operatic roles with a view to arranging some performances. . . . Mr. Fausto Cleva, well-known operatic conductor, is also interested in Mr. Lanza and has agreed to coach him. We seriously believe that intense study during the next few months is very necessary for Mr. Lanza in order that he may be able to start the fine career he has in store."[5]

A day later, the Countess, Lanza's benefactress, fired off a letter from her suite at the Hotel St. Regis in New York to Uriah Doyle, an influential associate in Washington, D.C., who had the ear of President Roosevelt:

> Knowing the admiration that our dear President has for your good-self . . . I felt that if there is anything in your power that you can do to help Mr. Lanza to be free to complete his studies you will *not* fail to try. Because of the account of the faulty condition of his left eye [I am] led to believe that this particular unusual case could be submitted to his Excellency the President or the Draft Board in Philadelphia. Everyone that hears Mario Lanza sing with his beautiful, glorious, rich, voluminous, unlimited voice truly believes that Mario could do duty to his country by giving delight and morale uplift to the army and civilians as well. . . . Just now Mario Lanza has the whole of New York to back him financially.[6]

It was all to no avail. Lanza was refused an extension and ordered to report to the armed services the following month. On 31 December 1942, shortly before he left New York, De Pace drew up a contract, which he and Lanza signed. With the exchange of one dollar between the two men, Michael De Pace officially became Mario Lanza's personal representative, advisor, and concert manager. Beyond that there was little either of them could do until the tenor's tour of duty had concluded.

A dispirited Private Alfred Cocozza eventually reported for duty to 1127 TSS army base in Miami Beach, Florida, on 5 January 1943. Things worsened considerably when he was transferred soon after to AB Squadron in Marfa, Texas. Lanza described the wretched conditions in a letter to De Pace soon after: "This place is worse than the kingdom of Mefistofile [sic] . . . in fact, it's worse than *Hell*. We breathe nothing but dust for air and believe me . . . my voice has not benefited from it. Oh how I wish I could have Robert Weede here now. . . . I sure could use some singing lessons."[7]

Lanza implored De Pace to use whatever influence the agent had to have him transferred to the Special Services Unit at Mitchell Field, where he would have the opportunity to concentrate once more on his singing. De Pace shot back a telegram saying, in effect, that there was nothing he could do. Lanza was on his own. Even without his manager's intervention, however, Lanza managed to make his superiors at Marfa aware of the musical gold mine the army had in its midst. He was given a three-day pass to attend a concert given by tenor Jan Peerce and came away deeply impressed by the man and his voice: "Jan sang magnificently and the audience was completely sold on him. It certainly was one of the finest programs that I have ever heard. He treated me like a brother and made me feel at ease the entire time I spent with him."[8]

Joining Lanza at the concert that evening was a five-foot-two ex-Burlesque comedian named Johnny Silver who had been charged with putting together variety acts to tour army bases throughout the United States. Silver knew Jan Peerce professionally and admired him as a singer, but he felt that Lanza had the greatest natural voice he had ever heard. He promised to do what he could to keep his friend out of active duty and get him back to singing. The perfect opportunity presented itself soon after when it was announced that impresario Peter Lind Hayes was to visit Marfa to audition talent for his traveling revue *On the Beam*. Hayes had written the musical with composer Frank Loesser, best remembered today for his work on *Guys and Dolls*. *On the Beam* was not in that league, but it did provide the moment Lanza had been waiting for. Silver lost no time in telling Hayes about the golden voice in their unit, and an audition was set up for the tenor the following day.

Lanza's own account of what happened next is straight out of a Mozart comic opera. The tenor awoke the next morning to find his throat inflamed by the red dust of the army base. Overnight the golden voice had been replaced by a croak. Even Silver was appalled by the sound but the ever-resourceful corporal immediately came up with an ingenious plan to save the hour. Lanza had a recording in his collection of Metropolitan opera star Frederick Jagel singing an aria, "E lucevan le stelle" from *Tosca*. Pasting a label with Lanza's name over Jagel's, Silver offered it to Hayes as a stand-in for his ailing friend. This, he maintained, was a test recording Lanza had made recently. In a short while when the throat had cleared, Hayes would hear the real thing. Lanza was accepted on spec that day and eventually sang for Hayes, who was heard to proclaim, "You sound even better in person!" It's a great story, but as with most accounts surrounding key moments in Mario Lanza's life, there is another take on the events of that day. Larry Adler's brother

Jerry, a talented harmonica player in his own right, was also cast in *On the Beam* and recalled a slightly less romantic scenario: "The whole story is completely untrue regarding the dry panhandle dust. Mario never did have a sore throat in Marfa and I was present when he sang his beautiful heart out in the base theater for us. The entire story is pure nonsense, though it looks awfully good in print."[9]

Whatever the truth, Lanza joined the cast of *On the Beam* and his singing career, in a manner of speaking, took off again. It was hardly the "fundamental training" that Noel Straus had encouraged after Tanglewood, but under the circumstances it would do. Lanza soon became tagged as the "Forces Caruso" and the show wound its way through army bases across the United States. He was featured in three scenes: in the first he reprised the "E lucevan le stelle" from his successful audition, and later he appeared in drag as the character Sylvia Storecheese in a number of comedy skits. He also joined Peter Lind Hayes, Jerry Adler, Johnny Silver, and six others for a number called "General Orders." High art it was not, but the entertainment provided much needed laughter in what were increasingly grim times.

One real casualty of Lanza's time in the armed forces was his weight. He had never been slim—stories are still told today in Philadelphia of Freddy Cocozza's prodigious appetite—but during his time in the army his waistline expanded out of all proportion. In a series of photos taken on base and during a visit to Los Angeles in 1944, Lanza is all but unrecognizable. His weight by some accounts topped 300 pounds, a far cry from the handsome young movie star the world would come to know in just a few short years.

One photograph has him prophetically standing on stage at the Hollywood Bowl in Los Angeles, arms outstretched and singing at the top of his magnificent voice. Barney Greenwald was one of several servicemen with Lanza at the Hollywood Bowl that day and, as always, the great voice made quite an impression: "There was no one around so Mario started hamming it up on the stage and Johnny [Silver] pretended to play violin. Then Mario began to sing. A group of us were sitting in the very last row and we couldn't believe the sound he made. The microphone was turned off but even at that distance the sound was thunderous. He had the most fantastic voice I've ever heard."[10] The only thing wrong with the photograph taken that day is the tenor's huge size. Lanza's fluctuating weight gains would become a contentious issue in times to come, but he was seldom if ever photographed at anything approaching this size.

Lanza was miserable when he allowed his weight to get out of control, and he expressed some interesting thoughts on the problem in a letter to Phil Sciscione from Marfa, Texas: "I'm really working hard to carve out a physique that will make everyone's eyes blink. . . . I'd like to kick myself in the ass for not taking your advice long ago when you worked so hard to make a better looking man of me. It's truly wonderful how you could see into the future. I always thought the voice was enough to carry a man through a singing career. But you knew all the time that appearance played an equal part in my business. . . . It's all clear to me now."[11]

It was during a stopover in Visalia, in the southern San Joaquin Valley ("a horse-trading center" was how Lanza later described it) that the tenor was offered a try-out for *Winged Victory*, a production that playwright Moss Hart was putting together. On 2 August 1943 the War Department approved Lanza's application for leave to appear in the new show. *Winged Victory* was a more ambitious undertaking than *On the Beam*, but the Lanza talent would not be center stage this time. Instead, he was relegated to the ranks of a fifty-man choral group under the direction of Lieutenant Leonard De Paur. Moss Hart would later make a point of telling everyone that he had no idea such a great voice was hidden in the chorus.

Hart's story dealt with the struggle of young air force men learning to fly B-17 and B-24 bomber planes and was probably best summed by reviewer Abel Green in *Variety* when he described it as "not a play, but a symbol." Hart's collaborator on *Winged Victory* was the legendary Hollywood agent Irving "Swifty" Lazar. Lazar, who was given his nickname by Humphrey Bogart after making five movie deals with him in a day, managed to assemble an impressive cast of movie stars who, like Lanza, were donating their talents to the war effort, including Karl Malden, Edmond O'Brien, Gary Merrill, Red Buttons, George Reeves, and Barry Nelson. Most of the actors worked for enlisted men's pay for the duration of the run, and their generous commitment to the production managed to bring in $25,000 a week for the Army Emergency Relief Fund, a considerable sum of money in those days.

Ironically, George Reeves and Barry Nelson would go on to play two of the century's most famous superheroes: Reeves (who tragically would later commit suicide) was Superman and Barry Nelson had the distinction of being the first actor ever to play the role of James Bond. The latter, admittedly, was in a show made for television but he was the first.

Winged Victory had its first dress rehearsal at the Shubert Theater in Boston and eventually opened at New York's 44th Street Theater on 20 November 1943, where it played successfully for seven months. Lanza was delighted to be back in New York, one of his favorite cities, but his outsized appearance continued to bother him. Lieutenant Bill Cahan, who went on to become a distinguished surgeon in New York City, recalled finding the tenor in a state of near collapse before a performance one evening. Lanza's parents were traveling from Philadelphia to see the show, and the singer, desperate to lose a few pounds before their arrival, had not eaten in days. Despite the glorious sounds he was creating in the theater, no one seriously considered Mario Lanza suitable for anything other than the opera stage.

During the run of the play, Lanza struck up a close friendship with Edmond O'Brien and Barry Nelson. Lanza spent occasional weekends at O'Brien's country home in nearby Scarsdale where, without too much persuading, he sang Irish songs to the actor's mother. There were many homes on the East Coast that welcomed the young tenor through its doors but none more so than that house in Scarsdale.

The Lanza entourage also included an army sergeant named Bert Hicks who hailed from Chicago. Hicks liked him from the start: "He really was quite a charming guy and had the most beautiful voice of anyone I ever heard—not well-trained but gorgeous, just gorgeous."[12] Hicks had shown Lanza a photograph of his sister, Betty, and the singer, immediately smitten, begged for an introduction. He would get his chance later when the entire cast of *Winged Victory* departed for Hollywood at the close of the Broadway run.

Lanza's return to New York also gave him the opportunity to prepare a special thank you to Maria Margelli for her friendship and continued support, which by now had included some financial remuneration. On 22 May 1944 the tenor booked time at New York's Melotone Studios to record a number of arias especially for his benefactor. In all, Lanza sang five selections that day, at a session that found him in robust voice. He began with Giordano's great aria from *Andrea Chenier* "Come un bel di di maggio," then followed it in quick succession with "E lucevan le stelle" from *Tosca*, the by-now-ubiquitous "Vesti la giubba,"

"Addio alla madre" from *Cavalleria Rusticana*, and the "Improviso" from *Chenier*. He started a sixth aria but broke down laughing and had to stop. Margelli in the background can be heard using a word that was invariably spoken whenever the young tenor sang: "Wonderful!"

Winged Victory ended its Broadway run on 20 May 1944 just as arrangements were being made to transfer Moss Hart's wartime extravaganza to the screen. Twentieth Century Fox had obtained the film rights to the show and the somewhat unlikely director put in charge of the production was George Cukor. Cukor was better known for his deft handling of such lighter fare as *The Philadelphia Story* and *Adam's Rib*, but in truth the very nature of *Winged Victory* called more for movie propaganda than movie classic.

Soon after the play closed, Lanza and the cast packed their belongings and moved to Los Angeles. If the tenor's career was still moving in fits and starts, at least he could say he had arrived in Hollywood. So too had George Burnstein, a burly Canadian bass-baritone who soon discovered a kindred soul in the oversized tenor from South Philadelphia. Burnstein, who as George London later went on to an illustrious career on the stages of the world's great opera houses, was supplementing his income at the time by appearing as an extra in films. Watch closely at the scene in *Casablanca* where the soldiers sing a spirited *La Marseilles*, and you will see the singer in the group. Lanza, who got many of his bookings through other people's recommendations, would provide a similar service a few years later for his Canadian friend.

As word started to spread throughout the movie capital of the great tenor voice on the Fox lot, Lanza began to receive invitations to some of the top celebrity homes in the district. All he had to do was sing for his supper, which he happily did, long into the night at one fabulous gathering after another. Frank Sinatra heard the voice one evening and exclaimed: "The kid knocked a hole through me. Talk about people swooning when I sing . . . there's no exaggeration in stating that for once in my life I really swooned!"[13] Lanza would later enjoy a spectacular working relationship with Sinatra's cousin Ray.

The free recitals eventually paid off when Lanza performed one of his impromptu sessions at the home of actress Irene Manning on North Knoll Drive in Beverly Hills. Among her stunned celebrity guests that night was a top Hollywood agent named Art Rush, who managed Nelson Eddy and cowboy star Roy Rogers. Rush was also the West

Coast representative for RCA Victor, and he was interested to learn that the tenor did not as yet have a recording contract. Calls were made to the RCA head office in New York the following day, and Lanza made a brief visit to the East Coast soon after for an audition with the record company. The RCA executives were suitably impressed; within months Mario Lanza would sign an exclusive recording contract with the company and never look back. Lanza felt this was a particularly good omen; RCA, after all, was the company that had recorded the great Caruso. The following summer he made a series of four test recordings for the Victor label: "Mattinata," "E lucevan le stelle" from *Tosca,* "Vesti la giubba," and Victor Herbert's "I'm Falling in Love with Someone."

By the fall of 1944, Maria Margelli had also moved to California and resumed her support of the tenor's lavish lifestyle. It was through an acquaintance of Margelli's, the Baroness Rothschild, that Lanza got to audition for company chief Jack Warner at Warner Bros. film studios. Warner thought the voice was fabulous, but he failed to see beyond the bulky frame at the time—Lanza had "opera singer" written all over him—and decided to pass. In truth, it was MGM and not Warner Bros. that was seen in those days as the home of the Hollywood musical, though Warner would make amends for the missed opportunity a decade later when he signed Lanza to appear in one of his films.

Lanza, meanwhile, was heading deeper into debt. He was notoriously generous with money and quickly spent whatever he earned. Maria bailed him out of his financial difficulties on more than one occasion, and within a year she was writing to Michael De Pace looking for some return on her investment. Maria formed a close bond of friendship with the Cocozza family in the years following Lanza's death, so it must be assumed that she was fully recompensed for her monetary contribution to the tenor's career.

Lanza's endless round of partying in Hollywood did have one unexpected side effect. In the fall of 1944 he was fired from the production of *Winged Victory.* In a letter to De Pace soon afterward, Margelli saw fit to warn him of the singer's reckless lifestyle. Lanza hadn't been making any money of note and De Pace had been content to await his return to New York. Maria's sincere if somewhat disjointed letter must have given him pause: "Mario has got in with a certain Mario Silver, Musical Director of Columbia Pictures. . . . I [asked] Mario Silver if Mario told him of his obligations with you and the contract . . . and he seemed surprised. In all honesty, he [Lanza] should not sign up with no one else [without coming] to an agreement with you first, but he [Lanza] goes ahead and signs with everybody. Now, Mr. De Pace, Mario has been kicked out of *Wing* [sic] *Victory* for bad behavior."[14]

The "bad behavior" Margelli referred to was the result of Lanza not turning up on the Fox set for two days when he was needed for reshoots. The all-night parties had finally taken their toll, and the singer was nowhere to be found. Disastrous though it must have seemed at the time, Lanza by now had become the eternal optimist, convinced that his fortunes had changed for the good. Something even better would turn up, he believed, something that would bring him out of the chorus and onto center stage. And, of course, something did.

CHAPTER THREE

A Voice Blessed by God

Following his abrupt departure from *Winged Victory*, Lanza found himself back in uniform again but his return to active duty did not last very long. On 29 January 1945 Private Alfred A. Cocozza received an Honorable Discharge from the U.S. Army base at McCaw General Hospital in Walla Walla, Washington, along with a pension of $69.00. The reason given for the disability was "defective hearing" resulting from the singer's war service, an odd rationale given Lanza's complete lack of engagement at the front.

Freddy Cocozza was Mario Lanza once again, but instead of returning to New York, the singer headed back to California. Several months earlier Bert Hicks had finally introduced the singer to his sister Betty. The young woman had been raised as a Catholic. Her mother, May, had been married to Irishman Jack Lyhan, who was Betty's biological father. Following May's divorce and subsequent marriage to James Hicks, Betty and her two siblings, John and Bert, legally adopted the Hicks name. Betty Hicks had moved to the West Coast with her brother's wife and family and was working as an expediter for the McDonnell-Douglas Corporation when she met Lanza. An attractive, soft-spoken brunette with a slim figure and beautiful eyes, she quickly lost her heart to the young man with the golden voice. The two were soon inseparable: "I didn't hear Mario sing until the night of my brother's birthday at a small Italian restaurant, Romeo's Chianti. Romeo, who has one of the most fabulous Caruso record collections in the world, put on 'Vesti la giubba.' When Mario began to sing, I sat back in amazement. Even the glasses tinkled on the shelves as he sang. I was so surprised that when he finished, I threw my arms around him and kissed him on the cheek. From that moment, I was his girl."[1]

Betty's relationship with the Italian-American tenor was a passionate one right from the very beginning. In late August 1944 over a romantic dinner at Romeo's in Hollywood, Mario Lanza had asked Betty Hicks to be his wife. She accepted. They would wait, though, until the war had ended. With little money in hand, Lanza was still struggling to kick-start a singing career. Marriage at that time was unthinkable, as was the idea of telling his parents. Maria Cocozza was fiercely protective of her only son and felt that nothing should be allowed to come in the way of a great career at the Metropolitan Opera House. Lanza knew that Betty would be only viewed as a threat, so he decided for the moment to keep quiet about the pending nuptials.

Romantic distractions notwithstanding, Lanza was anxious to head back to the East Coast and the resumption of his studies with Robert Weede. Lanza was living at that time at 1871 North Kingsley Drive in Los Angeles. In February 1945 he received a letter from J. W. Murray, general manager of the Record Division of RCA Victor. What was written on it opened all the doors:

> Confirming our conversation of this morning the Radio Corporation of America (Victor Division) hereby agrees to pay you $250.00 per month for a period of one year beginning 15 February 1945. The total payment of $3000.00 to be consideration for signing a five (5) year Red Seal contract with RCA Victor which will provide among other things a royalty of 10 percent of the list price on all records sold in this country; the number of selections to be recorded to be mutually agreed. A formal Red Seal contract will be prepared and forwarded to you within the next thirty days.[2]

Lanza could hardly contain his excitement. He was made aware that this was the first time in the RCA's forty-four-year history that a virtual unknown had been signed to their prestigious Red Seal classical label. It turned out to be a banner decade for the recording company, too. In addition to Lanza, RCA also added Bernstein, violinist Isaac Stern, baritone Robert Merrill, and the young mezzo-soprano Blanche Thebom to their burgeoning roster of classical artists. Still, another four years would pass before Lanza would step before an RCA microphone for his first recording session. RCA were content for now to allow the young tenor to develop his career on the concert platform and in the opera house. Later, when his name was enjoying a higher profile, the recording career would commence in earnest.

Lanza, Merrill, Thebom, mezzo-soprano Risë Stevens, and soprano Ann McKnight were captured briefly on record in the fall of 1945 singing "Happy Birthday" to RCA Chairman David Sarnoff—Lanza, for once, sounding somewhat subdued. Thebom, who enjoyed a successful career at the Metropolitan, would later join the tenor on the screen, though both their careers were very much in their ascendancy in the mid-1940s.

The $3000 advance from RCA took care of all Lanza's immediate financial problems, and he and Betty decided to get married. A license was obtained on 11 April 1945, and Lanza bought his bride-to-be a sterling silver wedding ring at Livingstone's in Beverly Hills for the princely sum of $5.95. (The Lanza's would accumulate considerable wealth in later years, but Betty Lanza never changed that ring.) Two days later, on Friday, 13 April 1945, and without the knowledge of his parents, Alfred Arnold Cocozza (the professional name change had not yet been legalized) and Elizabeth Janette Lyhan Hicks exchanged vows before Judge Charles Griffin at City Hall in Beverly Hills. Bert Hicks acted as best man and May Hicks stood by her daughter.

The happy couple boarded a train for the East Coast soon after, stopping first in Chicago, where Betty introduced her new husband to the entire Hicks family. Lanza, still fearful of his mother's reaction to the news, continued on alone to New York to look for an apartment. Temporary accommodation for the newlyweds came courtesy of Johnny Silver, who loaned them his apartment at the Park Central. Lanza then called his mother to say he would travel to Philadelphia but she insisted that she and Tony travel to New York to see their son. Loaded with food, Lanza's parents arrived at the Park Central, figured their boy was doing well, then promptly returned to Philadelphia. When Betty called from Chicago, Lanza sheepishly admitted he hadn't got round to telling them yet. Betty understood—an only child, married in a civil ceremony without his parents' knowledge, and to a woman he had met in Hollywood, of all places! Still, they had to be told. Betty arrived from Chicago at the end of May, and Lanza summoned his parents back to New York. While Betty was at a movie, the Cocozza's learned about their new daughter-in-law.

Given the circumstances of her son's marriage, it would be an under-statement to say that Maria Cocozza was taken aback by the news. The family had not been told of the wedding, had not been invited to the cer-emony and—worst of all—her son had not been married in a church! She was appalled and expected the worst from Freddy's new bride. All that changed when Betty walked in soon after. She was nervous about meeting her new in-laws, too, which immediately put Maria at ease. In the best Italian family tradition, Maria and Tony embraced the new member of their family and the four of them went to St. Patrick's Cathedral to pray for a long and a happy marriage. It is doubtful that Maria ever came to love her daughter-in-law—that deep feeling was reserved exclusively for her beloved son—but she did respect her and in time came to be fond of her.

Maria shared some of her feelings about her new daughter-in-law in a letter to Phil Sciscione soon after, though she was careful not to men-tion the fact that her son had already been through a civil ceremony: "Fred is getting married in a few weeks. . . . a girl he met in California and we met her a few weeks ago in New York. She is an American girl and seems to be very nice. I had the biggest surprise of my life when he told me. . . . Not that I don't approve of it, I most certainly do. But I wanted a big church wedding and so on and so forth. Instead he wants it to be very private and quiet, just his parents and hers, so that's what we are doing."[3] The second wedding ceremony of Freddy Cocozza and Elizabeth Lyhan Hicks eventually took place on 15 July 1945 at the Manhattan Catholic Church of St. Colombo in New York with the Hicks and Cocozza families in attendance.

Lanza by now had resumed his singing studies with Robert Weede. Despite his exclusive contract with RCA, the company was not yet ready to begin recording their new tenor. More vocal preparation was needed, and De Pace was encouraged to book recital work for his charge. Weede's generosity, meanwhile, continued to be extraordinary. Lanza had managed to deplete most of the $3000 advance from RCA, and financial conditions were tight once again. As soon as learned of the newly-weds' plight, Weede offered them the use of his exclusive four-room, fourth-floor apartment at 8 West Forty-ninth Street overlooking Rockefeller Center at a monthly rent of $75. In the summer of 1945, while Weede commuted from his home in Nyack, just outside New York, Mario and Betty Lanza enjoyed the sweet life in Manhattan.

Baritone Earl Wrightson was one of many visitors to the Lanza apartment that summer. Wrightson, who later had a hit recording with "They Call the Wind Maria" from *Paint Your Wagon*, recalled many happy evenings filled with good food and good wine and, of course, good music. Every night was party night at the Lanzas', and no one was ever turned away. Betty Lanza, always the perfect hostess, laughingly referred to her home as "The Bohemian Garret."

An important engagement for Lanza came in early fall when, following a recommendation by De Pace, Peter Herman Adler invited the tenor to join him for a one-off appearance with the NBC Symphony Orchestra at the Atlantic City Convention Hall in New Jersey. The occasion was a Labor Day conference of the Association of Broadcasters, and the Lanzas and the Cocozza's stayed at the Chalfonte Hotel. Lanza was paid the princely sum of $500 for the appearance, but he was more than a little intimidated by the booking. This, after all, was the orchestra that had achieved astonishing things under the great Arturo Toscanini, and Adler had established a considerable reputation for himself through his work on a number of touring opera productions—lofty company indeed for a young singer still trying to master his craft.

In the end, Lanza did not disappoint, though his performance that evening came at a high personal cost. Peter Adler was a merciless tutor, yelling at the top of his lungs and constantly berating the tenor for any perceived slip in his vocal preparedness. Lanza was never one to take criticism of any sort, especially when it came at him full-voice, but he respected Adler enormously and always did what was asked of him. Adler remained one of the few musicians involved with Lanza's career who was ever able to get away with outspoken criticism of the tenor's singing.

Back in New York, Robert Weede used his connections to get Lanza his first real career break on radio. Weede had been singing with Jan Peerce on the successful weekly Celanese Hour radio show *Great Moments in Music*. With Peerce on leave, Weede arranged for the producers to audition his young friend as a replacement. Lanza got the job, eventually appearing on six programs between 24 October 1945 and 20 February 1946 (see *Performance: Stage, Radio, and Television Appearances*). The format of the series—grand opera one week, popular songs the next— would anticipate the all-rounded style of singing for which Mario Lanza's career would soon become known. Lanza was paid $400 for each of the first four performances and $300 for each appearance on the remaining two, a considerable sum of money given the tenor's lack of experience. But the great voice by now was starting to open many doors, and the producers were well pleased with their choice.

The standard of Lanza's performance on the six shows was a mixed bag. The operatic excerpts found him struggling, especially on the *Otello* duets for which he was far too young and inexperienced, but the voice was heard to excellent effect on the more popular fare. The two selections from Lehmann's *In a Persian Garden*, "A Jug of Wine," on which he is joined by soprano Frances Yeend, and "Ah, Moon of My Delight," are quite lovely. Much would be said in later years of how Lanza seem to *live* everything he sang, and even at that early stage in his career that natural, informal approach to his craft was very much in evidence.

Of particular interest was his singing of selections from Sigmund Romberg's *The Student Prince*, his first encounter with a score he would eventually claim as his own. The broadcast also contained the only occasion when Lanza ever sang the lovely "Golden Days" as a duet, the way it had been written. His performance with Weede that day was deeply compelling.

Great Moments in Music was broadcast live every week, something that added to Lanza's vocal unease. On "America the Beautiful" he can be heard briefly forgetting the words but he recovered quickly and no major disasters were reported. He had been booked for ten appearances, but despite the steady income he decided to call it quits after only six. He recalled the reasons why in an interview with gossip columnist Hedda Hopper in 1948: "It wasn't a happy experience. I was required to sing things which were so difficult. . . . I needed years of experience before tackling them. . . . Verdi's *Otello*, for instance. After six programs I knew I couldn't go on."[4]

What Lanza had been most in need of at that time in his career was a personal manager. De Pace did an excellent job handling his concert engagements, but somebody else was needed to take charge of his financial affairs, especially now that he had signed with RCA. In addition to his work with Weede, Lanza was also studying repertoire with Maestro Renato Bellini and English songs with Polly Robinson. Robinson's studio was located in Room 802 at Carnegie Hall in Manhattan. A chance encounter there in December 1945 solved all problems and marked a significant turning point in the tenor's career.

Robinson had been coaching a successful realtor named Sam Weiler who, with his brother Jack, operated the Fairmont and St. Francis Hotels in San Francisco. But the entrepreneur's golden touch in the marketplace did not extend itself to the rehearsal room. He was an average student at best with a small and insignificant voice, but he did have an abiding passion for singing. One day, when Lanza and Weiler had met by chance in the Carnegie building, Robinson persuaded her more gifted pupil to sing an aria. Lanza by now had regained control of his weight and looked and sounded fabulous. The businessman could hardly believe what he was hearing: "I knew then and there that I had just heard the greatest voice in the world."[5]

Weiler never took another singing lesson from Polly Robinson. After the impromptu recital, he and Lanza adjourned to a nearby coffeehouse where they sat and talked for hours over endless cups of coffee. By the end of the evening Weiler knew just about everything there was to know about the struggling singer, where he had come from and, more importantly, where he wanted to go. One thing was certain: for Lanza to develop his extraordinary talent in the right manner, he would need proper handling. Lanza had the voice and Weiler had the money. It didn't take either man long to see where the possibilities might lead.

On 1 February 1946 Mario Lanza and Sam Weiler entered into a contract that would provide the singer with a weekly stipend of $70.00. Weiler also agreed to clear Lanza's current debts, which had run to several thousand dollars, and to take care of all expenses incurred through his singing lessons. In return, Weiler would be paid five percent of the singer's future earnings. Two years later, on 4 August 1947, the contract was amended to provide Weiler with ten percent of gross earnings. A third and final adjustment to the contract would be made in 1951, the net result of which would make Sam Weiler a very wealthy man.

One of Weiler's first tasks was to find the best voice coach for his new charge. He approached Peter Adler, who immediately recommended Enrico Rosati, former voice teacher to the great Beniamino Gigli. To Adler and many of his associates, Rosati was simply the finest voice teacher in the business. Weiler wasted no time in setting up an appointment, and within a week he and Lanza arrived at Rosati's studio on West Fifty-seventh Street. Lanza, understandably, was nervous. He was about to sing for the man who had coached one of his idols, a tenor second only in his mind to the great Caruso. What happened next has become part of the history books. Rosati sat down at the piano and began to play, Lanza sang and afterward, for a brief moment, all was quiet. Then, turning to the tenor, Rosati spoke softly: "I have waited thirty-four years for you [since Gigli]. You have a voice blessed by God."[6]

In the months that followed, Rosati set to work turning a rough vocal diamond into a polished stone. Lanza, overwhelmed to be working with the seventy-two-year-old maestro, initially did everything that was expected of him, but he soon fell back on his old habits. He was often late for rehearsal, which would send the precise and meticulous Rosati into a rage. His homework, carefully set out for him days in advance, would not be touched. But then, as always, Lanza would start to sing and the old disciplinarian's heart would melt. "To carve a work of art," Rosati later recalled, "you must have the tools and the proper piece of wood. In Mario I had the proper piece of wood. But he was rushed, rushed."[7]

Rosati soon came to realize how fundamentally insecure Lanza was about his vocal abilities. Many great singers suffer from stage fright before a performance, but Rosati sensed something deeper in his young charge—a deeper anxiety that might hold him back from pursuing a full-time career in the opera house. Rosati's concern was highlighted by an incident that took place during the singer's time at the West Fifty-seventh Street studio. Rosati had arranged for Lanza to audition for the incomparable Arturo Toscanini. For weeks he had prepared the tenor to sing an excerpt from Verdi's *Requiem*, but when the day finally arrived for him to appear before the legendary conductor, Lanza was nowhere to be found. He had called at the last moment and complained of being ill, he could not sing. Lanza would later speak of that time to his own conductor and accompanist Constantine Callinicos: "They were rushing me, Costa. Everybody was rushing me and I couldn't go any faster. I wasn't ready."[8]

Great mileage has been made over the years of Toscanini supposedly referring to Lanza's as "the greatest voice of the twentieth century." Establishing where and when this famous statement was uttered has proven difficult, if not impossible. It certainly was not at Rosati's studio in Manhattan, where the two men never met, and no other encounter between them has ever been reliably recorded. One theory has it that Toscanini made the comment after Manie Sacks at RCA played Lanza's RCA recording of the great *Bohème* aria "Che gelida manina" for him, but the likelihood of the conductor making such a remark on the basis of an electronic reproduction is suspect. In remains, however, an accolade inescapably linked to Mario Lanza's career.

Years later, when Lanza was beginning to make an impression in Hollywood, the tenor talked about his time with Rosati:

> It was both rich and difficult. Slowly and painstakingly he built my voice into what it is today, so I am able to sing for hours without tiring. Also, under Rosati, I had to practice every day to achieve what the Italians call Bel Canto. Eventually, Rosati and Edward Johnson [general manager] of Metropolitan Opera in New York invited me to join the company, but without the necessary time for me to prepare for it in peace, I did not think it would be an advisable step for me to take. I didn't want to be placed in front of the world's largest opera company without first completing an extensive study of the operatic works and until I had reached a reasonable standard of artistic representation and maturity.[9]

Lanza's claim that he wasn't ready to commit full-time to the classical stage would be revisited many times over in the years that followed. To some it was proof that the singer lacked the essential discipline critical for a serious operatic career. To others it simply reinforced their belief that the Lanza voice lacked the strength and the stamina to perform in full-length productions. Given the countless and undisputed accounts of the natural magnificence of the voice, the latter notion seems particularly fatuous, but it remains a theory that stubbornly persists in some musical circles to this day.

In all, Mario Lanza spent fifteen months with Enrico Rosati, months that profoundly shaped his thinking and his approach to singing. On his departure, the tenor presented his famous teacher with a signed photograph in gratitude for all he had come to learn at the tiny studio on West Fifty-seventh Street. Rosati, deeply touched, framed the photo and displayed it proudly next to his more illustrious clients: "To Maestro Enrico Rosati—any success I am having or will have in the future I owe 100% to you, the greatest voice teacher in the world, past, present and future. I love you and you will always be close to me wherever I am or in whatever I do. Especially on the stage however, you will always be there with the third register. All of my love for you, Maestro. Mario Lanza."[10]

One person who was not making any money off the Lanza career was Michael De Pace. Already stretched by his commitments to Martinelli, Weede, and the other artists on his roster, De Pace eventually, and some say reluctantly, agreed to sign Lanza's contract over to the more illustrious Columbia Concerts agency at 113 West Fifty-seventh Street. How much influence Sam Weiler exerted in this decision is open to question. Several years later, when Lanza's professional career was in full flight, De Pace's secretary Olga Troughton sought reimbursement for unpaid expenses owed to her employer by the tenor. If any monies did change hands, it was at Weiler's discretion.

Lanza's second audition for Columbia Concerts in 1946 was the one that secured him his contract. His accompanist for the short recital was pianist Thomas Martin, a coach and occasional conductor at New York City Opera. Martin had met the tenor at an "opera log" in Trenton, New Jersey, earlier that year. The opera log was a semiformal event sponsored by the local opera guild where members were treated to a discussion of a popular work interspersed with musical selections from a visiting artist. De Pace had arranged for Giovanni Martinelli to perform selections from *Otello* at the Trenton gathering, but the tenor was indisposed and Lanza was sent in his place. No one expected great things from a twenty-five-year-old singing *Otello*, but the vocal shortcomings were quickly forgotten the moment he began to sing. Martin was only too pleased to repeat his services at the tenor's Columbia Concerts audition later on.

Between 2 July and 17 December 1946, Lanza was booked for seven appearances on the concert stage, including his first appearance at Chicago's Grant Park Band Shell on 6 July with Frances Yeend. Claudia Cassidy reviewed the concert the following day for the Chicago *Tribune*:

[Lanza and Yeend] made debuts on the spectacular side with the Grant Park Symphony Orchestra last night, when competent Leo Kopp replaced Franco Autori as conductor. Most of an audience estimated at 25,000 got a shock of pleasant surprise. . . . What few of us really anticipated was the impact of those two voices. Mr. Lanza came first, a handsome, dark haired boy with wide shoulders and a disarmingly modest presence. With the two *Tosca* arias he left no doubt that he has a true Italian tenor. Beautiful, ardent and exciting . . . he has superb range and a crescendo to set susceptible folk shouting. When [Lanza and Yeend] sang the Love Duet from *Madama Butterfly*, it reminded me of the days of Mason and Hackett or the Ravinia night Raisa sang that duet with Martinelli. Not, of course, that they had reached such a goal but that it is not beyond their reach. Other things came later [including] "Cielo e mar" from Mr. Lanza, who took the soaring climax like a veteran.[11]

The Hicks family in Chicago turned out en masse to support the tenor's appearance at Grant Park and took time to pose for a charming family photograph on stage before the concert. Bert Hicks' eight-year-old daughter, Dolores, looked especially fetching in a smart check suit. A decade later, as the actress Dolores Hart, she would be responsible for giving Elvis Presley his first romantic kiss on screen in the film *Loving You.* "Uncle Mario and Aunt Betty came to my grandmother's house in Chicago. . . . I remember the moment when he was asked to sing and he hit the high note and all the glasses in the dining room began to tremble. I remember Grandmother running back and saying, 'Stop, stop! You're going to break every piece of glassware in my house!' It was really awesome to hear his voice and to hear that purity of sound. I've always heard that someone could break a glass with singing, and this [he] could do."[12]

On 13 November Betty accompanied her husband for an appearance with the Ottawa Philharmonic Orchestra. The couple stayed at the glamorous Chateau Laurier and, despite his new association with Columbia Concerts, the tenor still found time to dispatch a postcard to De Pace, written with all the enthusiasm of a young child: "The concert was a tremendous success. I sang very well and was in complete control all the way through."[13] And indeed he was. In a local newspaper review the following day, critic Lauretta Thistle wrote:

The enthusiasm of last night's concert of the Ottawa Philharmonic Orchestra had to be divided three ways: for Dr. Allard de Ridder, the conductor, for Gerard Bales, whose Nocturne was a feature of the program, and for Mario Lanza, a young tenor who bids fair to live up to all the glowing predictions made for him. Lanza has that golden quality to his voice which is given to few tenors, and he sings with ease and a welcome lack of affectation. Melodiousness and purity of tone are the most obvious qualities of his singing, but he has great reserves of power as well, and his range was indicated by the ringing high C he produced. He chose four familiar operatic arias: "E lucevan le stelle," "Che gelida manina," "M'Appari," and "Vesti la giubba." Another favorite *Tosca* aria, "Recondita armonia," was his first encore, and his second, "Mattinata," had to be sung twice to satisfy his audience.[14]

That "ringing high C" referred to in the review was in many respects the key to Lanza's success on those early concert tours. Columbia Concerts must have been particularly pleased with a letter they received following the tenor's Ottawa appearance: "Just a few lines to let you know what a tremendous impression Mr. Lanza made on our audience last night. It was impossible for him to leave. . . . From both an artist's and a personal point of view I don't think it will ever be possible for me to get such a thrill from presenting any artist. The privilege of having Mr. Lanza with us is definitely the high point of my career. I doubt it will ever be equaled. . . . For once don't chalk this up as the same old baloney. This is the real thing and we hope we'll have the thrill of presenting Mr. Lanza, many, many times down through the years."[15]

Under Rosati's tutoring the voice had clearly come into its own, and the rich lower register coupled with those dazzling top notes made for a thrilling combination. Lanza's pay for the tour averaged around $250.00 per recital, but the experience he was gaining in front of a live audience was priceless. Everyone who heard him sing was convinced that it would be only a matter of time before the great voice would be ringing out in the lofty portals of the Metropolital Opera House.

CHAPTER FOUR

The Road to Hollywood

Lanza's regular accompanist on tour was pianist Josef Blatt, a superb musician who, if called upon, could accompany a singer for an entire recital without recourse to a music sheet. On 14 April 1947 the two were booked for a recital at the State Teachers College Auditorium in Shippensburg, Pennsylvania, but at the last minute Blatt had to bow out. Zena Hanenfeldt at Columbia Concerts immediately sought a replacement. The man she chose eventually came to have the single most lasting impact on Mario Lanza's professional career as a singer.

Constantine Callinicos was a New York–born musician of Greek descent. A graduate of Manhattan's Juilliard Music School, "Costa," as Lanza affectionately came to call him, was a skilled pianist and some-time composer who had accompanied such luminaries as soprano Lily Pons and tenor Lauritz Melchior. Having just come off a grueling tour, an exhausted Callinicos was less than enthusiastic when Hanenfeldt asked him to stand in for the indisposed Blatt. For one thing, he had never heard of Shippensburg, and just who was Mario Lanza? Things grew even more ominous when he called Lanza at his apartment to arrange a rehearsal. "We don't need to rehearse," came the breezy reply, "I have confidence in you, Constantine."[1]

Mario Lanza and Constantine Callinicos met face to face for the first time in the town of Shippensburg just two hours before the start of their concert. Betty Lanza had accompanied her husband to Pennsylvania, and Callinicos was immediately struck by how young and charming they looked together: "He was just twenty-six with a simple, ingenuous vigor that I had rarely seen among professional artists. He had the build and the barrel chest of a heavyweight prizefighter and was in excellent shape. In the first few seconds I had to judge him uncomplicated and unspoiled, a press agent's delight. Betty was a lively brunette of medium height with a trim figure . . . as wholesome as 'the girl next door.' "[2]

In time, Callinicos would come to revise his initial assessment of the tenor's "uncomplicated" nature, but for now there was a concert to perform and he still had not heard Lanza sing. His sense of unease quickly returned when the tenor casually informed him that he had forgotten his tuxedo. The two would have to appear in business suits. In time Callinicos came to realize that the singer had an intense loathing of formality, and the "forgotten tux" excuse would reappear on numerous occasions over the years.

With some trepidation on the pianist's part, Lanza and Callinicos, resplendent in business attire, strode on stage to face an audience of close to 5000 people. The surprise that greeted Callinicos as he began to play banished all concerns: "As I started to play the introduction to 'Pieta Signore' by Stradella, a favorite of Enrico Caruso's, Mario turned his back on the audience. Leaning casually over the piano, he winked, then smiled at me. . . . Then he began singing, and I knew that the tux was unimportant and that the offensive, tradition-defying, back-to-the-audience was just a neophyte's lack of stage deportment. For as the rich, glorious tones flowed effortlessly through Mario's throat, I knew I was listening to one of the greatest voices since Caruso."[3]

Callinicos was so overcome after the concert that he hardly knew what to say. How do you tell someone that they have the most beautiful tenor voice you have ever heard? How do you explain to someone that after all the years you have studied and mastered your own technique, after all the singers you have coached and played for and listened to, that here—in Shippensburg, of all places—you have just listened to the greatest of them all?

Lanza responded by laughing loudly and embracing his new friend. Although neither man realized it at the time, a bond was formed between them that day that would develop and grow through all the fantastic successes—and all the unforeseen tribulations—that would become central to the career of Mario Lanza. Callinicos never doubted that his new friend was destined for greatness, not with a voice like that. And though his first reaction on hearing him sing was to think "an American Caruso," he knew in his heart that this was no carbon copy, no cheap imitation. This was the real thing.

In the golden years that followed, no accompanist or conductor would ever be closer to Mario Lanza than Constantine Callinicos. No other musician would ever come to understand him—and to forgive him—like the faithful Costa. No one else would share in all the triumphs and still continue to stand by when the troubles came. By doing so, of course, Callinicos helped carve his own special niche in the musical history books, but his involvement in Mario Lanza's career went way beyond the professional courtesy of one musician to another. It became, in the end, the deep and unconditional commitment of a friend: "Mario was like a brother to me. And it wasn't because he was generous to offer RCA Victor guarantees in order for me to start recording with him. It was that natural empathy and sympathy I had with the man. He had such a big heart that you couldn't help but love him."[4]

Lanza himself must have sensed something of that special empathy that day when he promised Callinicos that the two would work together again when the time was right. Two years would pass before their next engagement, but it would be an auspicious reunion. Lanza did return to the State Teachers College Auditorium in Shippensburg three months later, on 28 July, this time with Blatt in tow. Both men sported tuxedos for the occasion.

With rave reviews of Lanza's appearances flooding into Columbia Concerts in New York, Arthur Judson decided to expand the tenor's repertoire by sending him on an eighty-six-concert tour of the United States, Canada, Newfoundland, and Mexico. This time, however, he would travel as part of the Columbia Bel Canto Trio, with soprano Frances Yeend as lead singer. Judson had still to decide on the third member of the group, and at Lanza's suggestion, bass-baritone George London was brought on board. Under terms negotiated with the agency, Yeend was paid a fee of $500 for each appearance, Lanza just over $300, and London $275. Intensive preparations were immediately put in place for the tour.

On 8 July 1947 in Milwaukee, the Bel Canto Trio made their first appearance in concert before an enthusiastic audience of 6000 people in a "Music under the Stars" evening at the Emil Blatz Temple of Music. Music critic Edward P. Halline, commenting on the occasion for the *Milwaukee Sentinel* the next day, made it very clear which of the three stole the honors: "Three young singers definitely on the way up. . . . Lanza was the most impressive of all, with the kind of voice that is needed to get all the drama out of such emotionally charged arias as

'E lucevan le stelle' and 'Celeste Aida.'"[5] Richard Davis writing in the
Milwaukee Journal, echoed Halline's sentiments: "The favorite with
the audience was the tenor, Lanza, a singer unmistakably destined to
enjoy a handsome career . . . this youngster not only has a firm and ringing voice of adequate power, but he has set up standards for himself and
is eager to meet them. Clearly he is on his way."[6]

The program of songs chosen for the Bel Canto Trio was a particularly felicitous one. Lanza, Yeend, and London would open the evening
with "Qual volutta trascorere," from Verdi's *I Lombardi*. London would
follow with two arias: "In felice, e tu credevi" from Verdi's *Ernani,* and
"Quand la flamme de l'amour" from Bizet's *La Jolie Fille de Perth*.
Lanza and Yeend would return to the stage for "Parigi o cara" from *La
Traviata,* then it would be Yeend's turn for her two solos: "In quelle
trine morbide" from Puccini's *Manon Lescaut* and "The Jewel Song"
from Gounod's *Faust*. Lanza and London would return for a duet, "Ecco
il magico liquore" from Donizetti's *L'Elisir d'Amore*. Lanza would then
take center stage for his two arias: "E lucevan le stelle" from *Tosca* and
"M'appari" from Flotow's *Martha*. On occasion the tenor was forced to
repeat one of his solos but nobody, least of all Lanza, seemed to mind
very much. A good tenor voice is always irresistible and Lanza's was
very good indeed. Yeend and London would then return to the stage for
"Légères Hirondelles" from Thomas' *Mignon,* and the curtain would
come down on the first half with all three singing "Perdon, perdon,
Amelia" from Verdi's *Simon Boccanegra*.

Following an intermission, the trio would join forces for the
"Farewell Scene" from Mozart's *The Magic Flute,* Lanza would solo
with "Woman Is Fickle" from *Rigoletto* sung in English, and he and
Yeend would inject a little operetta into the proceedings with "Nobody
Could Love You More" from Lehár's *Paganini*. Yeend would return to
the stage for "Musetta's Waltz" from *La Bohème*—her performance
often giving Lanza a run for his money in the encore category—and she
and London would duet on "Bess, You Is My Woman" from Gershwin's
Porgy and Bess. London would return for one last solo "Slander's
Whisper" from Rossini's *The Barber of Seville*. The whole magnificent
evening would finally come to a close with all three glorious voices
singing the "Prison Scene" from *Faust*.

With the exception of the popular tenor solo arias and a live take of
"Parigi o cara" from a Hollywood Bowl concert, Lanza never recorded

any of these selections in his lifetime. In later years, when he was committing his talent to such questionable fare as "Boom Biddy Boom Boom" and "Pineapple Pickers," serious music lovers who had heard him in his Bel Canto Trio days would recall those past glories and wonder why.

One problem the trio occasionally encountered on the tour stemmed from Lanza's fear of flying. While Yeend and London regularly took flights to their next booking, Lanza always insisted on taking the train, often arriving at the stage door literally with minutes to spare before a concert. For the most part, though, the tenor was mindful of his behavior proving that when he was responsible to others, "temperamental" was not a word that applied to Mario Lanza. London, in particular, always felt that their time on the road together provided Lanza with the most intensive period of vocal development he would ever experience in his career.

On 20 July 1947 the trio arrived in Chicago for an appearance at the city's Grant Park. Despite a light rain, more than 55,000 concertgoers turned out to hear them sing. Critic Claudia Cassidy from the *Chicago Tribune* was on hand once again to join in the applause: "Young Mr. Lanza was something approaching a sensation. You are a sensation in opera when customers whistle through their fingers and roar 'Bravo!' . . . Mr. Lanza sings for the indisputable reason that he was born to sing. He has a superbly natural tenor, which he uses by instinct, and tho a multitude of fine points evade him, he possesses the things almost impossible to learn. He knows the accent that makes a lyric line reach its audience, and he knows why opera is music drama."[7]

Of the three, it was George London who went to the sort of career at the Metropolitan Opera House that everyone was predicting at the time for Mario Lanza. Lanza's eventual decision to travel a different road was especially felt by London: "If he could only have crawled out of his skin and listened to his own voice, he might have lived his whole life differently."[8] For Mario Lanza's journey to the Metropolitan Opera— his entire future as an opera singer—was about to take an unexpected detour.

While Lanza was touring the country with the Bel Canto Trio, Art Rush had seen to it that the tenor's RCA test recordings and many of his concert reviews found their way to the desk of Ida Koverman, personal secretary to Louis B. Mayer at MGM film studios. Koverman, an avid supporter of the arts, was a formidable woman who had once served as secretary to Herbert Hoover before he became president of the United States. When she had something to say, people usually listened, including her boss at MGM. Koverman had been deeply impressed with Lanza's recording and his striking good looks, an unusual combination she felt in an opera singer. By now, too, the glories of the Bel Canto Trio were common knowledge in classical music circles so with a little arm twisting, Ida Koverman set a plan in motion that would forever change the course of Mario Lanza's career.

Tenor Ferruccio Tagliavini, who was singing at the Met, had been booked to appear in concert at the Hollywood Bowl on the evening of 28 August 1947, but a scheduling conflict forced him to cancel. Rush, with Koverman's influence, suggested Lanza as a replacement. Eugene Ormandy would conduct and Frances Yeend would join the tenor on stage. London, on this occasion, would remain in the wings.

When word of Lanza's impending appearance at the Hollywood Bowl reached Rosati in New York, he offered to prepare his former pupil and Yeend for their *Traviata* duet, "O parigi o cara." Following a rehearsal one afternoon, Lanza bumped into Robert Merrill on Seventh Avenue. Merrill was on his way to a lesson with his own voice coach, Leila Edwards, a former rehearsal pianist for operatic stage director Armando Agnini. Lanza tagged along and without too much persuading agreed to sing "Ch'ella mi creda." Edwards' response was typical: "My God, what a voice! Where have you been hiding?" Merrill laughed and said, "He'll never be an opera singer, Leila. He suffers too much from stage fright."[9] The comment, made in jest, would prove more prophetic that anyone would have guessed at the time.

The main objective of the Hollywood Bowl concert, as far as Koverman and Art Rush were concerned, was to highlight the performance of Mario Lanza. Mayer agreed to attend, along with Koverman and his young singing star, soprano Kathryn Grayson. In addition, some of the stars from the *Winged Victory* troupe turned out to cheer Lanza on, Edmond O'Brien among them. All Freddy Cocozza had to do was sing like Caruso. What he did, in the end, was sing like Lanza and it was more than good enough.

Of all the people who sat in judgment of Lanza's performance, it is doubtful that anyone was more impressed than Louis B. Mayer, though George London would later claim that he ran him a close second.

"He sang that night like he had never sung before or has sung since," London recalled. The evening began with three arias from the tenor and by the time Frances Yeend had joined him on stage for a duet, the crowd was all but hoarse from cheering. The sustained climax he and Yeend brought to the conclusion of Puccini's great love duet from *Madama Butterfly* brought the entire audience to its feet. The critics raved: "The sort of tenor voice that every operatic stage has been yearning for, lo these many lean years. Lanza's is the warm, round, typically Italian type of voice that caresses every graceful phrase and makes the listener breathe with him as it models each curve of the melody."[10] "Lanza's voice is rich, full, warm and ringing. He has expression, emotion and good pronunciation. His operatic potentialities, if he works hard for a few more years, are unmistakably great."[11] "Electrified a large audience that cheered for several minutes. . . . He has truly a rare asset in a naturally beautiful voice, which he uses with intelligence, and a native artistry which, rightly developed, should proved to be on of the exceptional voices of the generation."[12]

In every respect imaginable the night was a triumph—the highpoint of Mario Lanza's concert career to date. It was also, conversely, its greatest tragedy. For if the tenor had been anything less than extraordinary that evening, if the voice had not been at its best, Louis B. Mayer might have chalked the whole thing up to little more than a pleasant musical evening spent under the stars. But like everyone else at the Hollywood Bowl, Louis B. Mayer was dealing with the not unpleasant sensation of feeling the hairs stand up at the back of his neck. Mayer simply could not believe what he was hearing—and, just as importantly—what he was seeing. Lanza was slightly overweight at the time but his dark good looks coupled with the magnificent voice made for a thrilling combination in Mayer's mind.

Within seventy-two hours Louis B. Mayer had arranged for Lanza to audition before a select group of veteran producers at his studio; people who would know in the cold light of day if his golden touch had once again proven infallible. Mayer was a master showman—loud, mawkish, pushy and more than a little vulgar. But he had a special ability to find and nurture talent, and it was not by chance that his studio boasted the slogan "More stars than there are in the heavens." Lanza, whom Mayer would later describe as "Clark Gable with a voice," would be his last great discovery.

On 30 August 1947 on the studio's mammoth Stage One soundstage, Mayer introduced his new singer to a select group of MGM dignitaries. With typical showman's panache, Mayer had the tenor stand behind a curtain while he made his announcement. Then, on cue, Lanza began to sing the two numbers chosen for him: "Che gelida manina" from *La Bohème* and Victor Herbert's "Thine Alone." Among those in attendance was producer Joseph Pasternak, the man who had nurtured the singing career of the young Deanna Durbin at Universal Studios. With Mayer's blessing he was soon to do the same for Mario Lanza: "It was the most beautiful voice I had heard in my life and he [Mayer] said this is our new discovery. A few minutes later the curtain parted and out walked Mario Lanza . . . bushy haired . . . he looked like a caveman."[13]

With one performance at the Hollywood Bowl, Mario Lanza had gone from being a struggling concert artist to someone who was actively being considered for a role in a movie—and a glamorous MGM musical at that. To the former Freddy Cocozza from the streets of South Philadelphia, it was an amazing experience. In truth, a lot of the producers present for Lanza's audition that day could not get past the "caveman" image so graphically described by Pasternak. But like Mayer, Joe Pasternak had a knack for seeing beyond the weight and the bushy eyebrows. Where others saw opera singer, he—at a stretch—saw movie star. If terms and conditions could be worked out with Lanza's management, Pasternak was determined to do for the tenor what he had done a decade earlier for Deanna Durbin.

Despite all the hype that was thrown at him at MGM that day, Lanza never really believed he would be sidetracked into a film career. He still had commitments with the Bel Canto Trio to fulfill, and it was only a matter of time before he would be trading the concert platform for the opera stage. But there was more to consider now. For one thing the money being waved at him by MGM was not to be dismissed lightly. And there was Sam Weiler to consider, too. Lanza had been anxious to start showing some sort of return for his benefactor's investment.

Sam Weiler was not present at the studio that day and cautioned his young charge to sign nothing, but Weiler was excited as well. By now the germ of an idea was starting to take hold in Lanza's mind. Nothing would be allowed to stand in his way of achieving stardom at the Met, but what if—just for the sake of argument—he could bring classical music to the screen? Wouldn't that reach a far greater audience than any performance he could ever give on the classical stage? No one had ever done it successfully before, but Mr. Mayer was already talking about letting him sing an aria or two in one of his pictures.

Lanza returned to MGM on 8 September 1947, when he made two test recordings for the studio: a reprise of "Che gelida manina" and a powerful take of "Vesti la giubba." The studio's resident musical prodigy, eighteen-year-old André Previn, accompanied him on piano, the only occasion when the two worked together. Previn thought the voice was magnificent but in time came to disapprove of the man and the way he was treating his exceptional talent. A gift like that, Previn believed, should be put to a much higher purpose.

While Weiler was sent to talk terms and conditions at MGM, Lanza rejoined the Bel Canto Trio for their tour. He also accompanied soprano Agnes Davis and pianist Josef Blatt for a concert at the Montcalm Palace in Quebec on 10 October 1947. The local newspaper at the time erroneously listed them as "artists from the Metropolitan Opera," though it is doubtful that anyone who heard Lanza's performance that evening would have seen fit to question it. The closing comment in the review that appeared the next day was both insightful and prophetic: "Mr. Lanza, though still very young, has a rich and expressive voice. The variety of his art, his interpretation possibilities, his magnificent voice, invited us to admire this exceptionally gifted tenor. He is able to interest even those who do not like classical music."[14]

On 2 November 1947, Lanza and Yeend took the stage with the Tri-City Orchestra for a concert at the Masonic Temple Auditorium in Davenport, Iowa. One member of the audience was impressed enough to scribble comments on the program "written in the dark during concert." Observing of Yeend that "she and her voice are lovely." The writer also wryly commented "you should have seen her gown. I was glad the arias didn't call for her to sneeze!" As for Lanza, "It seemed incongruous that such an angel's voice should come out of a burly football player. Our friend in the orchestra, Harry Garber, told us he—Mario—was a really talented performer. He also said he had a hole in his sock!"[15]

The Bel Canto Trio eventually headed to Mexico, where they ran into a most unexpected problem. Columbia Concerts had switched the last two dates, which now had them performing in Chihuahua on 27 November and Torreón the following day. Bill Judd later acknowledged that the eleventh hour switch was a mistake: "The Mexicans responded to this type of activity by putting on an income tax at the last minute. Obviously the Trio didn't have the money to pay its tax. The community monies had all been sent to New York direct, so they cooled their heels in the Mexican clinker the whole night. We couldn't get them out till the next day, when it all came clear that they weren't trying to get away with the national treasury."[16]

None of the Bel Canto Trio performances were ever captured on disc, though one recorded excerpt from *La Bohème* sung in English does survive. On 18 June 1948, one month after their final appearance together in concert, Lanza, Yeend, and London along with an unidentified soprano and a baritone sang part of Act IV of Puccini's masterpiece at the NBC studios in Manhattan. Peter Herman Adler had recruited the singers in an attempt to persuade David Sarnoff to green light an in-house opera company for NBC, which at that time was owned by Sarnoff's company RCA. Their audition, such as it was, had been organized by Samuel Chotzinoff, pianist and critic, in the Fifty-ninth Street apartment of Constance Hope, a public relations expert. The audience was small but select: Arthur Rubinstein, Jascha Heifetz, Sarnoff, and Adler. Sarnoff was enthralled and gave his approval on the spot but by the time the singers had assembled at the NBC studios for their recording, Lanza's career had already moved inexorably in a different direction.

Following negotiations between Weiler and MGM, Lanza signed a seven-year contract with the film studio, which, a first glance, seemed extraordinary. He was immediately given a $10,000 signing bonus with a starting salary of $750 a week for twenty weeks. Then, on the successful completion of the picture, he would receive a final bonus of $15,000. That completion bonus would be increased to $25,000 for the next picture and so on, right up to $75,000 for his seventh film: a fortune in those days to a singer who had yet to make his first professional recording. The contract—back-dated to 30 August 1947, the day of Lanza's audition—also allowed Lanza six months each year to pursue his concert and operatic engagements. What the singer and his manager failed to take into account was a small but critical provision in Paragraph 4. It stated that if the studio opted to suspend his contract or found him in default, Lanza would not be permitted to appear on stage or radio or make recordings until the dispute was resolved. It was a provision that would return to haunt him before his contract had run its course.

While plans were being readied for Lanza's film debut, the tenor set out to prove that he could handle the demands of simultaneously juggling an operatic and a movie career. Walter Herbert, general director of the New Orleans Opera Association, had heard Lanza sing at an outdoor pops concert in St. Louis and with the Bel Canto Trio in Chicago the previous year. An invitation to sing with his company in New Orleans was extended. By December, Lanza was being readied for his professional opera debut as Pinkerton in an April 1948 production of *Madama Butterfly*.

In later years when the subject of Lanza's lack of commitment to the opera stage became a regular topic of conversation in classical music circles, reference would often be made to the fact that *Butterfly* is not a "tenor's opera." Apart from an appearance in the opening act, the high-point of which is his glorious love duet with Cio-Cio-San, the tenor does not appear again until the close of the opera. The inference was, of course, that Lanza could not sustain a more demanding role on stage. In truth, Pinkerton was a comparatively straightforward part to launch the tenor's operatic career but it had nothing to do with any fear or reluctance to tackle heavier parts. In 1947 Lanza had every intention of singing Radames, Chenier, Canio, Dick Johnson, Don José—just about anything they threw at him. But Lieutenant Benjamin Franklin Pinkerton would do nicely for now; the weightier stuff would come later.

In preparation for the New Orleans engagement, Weiler arranged for Lanza to rehearse at the New York studio of Armando Agnini, the opera's stage director and nephew of Gaetano Merola, general director of San Francisco Opera. Problems began almost immediately when Agnini's Viennese pianist, Rudolph Scharr, started to correct the tenor on a number of minor musical points. "Correcting" Mario Lanza, even in those early days, was simply not done and he immediately demanded that Scharr be replaced. The crisis was averted when Agnini arranged for Leila Edwards to take Scharr's place. The memory of the tenor's impromptu recital in her studio the previous year was still fresh in her memory and she was delighted at the opportunity to work with him. In later years, Edwards would say, "Mario was a lovely, charming young man with the best, the most beautiful voice I have ever heard, and in my ninety-two years I've heard them all. Bob Merrill brought him to my studio one day and he sang 'Ch'ella mi creda' magnificently; whoever taught him that aria taught him well, there were no mistakes at all."

Lanza's idea of prepping for the role of Pinkerton was to listen to Beniamino Gigli's recorded performance of the score, a fact that Edwards immediately picked up on.

I knew he'd been listening to Gigli's recording because he made all the same mistakes! But he was the perfect gentleman, quick to learn and I never had any problems working with him. When I helped him prepare for New Orleans he would have me sing the part [Pinkerton] in my whiskey tenor voice—once, sometimes twice—then he would repeat it perfectly. Mario had an incredible ear for music and that's how he learned the role. And the words of the song were just as important to him as the music. He put so much feeling into whatever he sang, and the songs just came alive. I didn't travel to New Orleans to hear him in "Butterfly" because I thought it was only a matter of time before I'd see him at the Met. And make no mistake his voice would have filled the Met. I get so angry when I hear people suggest it was a small voice. It was magnificent . . . big and round . . . with limitless power. Mario could have sung in any opera house in the world, had he chosen to.[17]

In later years, when Lanza had achieved international stardom in Hollywood, he remembered his time with Edwards with a signed photograph that stands today in her gallery next to his more accomplished peers from the opera world. The fond inscription reads, "To Leila Edwards, one of the few people I really miss working with in New York, and a real friend. Until we meet again, which I hope is soon, I am . . . Mario Lanza."[18]

On 8 and 10 April 1948 at the Municipal Auditorium in New Orleans, Mario Lanza made what would be his first and final appearances on the professional opera stage when he sang the role of Lieutenant Pinkerton in *Madama Butterfly* for the New Orleans Opera House Association. Japanese soprano Tomiko Kanazawa was a fetching Cio-Cio-San, Jess Walters a commanding Sharpless, and the role of Suzuki was sung by Rosalind Nadell. Walter Herbert conducted the two performances.

Photos taken backstage after one of the performances depict an exceptionally slim tenor. Whether through nervousness or, more likely, in preparation for his forthcoming work at MGM, Lanza had lost all his excess weight and he looked and sounded fabulous. With Betty and Sam and Selma Weiler in the audience, Lanza made sure his singing would not go unnoticed. In a review for the *St. Louis News,* critic Laurence Oden wrote: "Mario Lanza performed his duties as Lieut. Pinkerton with considerable verve and dash. Rarely have we seen a more superbly romantic leading tenor. His exceptionally beautiful voice helps immeasurably—his combination of good looks and vocal ability should prove most helpful to Mr. Lanza in any of his more earnest undertakings."[19]

Those "earnest undertakings" would be on a movie soundstage and not another opera house, but no one gave much thought to that scenario in New Orleans that evening. Walter Herbert invited Lanza to return to the city the following season for two performances of *La Traviata.* Lanza enthusiastically agreed and a contract was drawn up, but by 1949 commitments to MGM were pulling him in a different direction and the appearance was cancelled.

One great and deeply significant part of Mario Lanza's dream had finally come true in New Orleans that April evening in 1948. He was now officially an "opera singer." In time, when his first film had been completed, he would take on the really tough roles, those that the great Caruso had claimed for his own. That "lucky aria" would finally be sung in its proper context, as part of Leoncavallo's opera and not just as an encore at the end of a concert. The Duke of Mantua in *Rigoletto* might have been written for Lanza, especially now that he had finally gained control of his weight, and just thinking of the dramatic possibilities he could bring to the role of the poet Chenier gave him chills.

Lanza was young, handsome, and singing like a god. Everything was possible, everything within his reach, just that one film to be completed. Maybe sing an entire aria on the screen—offer them a tantalizing glimpse of what they could expect from him in a full-length opera. Then back to his real home, here on the opera stage. Not as an American Caruso—never that—but as the first Mario Lanza. In time, if everything went according to plan, he would do it all.

CHAPTER FIVE

Movie Star

In just about every respect, 1948 was a groundbreaking year in the life of Mario Lanza. Shortly after the New Orleans engagement, the tenor reported for work at MGM only to be told that his leading lady, Kathryn Grayson, was pregnant. Everything was on hold until after the baby had arrived in the fall. Grayson did agree to one engagement, however. She and Lanza would appear at the Hollywood Bowl on 24 July at an MGM-sponsored concert, a gala evening with some of the studio's best talent on stage and in attendance. Lanza was meant to repeat his thrilling performance from the previous year, and he did not disappoint.

Veteran actor Lionel Barrymore joined the singers on stage that night for "The Halloween Suite," a sentimental piece he had written for orchestra and vocals. Why MGM saw fit to present a Halloween interlude in July is not clear, but the twelve-minute oddity was warmly received, more perhaps in tribute to its composer than to its musical merit, which was negligible. Mayer was especially keen to showcase Lanza's spectacular voice and with that in mind, the tenor chose to sing the perennial favorite "Nessun dorma" from Puccini's *Turandot*. Any tenor with a decent high B can make an impact with this aria but what Lanza did with it at that concert went beyond exciting. It was simply sensational.

Miklós Rózsa conducted the Hollywood Bowl Symphony Orchestra and some credit must be given to him for the quality of the singer's performance. In the end, though, it was Lanza who reached deep within to produce something he would never repeat on stage. He would record the aria in the studio seven years later but it would remain a pale imitation of his unforgettable singing that night. The Hollywood Bowl concert was also notable for Lanza's only recorded performance of Bizet's "Agnus Dei." Like everything else he performed on stage that evening it was beautifully sung; it remains a mystery why he never chose to revisit it in the recording studio.

While Kathryn Grayson took time off to have her baby, Betty Lanza discovered that she too was pregnant. A close and unshakeable bond quickly developed between the two women, with lots of happy parenting advice exchanged in the months that followed. It all augured well for a successful and trouble-free production.

Between 22 September and 19 December 1948, Lanza, at the studio's instigation, made a number of appearances on live radio. "Vesti la giubba" and "Thine Alone," a popular concert favorite, were featured on two "Salute to MGM" broadcasts in September. In November the tenor made a high-profile appearance on a Thanksgiving special hosted by actor Don Ameche with Jack Benny, Martin and Lewis, and Edgar Bergen and Charlie McCarthy providing the laughs. This time Lanza got to sing three selections: "Cosi Cosa," a novelty number previously sung by Allan Jones in the Marx Brothers' classic *A Night at the Opera*, "E lucevan le stelle" from *Tosca*, and the Thanksgiving hymn "All Ye Thankful People Come." Lanza, Bergen, and the dummy got together one more time in December when, in an unusually solemn moment, the tenor sang a powerful "Lord's Prayer." All the programs drew large audiences and all were there to showcase the studio's new singing star. The producers at MGM were delighted at the exposure, and Lanza did everything he could to please them.

Director Norman Taurog, an Oscar winner for his work on the little-remembered *Skippy* in 1931, was put in charge of the new film. Originally called *This Summer Is Yours*, the picture's title gradually morphed into the more marquee-friendly *That Midnight Kiss*. Though not a large-budget production by today's standards, the movie did have the benefit of being able to call upon the vast pool of talent on the MGM lot. Grayson had previously starred in pictures with Frank Sinatra and Gene Kelly and was given top billing, with veteran actress Ethel Barrymore offering sterling backup as her society aunt. Pianist José Iturbi was on hand to lend the film some musical class, Keenan Wynn played the tenor's best friend, Jules Munshin and Thomas Gomez provided the laughs, and Irish-American J. Carrol Naish played—what else?—Lanza's Italian father. But the real purpose of the picture, the reason that all of them were on the set, was to help launch the career of the Hollywood Caruso, Mario Lanza.

The musical director on the film was Charles Previn, picking up with Lanza from where his prodigiously gifted nephew André had left off the previous year. The elder Previn and Pasternak initially found Lanza a charming and cooperative student, though the tenor's first screen test at the studio had not been what Pasternak had hoped for. His hair looked wild and bushy and his suit emphasized his weight at the expense of his height. A quick visit to the hairdresser solved one of the problems, but Pasternak and Mayer decided that some physical toning was necessary before the singer was ready to appear before the cameras. Mayer turned to a physical trainer on the MGM lot named Terry Robinson, a licensed chiropractor and former "Mr. New York City" and Golden Gloves Champion of New York State, who had come to the studios to provide therapy for Mayer's wry neck.

If Callinicos came to serve the tenor's best interests in the recording studio and on the concert stage, Robinson provided a level of support and commitment to Lanza and his family that would go on well beyond the singer's lifetime. The extraordinary extent of that support was something neither man could have anticipated when they met for the first time in 1948.

I came out to meet a young man they had under contract named Mario Lanza. Mr. Mayer told me they were going to start a picture with him and asked me if I could take 25 lbs. off him in a month. Lanza already knew me because he used to read *Health & Strength* magazine and remembered me from a boxing tournament in Philadelphia. The first place I took Mario was to Muscle Beach in Santa Monica and he loved it there, loved the beach, and he lost the weight. I thought Mario and Betty were the cutest little couple I had ever met. They were living in a small little walk-up on Spaulding Drive in Beverly Hills. I had a better car than he had and so whenever we went out we used my car. They were the happiest two little people you would ever want to meet. I never heard of Mario Lanza the singer until one afternoon while we were having lunch Betty put some records on. I suddenly heard a voice and I said, "That's Caruso, right? My grandmother used to play Caruso all the time and she idolized the man but I never heard him sing that good." They started to laugh and Betty said "Hey, Stupid (her pet name for me) that's him! That's Mario!" Even though I don't know opera that well, I couldn't believe it. From that moment on the magnet attracted me.[1]

Kathryn Grayson's daughter Patty Kate was born on 7 October, the same day that Alfred Arnold Cocozza and Elizabeth Janette Lyhan Hicks legally changed their names to Mario and Betty Lanza in the Superior Court in the State of California. That date in October would have an ominous significance in all their lives, one that would be revisited in more tragic circumstances eleven years later.

Tragedy was far from everyone's minds, however, in those golden days of 1948. The Lanza's had been living in rented accommodations in the San Fernando Valley, but with the film work and a baby of their own now on the way, a residence closer to the studios was needed. In November, with the help of Terry Robinson and Robinson's friend George Eiferman, the current "Mr. America," the couple moved into their first Hollywood home, a duplex apartment at 236-1/2 South Spaulding Drive off Wilshire Boulevard. Betty remarked that they looked like a football team: she heavily pregnant, Lanza tipping the scales at 200 pounds, Eiferman at 210, and Robinson a trim 180. They laughed so hard that she was afraid their new neighbors would complain. Terry was soon a mainstay in the Lanza's lives and constructed a gym on the rooftop, where he and his charge worked out daily. By December the tenor was ready to begin recordings for the picture.

Mario Lanza's first movie soundtrack recording session took place at MGM on 1 December 1948. Working with the MGM Studio Orchestra conducted by Charles Previn, Lanza quickly ran through three popular selections, "Mamma Mia, Che Vo' Sapè," Jerome Kern's "They Didn't Believe Me," on which he performed a duet with Grayson, and a new song specially written for the production "I Know, I Know, I Know." For the Italian song, which would mark the tenor's first appearance on the screen, Lanza was accompanied on piano by maestro Giacomo Spadoni. Lanza had met Spadoni at a benefit appearance to raise funds for the Jewish Home for the Aged, an event held at Pickfair, the lavish home of Mary Pickford and Douglas Fairbanks. The concert had been organized by Louis B. Mayer's sister Ida Mayer Cummings, a woman known for her involvement with many charitable functions. It didn't hurt that she had the entire pool of talent at MGM to draw from, and her brother's newest star made a suitable impact that day. Lanza was equally impressed with his new accompanist.

Spadoni, a native of Bologna, Italy, had moved to the United States at the turn of the century. He eventually found work as a pianist for the

Chicago Opera Company. In 1935 he transferred to the Metropolitan Opera, first as a prompter and later as chorus master. Now semi-retired, Spadoni drew a steady income at MGM teaching voice and providing occasional piano accompaniment—the ideal musician, Mayer felt, to make their new singing star feel right at home.

A tall, elegantly dressed man in his sixties, Spadoni's introduction to the Lanza voice was an unforgettable one. The tenor had chosen to sing "Cielo e mar" with Spadoni accompanying him on piano, but halfway through the aria the old man stopped playing and sat for a moment in silence. His words moved even Lanza, who by now was used to the effect his voice had on those hearing it for the first time. "I never thought I'd live to hear a purer voice than Enrico Caruso's. You're so young, and you are American born. You have perfect pitch and beautiful Italian. I can't go on today. I'm all shaken up. . . . Please excuse me."[2] Spadoni and his wife, Helen, were soon regulars at the singer's household. Lanza would listen for hours as the old man recounted tales about his experiences in Chicago and at the Met and his friendship with the great Russian bass Feodor Chaliapin.

Lanza's next recording session at the studios was scheduled for 9 December but the day before, Betty suddenly went into labor. With Terry Robinson at the wheel, the couple drove to Cedars of Lebanon hospital. Betty's labor was long and difficult. Lanza, not wanting to cancel the studio time booked for him and the orchestra the following day, reported for duty as scheduled. While he was singing on the sound-stage his first child, a girl the Lanza's named Colleen, was born. Lanza had often referred to Betty as "my Irish Colleen," and both agreed it was a perfect name for the new member of their family.

In gratitude for all he had done for him, Lanza asked Sam Weiler if he and Selma would act as godparents to the child. They agreed. The Weilers were Jewish but gave assurances that Colleen would be raised as a Catholic in the unlikely event that anything happened to Mario and Betty Lanza. Colleen was baptized soon afterward in St. Paul's Catholic Church in Westwood, with the Lanzas, the Weilers, and "Uncle" Terry Robinson all in attendance. Father Paul Maloney presided.

Lanza now set to work on *That Midnight Kiss* with a vengeance, completing all recordings for the picture by the end of December. One additional track was added in January 1949 but did not feature in the final print. Previn and lyricist Bronislau Kaper settled on a wide-ranging selection of music to showcase the Lanza voice. In addition to the two operatic arias, the Kern standard, and a new ballad, Charles and André Previn cobbled together two duets from Tchaikovsky: "One Love of Mine" from the Andantino Simplice movement of the Piano Concerto No. 1, which was dropped later from the final print, and "Love Is Music" from the Fifth Symphony, used for the film's grand finale. Hollywood's fondness for bastardizing the classics aside, Lanza and Grayson performed all the selections beautifully.

As the daily rushes came in, it soon became clear that Mayer's celluloid Caruso was a natural in front of the camera. Though never anything more than a competent actor, Lanza had an easy charm that was well suited to the lightweight musical fare the studio had concocted for him, and his on-screen chemistry with Grayson was delightful.

That Midnight Kiss was scripted by Bruce Manning and Tamara Hovey and featured a sly nod at the singer's first meeting with Koussevitzky. Lanza played Johnny Donnetti, a Philadelphia truck driver with a magnificent voice who is discovered singing while helping to move a piano into one of the city's society homes. That "singing truck driver" tag would haunt Lanza for many years to come, a less-than-subtle put down, many believed, for his decision to direct his talents to Hollywood and not the opera house.

Columbia Concerts and RCA in New York, meanwhile, were both making plans to capitalize on Lanza's burgeoning celebrity. Columbia was first out of the gate. While *That Midnight Kiss* was being prepped for release, the agency booked the tenor for a twenty-seven-date cross-country tour of some of the smaller concert venues throughout the United States, the first time that the tenor carried the responsibility of an entire tour on his shoulders. Conversely, it would also be the last time that Mario Lanza would be viewed as a "classical artist" on the concert circuit, his subsequent successes as a film star moving him into another category entirely.

In preparation for the engagement, Lanza turned to Constantine Callinicos. The two had not met since their memorable appearance together in Shippensburg two years earlier, but Lanza had not forgotten his promise and Costa was only too thrilled to work with the great voice again. The tour, however, did not quite go as planned: "We opened with a cancellation in Bluefield, West Virginia, and closed with a cancellation in Lincoln, Nebraska. Out of twenty-seven dates,

Mario was on hand for twelve. He ducked out of some dates without giving a reason. For others, he pleaded a cold—'pneumonia' he insisted on calling it."[3]

It was a disturbing trend that Callinicos put down to his friend's sense of imminent stardom. Lanza, he believed, resented the idea of playing the "tank towns" for so little money. A voice like his was better suited to the great concert halls of all the major cities. Arthur Judson at Columbia felt that Lanza still had much work to do to shape the voice and perfect his technique on the concert platform, but by now the tenor had other ideas.

Most of Lanza's on tour appearances were in recital with Callinicos providing musical support, but occasionally he crossed over to a full-fledged concert with symphony orchestra. On 22 March 1949 he performed with the Oklahoma State Symphony and, not surprisingly, the marriage of the Lanza voice with an orchestra drew an ecstatic response from audience and critics alike: "One of the largest crowds of the season gathered to hear Mario Lanza, 27-year-old tenor, stop the show cold every time he sang . . . possibly the greatest of our young tenors who might possibly fill the long-vacant shoes of Caruso. All the Italian fervor, the clear bell-like tones of the almost extinct bel canto style are present in this fine American's voice. . . . One was left only with the desire to make him sing again."[4]

The tour was interrupted at the beginning of May when Lanza returned to New York to prepare for his professional recording debut with RCA Victor. The company had booked the outsized Manhattan Center on West Thirty-fourth Street for the session and a forty-five-piece orchestra comprised largely of musicians from the New York Philharmonic was recruited for the occasion. Two arias and two Neapolitan songs were chosen for the tenor to sing that day: "Celeste Aida" from Verdi's masterwork *Aida*, "Che gelida manina" from *La Bohème*, "Mamma Mia, Che Vo' Sapè," and "Core'ngrato," an eclectic mix to launch the tenor's recording career.

The vice president of RCA Records during the post–World War II years was Emanuel "Manie" Sacks. Much like his counterpart Louis B. Mayer at MGM, Sacks was a legendary figure in the recording business, noted for his ability to spot and nurture new talent. Lanza was someone he had taken a keen interest in and he arranged for Richard Mohr, RCA's top A&R (artist and repertoire) manager to take charge of the session. Jean Paul Morel of New York City Opera was assigned to conduct the orchestra.

Mohr made arrangements for Morel and Lanza to rehearse at the New York City Center, and it was agreed that the two would give particular attention to the operatic arias chosen for the recording session. Morel, a consummate professional, was only too aware of Lanza's minimal experience on the opera stage and felt it his duty to correct his young charge whenever he saw fit. For Lanza, that quickly became too much too often. After one particularly contentious rehearsal, Lanza stormed out and informed the company that he would not record with Morel on 5 May as scheduled. He proposed instead that they engage Callinicos, who at that time had never conducted a full orchestra at a recording session.

Not surprisingly, RCA balked at the suggestion. Lanza had still to prove his abilities in the recording studio and Callinicos had no experience at all. The cost, if anything went wrong, would be considerable. In the end, Lanza generously offered to cover expenses if Costa did not live up to the task. At two o'clock on the afternoon of 5 May 1949, everyone assembled at Manhattan Center for the first RCA recording session of Mario Lanza's career.

With little time to prepare beforehand, Callinicos was more nervous than Lanza. His apprehension was further aggravated by the tenor's habit of occasionally closing his eyes when he was singing. Eye contact between them was essential if Costa was to remain in control of voice and orchestra. In the end, though, the quality of work produced at the session exceeded everyone's wildest expectations.

It is no exaggeration to say that Lanza produced some of the best singing of his career that day, with the two Neapolitan songs and the two arias all recorded in single takes. The Puccini aria, "Che gelida manina," was subsequently voted operatic recording of the year by the National Record Critics Association, and RCA later added it to their "Hall of Fame" catalogue of historical recordings. Given the high standard he managed to achieve every time, Lanza's ability to record in single takes was extraordinary. Some would suggest that a little more attention to the music's finer points would undoubtedly have resulted in more polished performances, especially on the operatic recordings, but Richard Mohr, for one, was always ready to spring to the tenor's defense: "The magnificence didn't change. The problem was one of energy. When Mario was heavy he felt he could sing as much as he wanted, so he would do numerous 'takes' for us. When he was thin, one 'take' was all he would do. The orchestra was always well rehearsed and we got spontaneous performances from Lanza. Either way he was fine— it was just that he was more comfortable heavy."[5]

RCA was particularly struck by how polished and completely assured Lanza sounded at that first session. It often took years for singers to master recording techniques, but Lanza had it down pat literally from day one. Callinicos had also performed his duties well and everyone was thrilled with the results. Later, Lanza and Costa posed for a photograph, with the tenor holding the music sheet to "Mamma Mia, Che Vo' Sapè?" Embracing his friend after the recordings had been completed, Lanza beamed and remarked that they had been captured for posterity on record. All in all it was an auspicious start to what would prove to be a great and prodigious recording career.

With *That Midnight Kiss* scheduled to open in September, MGM arranged for Lanza to make another appearance at the Hollywood Bowl, this time on 16 August 1949. The evening, "Salute to MGM," was another hodge-podge of musical and comic entertainment from the studio: Eleanor Powell danced, the younger Previn played, Carmen Miranda and her basket of fruit provided the laughs, and Lanza, as always, brought the house down with a full-voiced rendition of "Celeste Aida." He also thrilled the crowd with a sustained and dazzling D flat at the close of the "Addio, addio" from *Rigoletto* on which he was partnered by soprano Mary Jane Smith. His performance that night marked the last time he would appear at that famous venue.

After the show Lanza and several of the performers headed to Ciro's nightclub, where Dean Martin and Jerry Lewis were topping the bill. Shortly before the end of their act, Lewis called Lanza to the stage and asked him to sing. Lanza, in an expansive mood after his triumph at the Hollywood Bowl, obliged with his "lucky" aria, "Vesti la giubba." The applause was thunderous, prompting Lewis to call an abrupt end to the evening's entertainment. "The show's over for tonight, folks. No one can follow that performance."[6]

One week after his stunning appearance at the Hollywood Bowl, Lanza reported for his second recording session for RCA, this time at Hollywood's Republic Studios. Three songs were chosen, including a close-to-definitive rendition of "Mattinata." Once again each was completed in a single take. With separate contractual agreements between MGM and RCA, it was agreed that the tenor would re-record music from his films for commercial release, a practice that would change in years to come as the idea of releasing actual soundtrack recordings became more commonplace. For this second session Lanza worked with conductor Ray Sinatra, cousin to another great recording artist and a skilled musician in his own right. Sinatra enjoyed an excellent working relationship with Lanza, and within a year the two would produce what is arguably Mario Lanza's most famous recording, "Be My Love."

The 23 August session was also a marvelous example of how Lanza was able to move with consummate ease from singing at the top of his voice to interpreting a standard—in this case "They Didn't Believe Me"—in a delicate and tasteful manner fully befitting the song's origins. That amazing ability to crossover between the two musical worlds goes a long way toward explaining why Lanza's legacy endures. It wasn't just that he did it—even Caruso had taken a spirited vocal swipe at George M. Cohan's "Over There" in 1918—it was that he did it so well. His phrasing was impeccable, his diction beyond reproach, and he knew how to master the difficult musical nuances that separate Giuseppe Verdi from Jerome Kern. Whatever the tenor's shortcomings in the classical field—and those were clearly due to his lack of full-time exposure to the medium—Lanza's skills as a crossover artist have never been surpassed.

That crossover ability was shown to particularly good effect in *That Midnight Kiss*. The highpoint of the picture as far as Lanza and many critics were concerned was the tenor's rendition of "Celeste Aida," the song he had recorded on the day his daughter Colleen was born. Before Lanza, opera on the screen generally came in very small doses. If an aria was featured at all, it was invariably an excerpt; no opera singer was ever trusted with holding his audience for an entire song. This time, MGM took a chance and allowed Lanza to sing the complete aria, though they did insist on dropping the recitative. That, they felt, might be pushing it. They need not have worried. When the film previewed at the Picwood Theater in Westwood, Los Angeles, on 25 August 1949, Lanza, Betty, and Robinson sat quietly in the back stalls, each of them thrilled as teenagers when the crowd broke into applause after "Celeste Aida." Lanza's belief that he could bring opera to the masses, though as yet on a trial run, was triumphantly proven. Even then, a comparative novice to moviemaking, Lanza was already dreaming of bringing full-length operas to the screen.

On 29 August the Lanzas, Kathryn Grayson, her husband Johnny Johnston, and Giacomo and Helen Spadoni traveled to Philadelphia to attend the world premiere screening of *That Midnight Kiss* at the city's Boyd Theater. Lanza was also booked to sing for President Harry S. Truman at Philadelphia's Bellevue-Stratford Hotel later that day. The tenor's parents, Kathryn Grayson, and Johnny Johnston were also in attendance, but unfortunately Truman had to leave to attend another function before Lanza was called to the podium to sing. Truman expressed his regrets at not hearing Lanza sing, a feeling acutely shared by the tenor and his entourage.

Lanza and Grayson made an even more high-profile appearance at the city's Labor Day Parade, traveling in high style in a motorcade through downtown Philadelphia. Maria Cocozza, still living in Mercy Street, joined her son in his limousine, with Betty joining Kathryn Grayson in another car. In Maria's eyes Freddy Cocozza had overnight gone from operatic hopeful to bona fide superstar. In a sense she was perfectly correct, though it would take another year before that particular mantle could be confidently hung on her son's broad shoulders.

One of the many thousand people who saw Lanza in the limousine driving down Broad Street that day was a young local entertainer named Al Martino, then trying to get a break in the business. Seeing the local-boy-made-good passing by inspired Martino to stick with it and within a few short years Lanza would do him a personal favor that would catapult his career into the mainstream. Lanza was offered a song called "Here in My Heart," which Martino had wanted to record. On learning of his interest in it, Lanza decided to pass on the number and gave it to Martino instead. "Here in My Heart" eventually sold more than one million copies, making Al Martino a household name. Martino never forgot the gesture and seldom fails to honor Lanza whenever he appears in concert to this day.

The Lanzas and the Graysons also paid a visit to Little Italy, spending time at the Christian Street and Mercy Street homes. The entire neighborhood turned out to greet them and many were shocked at Freddy Cocozza's transformation from overweight, streetwise kid to glamorous movie star. At a packed reception later in nearby Palumbo's

Restaurant, Eddie Durso caught up with his pal. He was just as astonished at the makeover, but it was soon obvious that it was the same old Freddy. The two promised to keep in touch but it would be another two years before they would see each again and then for the last time.

The campaign to promote *That Midnight Kiss* moved into high gear when Lanza and Grayson were dispatched together on a nationwide tour to sing and talk about their respective careers. On 29 September 1949 the two appeared on the *Screen Guild Theater Program*, which was broadcast on NBC radio. Every word, every pause, every casual remark was carefully rehearsed but the singing was free and relaxed. Lanza's soloed on "Mamma Mia, Che Vo' Sapè?" and "I Know, I Know, I Know" and his partner joined him for "They Didn't Believe Me" and "Verranno a te sull'aure" from *Lucia di Lammermoor*. Grayson, admittedly, was more at home with Kern than Donizetti, but the voices were young, fresh, and powerful and the audience for those shows none too discerning. Interestingly, of the musical selections sung on their promotional appearances, Lanza and Grayson did not reprise the Donizetti duet in *That Midnight Kiss*, though the number did surface briefly in the picture as part of a comic interlude with Grayson and character actor Romo Vincent, with Richard Charles providing Vincent's singing voice.

That Midnight Kiss opened to generally good reviews and a healthy return at the box office. The picture that introduced Mario Lanza to his public garnered him some excellent notices, particularly from the influential *Variety*, who with typical *Variety*-speak wrote: "The film introduces a potentially smash box-office draw in tenor Mario Lanza. His standout singing and capable thesping should provide an extra word-of-mouth fillip for exhibitors. His voice, when he's singing opera, is excellent. In addition, far from resembling the caricatured opera tenor, he's a nice-looking youngster of the average American boy school, who will have the femme customers on his side from the start."[7]

Even before *That Midnight Kiss* had opened, plans were well underway for Lanza and Grayson to return to the screen in *Kiss of Fire*. The film would also reunite the two stars with director Norman Taurog, who would later direct several eminently forgettable Elvis Presley vehicles in the 1960s, and producer Joe Pasternak. J. Carrol Naish rejoined the group, with the young Rita Moreno making one of her first appearances before the cameras. A mixture, in others words, much as before. Sy Gomberg and George Wells were assigned to write the screenplay, which this time cast Lanza as Pepe Duval, a brawling Louisiana fisher-man who charms opera singer Grayson with his powerful voice. Not exactly high art, everyone agreed, but Lanza was still learning and at least this time he would receive top billing. The one difference—and it was a significant one—was that MGM decided to allow the tenor to experiment with a more liberal sprinkling of opera. Lanza would sing excerpts from a number of arias and he and Grayson would duet on the popular drinking song from *La Traviata*. Best of all, in lieu of warmed-over Tchaikovsky, *Kiss of Fire* would conclude with the magnificent love duet from *Madama Butterfly*, an abbreviated duet, to be sure, but still full-flight Puccini.

There was also talk around this time of Lanza making a picture with Ezio Pinza, in which the great bass would play his father. The project, entitled "Deburau," was based on a story by Sacha Guitry with the two men cast as opera singers competing for the hand of the same girl, but nothing ever came of it. Pinza instead went to make a number of for-gettable pictures at MGM, one of which happened to be shooting at the same time Lanza was on the set. Hearing his famed colleague nearby, the tenor launched into a pitch-perfect imitation of Pinza singing "Some Enchanted Evening" one that drew roars of laughter and applause from his friend and everyone who heard it.

MGM in those days had two schools of film musicals. Louis B. Mayer's idea of class was to have an orchestra play an excerpt from *Swan Lake*, followed promptly by his new discovery singing "Celeste Aida." Scripts were always of secondary importance, something merely to set the stage for the next big number. Arthur Freed, on the other hand, saw other possibilities. Working with directors like Vincente Minnelli and Stanley Donen, Freed dug deep into the genre to mine such masterpieces as *An American in Paris*, *Singing in the Rain*, and *The Bandwagon*. Terry Robinson always believed that Lanza would have been better served working with the Freed unit at MGM, but it remains open to question whether the tenor had the discipline to work with such a demanding taskmaster.

On 28 October 1949 Lanza and Ray Sinatra returned to Republic Studios to capture what many consider to be the definitive recording of "Granada." Among those people was the song's composer, Augustin Lara. Terry Robinson was present when Lanza and Lara met for the first and only time: "Mario had recorded 'Granada' and he loved the song.

The composer, Mr. Lara, happened to be in California and he told some-one at the MGM Music Department that he would love to meet Mario. When the two met they communicated in a mixture of broken English, Italian and Spanish—you should have heard them! Mario was not the first to record 'Granada' but when his rendition came out, that was the one for Mr. Lara. He couldn't believe it! Lara told Mario that he had sung his song better than any one else."[8] It is surely no exaggeration to say that to this day, Mario Lanza's recording of "Granada" remains the standard by which all performances of this song are judged.

Lanza reported for work at MGM on *Kiss of Fire* on 20 October 1949. Joining him and Grayson on the set was the debonair British actor David Niven. Niven's career was in a slump and he was glad to be employed, even if it meant working on a lightweight Mario Lanza movie. Despite the obvious differences in their ethnic backgrounds, Lanza and Niven got on well for the duration of the shoot. The same, unfortunately, could not be said for the actual filming. Niven intro-duced Lanza to a new drink, Chivas Regal scotch, and he, Lanza, and J. Carrol Naish would enjoy a discreet beverage throughout the daily shoot. By four o'clock in the afternoon, Naish would often be asleep and Lanza would be feeling drowsy, but the alcohol never affected Niven. The British actor was also a great opera lover, and he and Lanza would spend many of their lunch hours listening to Caruso records in the tenor's dressing room.

Despite Terry Robinson's best efforts to keep him in shape, Lanza had clearly put on quite a few excess pounds. The tenor's eating habits were truly prodigious. Although he never looked obese in any of his public appearances, stories were soon flying around Hollywood of huge eating binges both on and off the set. Accounts of these sessions varied wildly and were always open to question. Stories of Lanza consuming twenty pieces of chicken at a sitting vied with similar reports in the news media of him consuming twenty whole ones. And did he wash down the entire meal with twenty bottles of Coca-Cola or a mere fif-teen? That depends on which account you read. Those stories, which more or less persisted throughout his career, became a very real source of annoyance to the singer, as Robinson recalled, "Mario hated it when the Press kept on at him about his weight. He wanted them to talk about his singing instead. Mario was born big—he had a 50″ chest. When he'd lose weight it wouldn't always show and the Press would keep on asking him how many pounds he had to lose for his next picture. The questions never stopped and it really used to upset him."[9]

Joe Pasternak also noticed a less-than-subtle change in the tenor's attitude to his employers. Mario Lanza had a very real problem with authority figures, one that soon manifested itself on the production of *Kiss of Fire*. He was often late on the set, sometimes arriving hung over from an all-night party, and Grayson and Niven had to scramble with pots of strong black coffee to get him in shape for the shoot. At other times Lanza would deliberately fluff a take, with the resulting overtime going to an increasingly appreciative crew of technicians and extras. If the "little people" on the set loved him—and most of them did—the studio chiefs by now were starting to wonder what they had gotten themselves into. In time, they would all find out.

CHAPTER SIX

The Great Lanza

In addition to the operatic selections chosen for Lanza's new picture, MGM engaged songwriters Sammy Cahn and Nicholas Brodszky to write six new numbers for the production. One of those songs would eventually give the film its new title: *The Toast of New Orleans*. Sammy Cahn had already established a reputation as a superb lyricist, and his work over the years with Frank Sinatra would become legendary. For the Russian-born Brodszky, the chance to write for Lanza was an opportunity he would not treat lightly. Along with the title song, the Cahn-Brodszky team came up with two pleasant if unexceptional ballads, "I'll Never Love You" and "The Bayou Lullaby." This being an MGM musical, the songwriters also produced a couple of novelty numbers, "The Tina-Lina" and "Boom Biddy Boom Boom," the title of which really says it all. Still, all were rich in melody and all were performed with astonishing brio by the tenor. The script also called for a love song that Lanza and Grayson would perform as a duet, and it was here that Cahn and Brodszky finally struck gold. As Sammy Cahn remembered:

> Brodszky had patent leather hair and the kind of shape that if you pushed him over he would roll back up—which is good if you are going to compose. On the piano, he had a printed sheet of music—not a handwritten manuscript, but printed. No chance of changing a note with this man! It was titled "Love Theme for Mario Lanza." Could I write words for it, they asked? I started to write and what gradually came out was: "Be my love, for no one else can end this yearning. . . ." If you've only heard Mr. Lanza on a record or a tape, you've never heard him at all, because no mechanical reproduction could capture the brilliance of that voice. It scared the hell out of you."[1]

With the marriage of Sammy Cahn's magical words to Brodszky's sumptuous melody, Mario Lanza had found his theme song. Though featured as duet in the film, it was Lanza's benchmark solo performance later that set the seal on his career as a recording artist. If it can be said that every operatic tenor has a take of "La donna e mobile" in him, it is equally true that most of them nurture a desire to tackle "Be My Love." However, it remains first, last, and always Mario Lanza's song, so closely associated with him that any other tenor's attempt at it invariably fails. Indeed, the only recordings of the romantic ballad comparable to Lanza's are from crooners Andy Williams and Matt Monro, both of whom took a different approach to the song altogether. Brodszky and Cahn eventually received an Oscar nomination for their song, but it lost on the night to Jay Livingston and Ray Evans' "Mona Lisa."

Between 5 December 1949 and 17 February 1950, Lanza completed all of the soundtrack recordings for *The Toast of New Orleans*. His singing was robust and spirited throughout, though the picture does not contain any defining vocal moment from the tenor. He would have to wait until his studio date with Ray Sinatra four months later before immortalizing "Be My Love." Lanza's first recording at MGM for the new picture was the *Butterfly* duet, which he sang with Kathryn Grayson under the orchestral direction of Johnny Green, MGM's resident classical conductor at the time, with Georgie Stoll handling the more popular fare. Both were Academy Awards winners—Green for his scoring on *Easter Parade* and Stoll for his work on the Gene Kelly/ Frank Sinatra classic *Anchors Aweigh*. Stoll, with one exception, would go on to work on all of Mario Lanza's films in the years that followed.

Still wary of opera's appeal to a mainstream movie-going audience, the truncated *Butterfly* duet was presented in part as a comedy routine for Lanza and Grayson, with the tenor spending most of his time struggling romantically with his costar on stage. It was certainly not the way Puccini had intended it but at least the two stars were getting to sing a sizeable chunk of classical music, something unheard of before Lanza. The scene works best in their close ups together, with Lanza emanating all of the sexual magnetism that had already begun to thrill moviegoers the world over.

A return to the opera stage was briefly considered in 1950, when Lanza was approached by Victor de Sabata, artistic director of La Scala opera house in Milan, and Gaetano Merola, general director of the

San Francisco Opera. Both men were interested in having Lanza appear in productions of *Andrea Chenier*, and for a time the tenor did consider traveling to Italy. In April, however, Betty discovered she was pregnant with her second child and Lanza graciously declined the offer. The San Francisco engagement still remained on the table, with the added incentive that Lanza would be joined on stage by the great Italian diva Licia Albanese. Albanese was one of Lanza's favorite sopranos, and it seemed for a while that something might be arranged. In the end neither singer appeared. Instead, the fall season of the San Francisco Opera opened with a production of *Aida* with Renata Tebaldi and Italian tenor Mario Del Monaco, both of whom were making their American opera debut. Robert Weede, Lanza's old friend, sang in the role of Amonasro.

In his defense for opting out of the engagement, Lanza maintained that he needed more time to prepare for his return to the classical stage. Right now there were too many demands being made on his career: demands to appear in concert and on radio; demands from MGM for more film work; demands from RCA for more recordings. "Next year" he would be ready. "Next year" he would sing Chenier, or Cavaradossi, or Don José, or whatever they wanted. "Next year" he would do it all! Those "next year" excuses would be revisited many times over in the years that followed until, in the end, even Lanza himself began to believe them.

Mario Lanza was more than qualified to sing at La Scala or San Francisco in 1950, and there is ample evidence to suggest that he would have been sensational in the role of the doomed poet. However, the time needed to prepare for the opera would have meant a major commitment on his part, a commitment to study and immerse himself completely in the chosen role. A commitment to stay away from all the distractions that Hollywood was throwing at him daily. A commitment to turn his back on the huge sums of money he was receiving for his film and recording contracts. A commitment, in a sense, to be humble again. In those heady days of 1950, he was simply not ready or willing to take that step.

In fairness to Lanza, of course, the distractions were considerable, as Joe Pasternak recalled: "Success is harder to take than failure. He was not equipped to be very successful and overnight he became the sensation of the world. I don't think he could take it. He came to me one day with a check for $1 million royalties from his recordings. You know if a man didn't have $10 and you get a check like that, very few of them could stay sober."[2]

Pasternak's reference to staying sober was meant literally as well as figuratively. One unpleasant side effect to all the riches and acclaim that came the singer's way was his increasing dependence on alcohol. Lanza loved the sweet life and all the benefits that came with it. One of those benefits, as he saw it, was a regular supply of champagne, usually on tap for breakfast, followed by a steady consumption of beer throughout the remainder of the day. The mix was a lethal one as far as his weight was concerned, and as his waistline expanded so too did his temperament. MGM wanted a svelte movie star. Lanza saw himself first and foremost as an opera singer who happened to be taking a leave of absence in Hollywood. He further maintained that he sang better at a heavier weight than he photographed, so there was always a battle to find a happy medium between the two. In this particular war, Mario Lanza was always the loser.

On 20 March 1950 the Lanza entourage, which included the Weilers, Joe Pasternak's wife Dorothy and Callinicos, traveled on the steamship *Lorelei* to Hawaii, where the tenor was booked for three concerts at McKinley Auditorium in Honolulu. Tyrone Power and his Mexican-born wife, actress Linda Christian, en route to film Power's movie *An American Guerilla in the Philippines,* joined the group for what in effect was a working vacation. On his arrival Lanza was given the key to the city by Mayor John H. Wilson. Movie star Esther Williams—dry for the occasion—was also on hand to present the tenor with an award on stage after one of the performances. Tyrone Power was one of Hollywood's best looking leading men at the time but Lanza, slimmed down, fit and singing magnificently, was the toast of the town.

Lanza also enjoyed giving his friends nicknames. He was the "Tiger" and he had a sign put on his dressing room door that read "Don't F**k with the Tiger." Terry, who was responsible for keeping all the unwant-eds at bay, was "Terry the Terror," and Callinicos was quietly and ominously referred to as "J. P. Snake." If Costa knew about the nickname, he never let on.

The year 1950 also marked Callinicos' return to the conductor's podium. On 8 April he joined Lanza at Republic Studios to record a number of arias for a tie-in compilation album to *The Toast of New Orleans.* The *Traviata* and *Butterfly* duets were recorded three days later, with soprano Elaine Malbin providing more qualified vocal support than her movie counterpart on the two selections. Lanza's one-take recording practice was not always on target when there was a partner involved, and both selections were recorded several times. Though very young, Elaine Malbin had already embarked on a professional opera career, and everyone was pleased with her studio work with Lanza that day. In years to come, when her career in the opera house had moved forward and Lanza's had remained static, she would vigorously spring to his defense whenever condescending remarks about his supposed lack of vocal skills were brought up.

Lanza made a brief but impressive return to the stage on the evening of 22 April 1950, when he appeared at the Shrine Auditorium in Los Angeles. The Friars Club of California, a charity organization that drew on the talents of every major star in Hollywood, was staging their yearly gala, "The Friars Frolic of 1950." The list of entertainers featured that night was extraordinary. Jack Benny and Harpo Marx brought their unique blend of humor and music to the proceedings. Isaac Stern, billed as "The World's Well Known Violinist," showed why he would soon become known as the world's best. Dean Martin and Jerry Lewis confirmed their status as premier movie clowns, and the legendary Al Jolson, nearing the end of his own incredible career, had everyone singing along. Lanza, accompanied by Giacomo Spadoni on piano, appeared near the close and almost stopped the show with his powerhouse renditions of "Vesti la giubba" and "O Sole Mio." Terry Robinson, who was present for most of the tenor's concerts and virtually all of his studio recordings, felt that Lanza outshone everyone at the Shrine Auditorium that night. Ann Helming, reviewing the concert for the *Citizens-News,* concurred: "Mario Lanza singing 'Vesti la giubba' from *I Pagliacci* and 'O Sole Mio' shone brilliantly in spite of the stiff competition from older, more experienced hands. Lanza, in fact, came closer than anyone else to stopping the show cold."[3]

Lanza shared a dressing room that night with Isaac Stern, who took the time before the concert to run through his selections. The rehearsal came to an abrupt end when actor Errol Flynn stopped by, bottle of Smirnoff vodka in hand, to regale the tenor with a litany of bawdy stories. Stern, his concentration gone, grabbed his violin and retreated to the men's room to complete his preparations.

Lanza's 1950 RCA sessions were evenly divided between Callinicos and Sinatra. With Callinicos on the conductors' rostrum, Lanza concentrated on classical selections, producing two superb recordings from

Andrea Chenier and a deeply intense reading of the great *Tosca* aria "E lucevan le stelle." Sinatra took charge of the lighter fare, and it was through working with him that Lanza finally vaulted from successful movie star to recording superstar.

On the evening of 27 June 1950 Lanza, Sinatra, and the Jeff Alexander Choir joined forces at Republic Studios to record two songs from *The Toast of New Orleans*, "The Tina-Lina" and "Be My Love." Henri René was in charge of the session and, in keeping with past practices, both recordings were completed in single takes. First out of the gate was "The Tina-Lina," a song saved from utter banality by Lanza's joyous singing and the glorious high C that wraps the whole thing up. Then came "Be My Love."

Over time, certain singers develop a close association with particular songs, performances that are identified the moment the orchestra starts the introduction. Think of Gordon Jenkins' lush and lovely string opening to Nat King Cole's definitive recording of "Stardust." Or Nelson Riddle's gently swinging chart that leads into Frank Sinatra's equally fabulous take on "I've Got You Under My Skin." Just the hint of those great introductions prepares the listener for the glories that are about to follow. Ray Sinatra's shimmering-string lead into "Be My Love" joined that very select group that day in June 1950. What Lanza did with it after that was pure magic.

Golden, effortless, utterly convincing, and meltingly romantic, Lanza's recording of "Be My Love" found the singer at the absolute top of his game. The dazzling high C that brings the song to a close confirmed his status as the most exciting tenor voice in the world. Other tenors attempt the C on occasion but usually at the interpretative expense of all that comes before. Lanza treated the high note almost as an afterthought. What pulls you into the recording, what makes you feel every one of Sammy Cahn's words, what makes it in the end a bona fide masterpiece, is Mario Lanza's total belief in what he is singing. Every carefully nuanced word, every beautifully crafted phrase, is given the same level of intense commitment by the tenor. No song was too great or too small for the full Lanza treatment.

"Be My Love" went on to give Mario Lanza his first million-selling gold record and firmly established his worldwide status as a major recording artist. The record was also the first RCA Red Seal single to hit the magic million mark, a remarkable achievement in those less media-hyped days. In time Lanza would have no difficulty in surpassing even those sales. By now he was being referred to as the "man with the million-dollar voice," and any association with Caruso was hardly mentioned. All that would soon change.

One unusual performance of "Be My Love" was captured on record in November 1950 when Lanza appeared on *Hedda Hopper's Hollywood*, the gossip columnist's weekly radio show. The singer was in magnificent voice opening with a particularly thrilling "Vesti la giubba," but the version of the Brodszky-Cahn ballad that followed it had a completely different arrangement than Ray Sinatra's million-selling recording. Lanza seldom strayed from arrangements he was comfortable with, and it is unusual that he was persuaded to do so on this occasion. The show gave the impression of being broadcast live but given the accepted trickery of recordings and added applause tracks, it seems probable that the song was already in the can before the show aired. Because of its dramatic one-of-a-kind arrangement, that recording of "Be My Love" on *Hedda Hopper's Hollywood* remains a real curiosity in Mario Lanza's career.

Just about everything Lanza touched in those days turned to gold. RCA would have had him in the recording studio every day of the week if they could, and MGM was also deeply immersed in plans for his next picture. For years Lanza had pleaded with the company to consider bringing the life of Caruso to the screen, always to no avail. Studio executives admitted that the tenor could "sell" the occasional aria but the Caruso story would mean in effect an all-opera picture, unthinkable even for their box-office star. Besides, television was starting to make significant inroads on their business and movie attendance was falling daily. It was certainly not the time to be considering high-brow fare.

MGM in fact had acquired the rights to Dorothy Caruso's biography of her husband in 1949. The idea of filming the great tenor's life had been brought to Louis B. Mayer by veteran producer Jesse Lasky, founder member of Famous-Players Lasky Corporation, which later became Paramount Pictures. Lasky had produced a number of silent films with Caruso at the turn of the century, for which the celebrated tenor was paid a then staggering $100,000 per movie. In the decades that followed, Lasky had searched in vain for someone to capture the essence of the man and his voice on the screen. After hearing Lanza sing at the Hollywood Bowl in 1947, he knew he had finally found his man. By the time Lanza and Grayson had brought *The Toast of New Orleans* to an operatic close, even Mayer was beginning to think that Lasky's idea might be a good one. If anyone could pull it off, it was Lanza. The problem they all faced was how to convince a skeptical studio that such a project might actually turn a profit.

The situation was further complicated by Mayer's rapidly diminishing standing at MGM and the increasing influence of producer Dore Schary. Schary had previously worked at the studio as a writer and won an Oscar for them in 1938 for his screenplay for the Spencer Tracy classic "Boys' Town." But he soon fell out of favor with Mayer for what the latter perceived as his arrogant and intellectual notions. Mayer, very much a product of the meat-and-potatoes school of filmmaking, deeply resented Schary's lofty ideas for "quality" pictures. Their mutual dislike of one another was intense, and by 1945 Schary had had enough and moved to RKO Pictures. He was brought back to MGM three years later by Nicholas Schenk, president of Loew's, Inc., the company that had financial control of the studio. Schenk had lured him back with the promise of more creative control, and by 1950 Schary was poised to take over Mayer's job as studio chief. Mayer, refusing to deal with him on any level, offered an ultimatum to head office: either Schary went or he would. Regrettably, Schenk accepted Mayer's resignation and Dore Schary stepped into the company founder's shoes. Time would show just how disastrous that decision would be for MGM—and for Mario Lanza.

Louis B. Mayer was deeply proud of the stars and technicians who worked at his studio, memorably observing that MGM was the only company whose assets walked out of the gate at night. To Schary it was just business. People had a job to do and they all got paid very well for it. Beyond that, he just did not care. Lanza was surprised and angry to hear of Mayer's firing and immediately called him to see if there was anything he could do. Mayer, touched by the gesture, thanked him for his kindness and assured him that, despite the early retirement, he would still do all that he could to bring the Caruso project to the screen.

Lanza had crossed paths with Schary before. Following a preview of *The Toast of New Orleans*, Schary had dismissed it as a $3 million lemon, hardly the sort of comment destined to endear himself to one of the studio's biggest box-office draws. Now, with Mayer gone, Lanza made no effort to hide his intense dislike for his new boss. The feeling from Schary was mutual. He viewed Lanza as little more than an uncouth, temperamental, and overpaid opera singer who was about as far removed from Schary's intellectual circle of friends as could be imagined. But even Dore Schary was smart enough to realize that in 1950 Lanza was quickly becoming the studio's biggest money-making star, and it was tacitly agreed that both men would learn to live with their mutual animosity. Just as importantly, the Caruso project was suddenly and unexpectedly given the green light. Lanza would finally be able to live his dream by bringing the life of his idol to the screen.

Work commenced on the *Life of Caruso,* the film's working title, on 11 July 1950, several months before *The Toast of New Orleans* was released. MGM had assumed that Johnny Green would take charge of the many operatic selections chosen for the picture, but Lanza immediately made it clear that he had someone else in mind, someone who would do full justice to the greatest tenor who ever lived. Green was good—Callinicos even better—but Lanza wanted Peter Herman Adler on the conductor's rostrum. He also wanted soloists from the Metropolitan Opera Company to come on board—nothing but the very best would do for the great Caruso. Surprisingly, Schary and the board of MGM agreed, though they cautioned Lanza against any on-set tantrums and warned that the budget would be strictly enforced on the planned eight-week shoot.

In preparation for the role, Lanza headed to Ginger Rogers' ranch in Medford, Oregon, where for six weeks he underwent a rigorous training session supervised by Terry Robinson. Conditions at the ranch were far from Spartan, and Lanza was joined by Betty, pregnant with her second child, their daughter Colleen, a butler, a cook, and his public relations agent, Jack Keller, who was there to deal with all the lucrative offers that were rolling in daily. The work-out regimen prepared by Robinson was sheer torture—skimpy meals, weightlifting, and roadwork every day—but Lanza persevered and by the end of the six weeks he was forty pounds lighter and fitter and happier than he had felt in years. Ready, in other words, to embark on the performance of his career—the ultimate and supreme tribute to the man, the tenor, who had brought him to where he was today.

In this happy frame of mind Lanza returned to Hollywood where, on 17 July 1950 he and Adler made their first recording together for the *Life of Caruso.* Whether by accident or design, the one they chose for the opening session was Lanza's "lucky aria" and Caruso's signature piece, "Vesti la giubba." Lanza would sing and record this aria many times in the course of his career, but it is arguable whether he ever improved on his performance with Adler that day. It would, in any event, provide a standout moment in a film that would boast of many. The aria is featured in the Liberty Loan Drive sequence where Caruso auctions his voice for charity. The maestro on the podium in the picture was Richard Hageman, an accomplished conductor and composer in his own right, but it was Adler's hand that guided the tenor's performance.

Bandleader Irving Aaronson, who had worked with Lanza on *That Midnight Kiss*, provided piano accompaniment for a number of Neapolitan songs featured in the picture. More importantly he also contributed a new song, "The Loveliest Night of the Year," which would be sung on screen by Lanza's costar Ann Blyth. Aaronson had adapted the song with lyricist Paul Francis Webster from a popular melody called "Over the Waves." In time it would provide Mario Lanza with his second million-selling single.

Lanza's instincts to have Adler on the recording soundstage proved well founded, and the two men produced a superb body of work for the picture. Adler showed no mercy when the tenor missed a cue or fluffed an entrance, and the tenor was often berated in front of the other musicians. But the criticisms were always constructive and never for show. On 18 August singers from the Metropolitan Opera Company showed up for the recording session, and Lanza knew whatever reputation he had developed for himself was now on the line. He need not have worried. Joining him for excerpts from *Tosca* and *Aida* were soprano Dorothy Kirsten, who would play an important role in the picture, mezzo-soprano Blanche Thebom, baritone Giuseppe Valdengo, and soprano Teresa Celli. Other artists who would join Lanza in the days that followed included bass Nicola Moscona, tenor Gilbert Russell, and sopranos Jarmila Novotná, Lucine Amara, and Marina Koshetz. All expressed surprise at the tenor's natural abilities and all implored him to report to the Met for try-outs; MGM was no place for a voice of that stature and size. In a sense, however, it was already too late. Adler, for one, saw the tragedy for what it was, "Opera singers are like wild animals. They must be trained, kept in strict discipline. Ten years with the right Opera Company and no one could compare with him. But after being a star, how could he go back to training?"[4]

Adler worked with Lanza on the operatic recordings until August, when his services were needed elsewhere. Johnny Green stepped in for two sessions after that and by 18 December 1950 all recordings for the picture had been successfully completed. Lanza's singing throughout, particularly his work with Adler, was superb. In addition to the duets, twelve popular arias and six Neapolitan songs were carefully chosen to highlight the Lanza voice at its best. Everything from "La Danza" to "Torna a Surriento," "La donna e mobile" to "Vesti la giubba" was handpicked for maximum effect. "Because," one of the very few songs Lanza got to sing in English, became a hit all over again on the strength of the tenor's impassioned performance. In every way, shape, and form, the *Life of Caruso* was crafted to make Mario Lanza a superstar.

The script for the *Life of Caruso* was adapted—very loosely—from Dorothy Caruso's biography *Enrico Caruso: His Life and Death*. Jesse Lasky had acquired the rights to the story from Caruso's widow for the vastly inflated sum of $100,000. Under his subsequent contract with MGM, Lasky made sure that he would act as executive producer on the Lanza picture, though his principal concern was not merely financial. He had not waited for almost thirty years to simply hand over the project to another studio. This, to him, was more than a commercial enterprise. Lasky had worked with and admired the great Caruso himself. This was personal.

Unfortunately, while the singing was sensational and the staging of the operatic excerpts more than lived up to the lush treatment MGM lavished on its musicals at that time, the storyline itself was wanting in just about every respect. Screenwriters Sonya Levien and William Ludwig took such liberties with the Italian tenor's life that the Caruso family eventually felt compelled to institute an action against the film studio. Considering Levien and Ludwig's source of inspiration, to say nothing of the political climate of the early 1950s, it was hardly surprising that no mention was made of Caruso's common-law wife, Ada Giachetti, or the two sons he fathered with her. Instead, *The Great Caruso*, as it would become known, concentrated in fairy-tale fashion on the tenor's love affair with society hostess Dorothy Park Benjamin and the efforts of her pompous father to stand in the way of true love. In keeping with the practice of racial stereotyping at the time, American actors were saddled with broad Italian accents and forced to speak such deathless lines as "It's-ah good to see a face from-ah Naples."

In a nod to that real-life incident that occurred at the Brooklyn Academy of Music in December 1920, when Caruso was taken ill during a performance of *L'Elisir d'Amore*, the film concluded with the suggestion that the great Italian tenor expired on stage. Instead of Donizetti, however, *The Great Caruso* galloped to a musical close with Lanza, Kirsten, Nicola Moscona, and chorus singing the finale to Flotow's *Martha*—at full-voice!

As an accurate telling of the life and times of Enrico Caruso, the film failed in just about every way imaginable. Dorothy Caruso reportedly hated it, though that probably had more to do with the subsequent success of its young star than the fanciful account of her husband's life on the screen. Lanza by now was being increasingly referred to as an "American Caruso," an accolade that Dorothy Caruso found deeply objectionable. Caruso had devoted his life—*given* his life—to an unparalleled career on the opera stage. Lanza had only sung Pinkerton in *Madama Butterfly*—and a mere two performances at that. The suggestion that he was somehow viewed as Caruso's heir incarnate was highly offensive to her. It was also rumored that Dorothy Caruso wanted herself played on the screen by Joan Fontaine, though it is hard to see how she could have objected to Ann Blyth's sympathetic portrayal.

In the end, though, none of the negativity really mattered. Dorothy Caruso's grievances and the bad script notwithstanding, *The Great Caruso* was a landmark motion picture, one that captured the spirit, the very essence of the great Italian tenor through the unforgettable performance of one man—Mario Lanza. In preparation for the role, Lanza *was* Caruso: studying his mannerisms endlessly on Jesse Lasky's old silent movies, dressing like him, walking like him. *Being* him. In rehearsals with Peter Herman Adler he suffered all the criticisms, all the constructive barbs that Adler threw at him from time to time, just to be better. Just to be the *best*.

And that, when all was said and done, is what he was, for the one thing that Mario Lanza did not try to emulate in any way was Caruso's singing style. By staying true to his own voice and his own identity, Lanza delivered a larger-than-life performance that managed to capture the soul of the great Italian tenor and all he that had come to represent in classical music. In that sense Mario Lanza paid a peerless and unsurpassed tribute to his idol, one that reverberates to this day whenever the film is screened. By giving his all to *The Great Caruso*, he became by definition the great Lanza.

The Great Caruso was directed at a brisk, professional pace by Richard Thorpe. Despite Lanza's absence for twenty-one days during the shoot due to illness—thirteen of which the tenor spent with his ankle in a cast—the picture was completed on time and under budget. Thorpe's best work was behind him, notably his 1938 adaptation of Emlyn Williams' play *Night Must Fall* with Robert Montgomery, but he knew how to bring out the best in Lanza's limited acting skills, and the results showed on the screen.

Mario Lanza completed work on *The Great Caruso* on 6 November 1950, confident that if the picture proved a success it would surely be only a matter of time before MGM agreed with his plans to bring complete operas to the screen. RCA, meanwhile, quickly cobbled together a selection of eight operatic recordings that Lanza had completed earlier in the year and rushed them out on an album under the movie's title. No one seemed to care that only four of the selections were actually featured in *The Great Caruso*. The record quickly sold more than 200,000 copies on its initial release, and eventually became the first collection of operatic arias ever to sell more than one million copies. RCA enjoyed a further bonus when the curious, brought to the real Caruso by Lanza, sought out recordings by the great master himself.

By now, the Lanza's had rented a house at 810 North Whittier Drive, a beautiful home in the Beverly Hills suburbs well in keeping with the tenor's status as a world-class entertainer. The Lanza's hired an African-American cook from Arkansas, a woman named Johnny Mobley, who became an integral part of the Lanza household. "Grandma Johnny," as she was affectionately referred to, was a great lady and loved by all the family. Lanza liked to fill his house with people, though as he pointed out to Terry Robinson, it had nothing to do with any grandiose notions of super-stardom: "Mario had everyone who worked for us live at Whittier Drive. He had Mrs. Nordquest, or 'Nordie,' a nurse to help with the babies, and Marion Rigsby who helped out too. When I asked Mario why he surrounded himself with so many people he said he was an only child and he was going to have a full house of people. I was 'Uncle Terry' . . . Everybody was an 'Uncle.'"[5]

On 3 December 1950, Betty gave birth to another girl at the Cedars of Lebanon Hospital. This time the family opted for a name that reflected the Lanza heritage and the child was christened Ellisa, after Mario's beloved grandmother, whom he adored. Ellisa's godparents were singer Andy Russell and his wife, Della, longtime friends of the family. Lanza confided in Terry Robinson that he had a crush on the blonde and glamorous Della, a small infatuation that manifested itself in an amusing way later on. Andy Russell had a hit recording in the late 1940s with "Besame Mucho," and Lanza used to tease him by saying that he would record a better version especially for Della. True to his word, Lanza did just that two years later, and it remains one his very best and most romantic recordings.

Tony and Maria Cocozza, meanwhile, had moved to California to be near their son, and for a time everyone lived at the house on Whittier Drive. It was not an ideal arrangement. Betty liked her mother-in-law, but there was always a sense of quiet friction between the two women. Lanza, after all, was Maria's only child and no woman in the world could ever fully live up to her expectations for him. Lanza eventually solved the problem by renting a home for his parents at Crescent Drive. Terry Robinson, who was genuinely fond of the Cocozza's, moved in with them. The house became a family stopover whenever guests such as Callinicos or Peter Herman Adler were in town. Lanza liked to share his deep sense of family with his friends and professional colleagues, and few objected to the arrangement.

Mario Lanza now looked to 1951 secure in the knowledge that his greatest triumphs were still to come. Under his present contract with MGM he was still committed to two more movies, and Joe Pasternak was already making plans to bring the Sigmund Romberg operetta *The Student Prince* to the screen. Lanza loved the score, and everyone agreed it would provide a tasteful musical counterpoint to the all-opera content of *Caruso*. In a life ultimately filled with what-might-have-been moments, however, none would prove more telling, more dramatic, or more costly to Mario Lanza's career than his involvement with *The Student Prince*.

CHAPTER SEVEN

Glory Days

In preparation for the release of *The Great Caruso,* Columbia Concerts lined up a twenty-two-city concert tour of the United States for Lanza and Callinicos. The tour was scheduled to commence in Scranton, Pennsylvania, on 16 February, but Lanza had gained weight in the two-month lay-off since completing *Caruso;* too much, it was felt, for a movie star appearance at the selected concert venues. In January 1951, the Lanzas, Weiler, Callinicos, and Terry Robinson headed down to a secluded ranch house just outside Palm Springs.

On 12 January, shortly before they departed, Sam Weiler was further rewarded for his services to Mario Lanza's career when his contract was amended to twenty percent of the tenor's income plus a perpetual income from Lanza's recording royalties. Weiler would continue to invest the singer's money through a company, MarSam Enterprises, formed in their name. Weiler was the president of the company, Selma Weiler acted as vice president, and Jules Berliner, Sam's brother-in-law, was secretary-treasurer. Kathryn Reitzle, a close friend of the Lanza's from their days in Rockefeller Center, was flown in from New York to act as secretary. No member of Lanza's family acted on his behalf in the running of the company. It was an extraordinary act of faith and generosity on Lanza's part. It was also one he would bitterly come to regret later on.

Weiler also made a deal with top agent Lew Wasserman, president of Music Corporation of America (MCA), to represent the singer's interests. Wasserman assigned Arthur Parks, Johnny Dugan, and Jerry Parencheo to take care of their new client's needs. All were there to see to it that Lanza was treated like the superstar he was.

In Palm Springs Terry Robinson worked his magic transforming an overweight tenor into a movie star. According to Callinicos, Lanza had to lose at least two and a half pounds every day for twenty-one days if he was to get in physical shape for the tour. By the time they were ready to return to Hollywood, Mario Lanza was fifty pounds lighter. That mad pattern of rapid weight gains followed by Spartan dieting and grueling roadwork would be repeated many times over in the years that followed—a cruel and unnecessary lifestyle that would play havoc with the singer's health in years to come.

Terry Robinson often referred to the "Great Caruso" tour that followed as a "Lanza Bonanza." The tenor's discipline throughout was exemplary, his singing sublime. In an unusual turnaround, Lanza missed only one date on the itinerary, a scheduled second appearance in St. Louis. *Variety* headlined "Lanza Proves Hottest Draw with $177,720 Gross in 22 Concerts." The only other tours that came close to matching those figures at that time were appearances by Toscanini and the NBC Symphony Orchestra, Sadler's Wells Ballet, and the Royal Philharmonic. As a solo performer, Lanza was in a class all his own. Every venue sold out as fast as the tickets went on sale, and all of this before *The Great Caruso* had even opened.

Lanza's program for the tour was fundamentally the same as the one he would sing for his European audience seven years later (see *Discography: The Complete Film Soundtrack and Studio Recordings, 1948–1959*), though in those days, when the voice was a little freer, "Be My Love" and "Because" would invariably be included in his list of encores. A favorite word used by Lanza at that time was "fractured," one that amply summed up the effect he was having on audiences everywhere he appeared.

For a scheduled appearance at the Syria Mosque in Pittsburgh on 6 March, Callinicos was given the night off. Instead, Lanza would be backed by the Pittsburgh Symphony Orchestra conducted by Vladimir Bakaleinikoff. With the concert completely sold out weeks in advance and people still clamoring for tickets, Lanza was persuaded to open his afternoon rehearsal to a paying audience. Edward Spector, manager of the Pittsburgh Symphony, promptly placed an advertisement in the morning newspapers: "Due to the fact that the Pittsburgh Symphony Concert on Tuesday evening, March 6th, with Mario Lanza as soloist has been completely booked out, and because of the continued and overwhelming demand for tickets, the rehearsal for the concert will be open to the public at general admission prices."[1]

"Rehearsal" is probably too refined a word for what took place at the Syria Mosque that afternoon. Sensing the informal atmosphere, the audience could hardly contain themselves. When the tenor sang, everyone was quiet—not a sound. When the orchestra tried to rehearse without him, pandemonium broke out. "Be My Love, Mario." "Sing Because." It was impossible to control them and Bakaleinikoff was furious. "This is a symphony orchestra," he roared. "I insist that you be very respectful. Shut up!"[2]

For the evening performance 4100 people were seated and several hundred more stood crammed into every available space in the auditorium. Terry Robinson, who took it upon himself to help with the program sales, had never seen anything like it, an opinion shared by the music critic of the Pittsburgh press the following morning: "Mario Lanza and the Pittsburgh Symphony Orchestra rocked the Syria Mosque last night until the building itself blew a fuse or something. The Mosque was packed for the event. About the only place you didn't see a face was in the huge chandelier above the auditorium. For when you jam 4000 people into the Mosque, you are jamming. But jammed or not the auditorium cheered, and cheered and cheered and each went home singing 'Be My Love' after their own fashion. That's about the time the lights went out."[3]

Three days later the tour had moved to Columbus, Ohio. The date, 9 March, also marked Terry Robinson's thirty-fifth birthday.

We were in Columbus, Ohio, and Mario happened to be singing there on my birthday. Mario wanted to give me a party but I told him that if he got a chance on the encores, maybe he would sing "Because." I love that song. Anyhow, when he came out for the encore after the concert, they were all calling for "Be My Love" or "O Sole Mio." Mario stopped them and made a little speech: "Ladies and gentlemen that man you see selling the programs there? That's my friend Terry Robinson. He's like a brother to me and today's his birthday. He has a favorite song, 'Because.' Can I do that one for him instead?" The whole place erupted in cheers so he sang it—just for me. When we came to town we used to have the Boy Scouts help me sell programs. We'd give them 10 cents for every one we sold, plus a donation to the Boy Scouts organization. Well, after Mario's performance that night we sold every program and he decided to make me a part of the show after that![4]

The "Tiger" repeated his impromptu tribute to his friend four days later on 13 March when he appeared at the Academy of Music in

Philadelphia, the same venue where Koussevitzky had first heard him sing a lifetime ago. It was a fabulous homecoming for a local boy made good, but one surprise awaited him at the stage door. Shortly before the concert started, Lanza was served with a summons demanding payment for breach of contract, a problem compounded by the fact that no one seemed to recognize the name on the summons, Mrs. Arthur E. I. Jackson. It didn't take long before the mystery was solved. Irene Williams, her "contract" with Lanza filed with the courts, had served notice on her former pupil using her married name. It was time to pay. The claim was eventually settled before Judge Stanley Barnes at the Superior Court of Los Angeles, with Ms. Williams pocketing a handsome $10,000 for her efforts—the first of many chickens that would come home to roost as Mario Lanza's career took off into the stratosphere.

Lanza's performance at the Philadelphia Academy that evening was one of his very best. He was acutely aware of the importance of the occasion and the deep significance of the venue. The following morning, Marion Kelley in the *Philadelphia Inquirer* observed that "Mario Lanza came home last night . . . and the old Academy of Music has not seen or heard such applause for a singer in many a day." His appearance too, matched the voice, as Callinicos recalled, "Slimmed down, vigorous and athletic in manner . . . Mario would have been attractive in any crowd. With the voice at center stage, he was truly magnificent."[5]

Ensconced in a suite at the Ritz Carlton across the street from the Academy, Freddy Cocozza held court, warmly greeting friends from the old neighborhood including Eddie Durso and Joe Siciliano, who was now on the police force. Durso drove with Lanza to the Thirtieth Street train station the day after the concert to wish him safe journey. Tragically, Mario Lanza would never set foot in the City of Brotherly Love again and that handshake and embrace between the two friends at the station would prove to be their last farewell.

Some understanding of how well Lanza was singing on the tour can be gleaned from a number of recordings he made at that time for RCA. On 12 February 1951, Lanza, Callinicos, and producer Richard Mohr made a one-day return to the Manhattan Center in New York to record three selections, all of which had been featured in *The Great Caruso*. Each song was recorded in a single take and each in its own way was a small masterpiece. The session began with "The Loveliest Night of the

Year," the song that would give Lanza his next million selling single. The voice, soaring, supple, and powerful, was simply fabulous—the recording as fresh today as when it was recorded. Lanza followed it with two popular Neapolitan favorites, "'A Vucchella" and "Marechiare." If there are two better performances of these songs available on disc, this writer has yet to hear them. The beauty of Lanza's mezza-voce is heard to exquisite effect on "'A Vucchella," while his dazzling take on "Marechiare" captures all the passion inherent on that type of expansive Mediterranean song.

On 7 April 1951 Lanza and Callinicos performed at Orchestra Hall in Chicago. As usual, the crowd was ecstatic but reviewer Felix Borowski writing for the Chicago *Sun-Times* took a more jaundiced view of the evening. Where before the natural beauty and power of Lanza's voice were enough to win over the critics, his current acclaim as a latter-day Caruso was prompting even the most generous of scribes to take a closer and more caustic look at everything he did. Even Costa was not spared on this occasion.

> As a legitimate artist Lanza can make only the mildest appeal to a serious concertgoer. There can be no doubt, however, about the natural magnificence of Lanza's voice. A splendid voice is a notable asset but alas, there is more to singing than voice. Where an aria asks for the high notes at the end and some kind of dramatic impact in the middle, Lanza roars throughout like the Bull of Bashan. . . . All this is a matter of pity for there are moments when Lanza did not shout and his mezza-voce, as in Scarlatti's "Già Il Sole Dal Gange" and "Pietà, Signore," was ravishing to hear. Given musical sensitivity above all better taste, even a better vocal production, then Saturday's artist might well achieve an approach to Caruso. . . . "Vesti la giubba" brought the house down. The concert was shared by Greek pianist Constantine Callinicos, who played no fewer than seven solos with tremendous pounding of his innocent instrument and often with an astonishing inaccuracy of execution.[6]

The "Lanza Bonanza" tour concluded on 13 April 1951, which was also Mario and Betty's sixth wedding anniversary. Lanza, flush with money and success, promptly bought Terry Robinson a new Chevrolet convertible and rewarded his parents with their own home at 622 Toyopa Drive in Pacific Palisades. Robinson, who was now viewed as an integral part of the family, moved with the Cocozzas to their new home, happy to be on call whenever he was needed.

On the evening of 29 May 1951, the Lanza family headed to the Egyptian Theatre on Hollywood Boulevard for the invitational premiere of *The Great Caruso*. The forecourt of the theatre had been specially decorated to represent the year 1905, when Enrico Caruso first came to America, with gas lights and red plush velvet everywhere. Lanza had also insisted that Jesse Lasky accompany him and Betty to the screening. It was Lasky's dream that had helped make *The Great Caruso* a reality, and the tenor made sure that the old man was a special guest of honor on the night. Terry Robinson and the Cocozzas made up the rest of the Lanza party. Celebrities at the premiere included Mr. and Mrs. Arthur Rubinstein and the actress Deborah Kerr. The standing ovation that greeted the film and its dazzling star at the conclusion convinced everyone that the studio had a major hit on its hands. Dean Martin, sitting directly behind the Lanzas, summed up everyone's feelings that night: "Lanza just made the screen come alive."[7]

The Great Caruso opened to the public at Radio City Music Hall in New York, grossing $1.5 million and breaking all box-office records during its ten-week run. Radio City enjoyed the distinction of being the world's largest cinema auditorium, and newsreel photos taken at the time show lines stretching right back to Rockefeller Center. Audiences regularly broke into applause after the arias and, to Lanza's delight, attendance at opera houses increased in cities whenever the film played. *The Great Caruso* went on to become MGM's most profitable film for 1951 and one of its biggest money-makers of all time. The movie also garnered an Academy Award for best sound recording, which went to Douglas Shearer. Adler and Green received Oscar's nod for scoring for a musical picture, along with Helen Rose and Gil Steele who were nominated for costume and design. All these categories lost out to another MGM smash, *An American in Paris*.

To everyone's delight, critical reviews of *The Great Caruso* were overwhelmingly positive: "Lanza has a handsome, becoming appearance, his voice reminiscent of the rare magnificence of the lyrical emotions expressed by Caruso. He comes astonishingly close to the original."[8] "Lanza dominates the whole screen when his commanding voice sings the great arias."[9] Still, it was left to Bosley Crowther writing in the *New York Times* to touch on the obvious: "Mr. Lanza has an excellent young tenor voice and he uses it in his many dramatic numbers with impressive dramatic power. . . . Something better—much better—as a story might have been contrived for the biography of Caruso, and something more subtle too."[10]

One unexpected offshoot of the film's worldwide success was a legal challenge from Caruso's heirs in Italy. Angered by the failure of *The Great Caruso* to even acknowledge their existence, Caruso's sons Rodolfo and Enrico Caruso Jr. instituted a lawsuit against MGM for "offense to their honor and private life." The insult to their family name was further compounded when Tirenna Film Associata of Rome, in an attempt to cash in on the success of the American film, rushed into production an Italian account of the great tenor's early years. Clumsily titled *Enrico Caruso: La leggenda di una voce*, the picture starred a young Gina Lollobrigida, with Mario Del Monaco providing the singing voice of Caruso. To the family, *Enrico Caruso: La leggenda di una voce* was a travesty, a film that took even more liberties with the truth than its American counterpart, and the producers of the Italian film were soon facing a lawsuit similar to the one filed against MGM.

The courts eventually ruled in the family's favor in both actions, though it would be several years before a final settlement with MGM was reached. In 1953 the company was ordered to pay five million lire to the Caruso heirs plus all resulting court costs. Worse still, MGM was forced to withdraw *The Great Caruso* from circulation in Italy, though by that time the film had already made a fortune for its distributors. Del Monaco's take on Caruso was released briefly overseas as *The Young Caruso*, but sank without a trace soon after.

Legal wrangling aside, the Caruso family bore no ill will toward Lanza or Del Monaco. Indeed, the extraordinary success of the Lanza film was already resulting in increase sales of Caruso recordings and all the resulting royalties that came with it. Enrico Caruso Jr. was particularly aware of Lanza's personal dedication to his father's legacy and paid gracious tribute to him many years later in his richly detailed and fascinating memoir *Enrico Caruso: My Father and My Family*, "It was Lanza who made the picture a success. . . . Mario Lanza was born with one of the dozen or so great tenor voices of the century, with a natural voice placement, an unmistakable and very pleasing timbre, and a nearly infallible musical instinct conspicuously absent in the majority of so-called 'great' singers. . . . Let it not be forgotten that Mario Lanza excelled in both the classical and light popular repertory, an accomplishment that was beyond even my father's exceptional talent."[11]

Perhaps the most enduring legacy of *The Great Caruso* is to be found in the influence the picture had on the careers of countless musicians. José Carreras, Luciano Pavarotti, Plácido Domingo, Richard Leech, Jerry Hadley, and Roberto Alagna—to name but a few—all attest to the impact the film made on their lives. While serious opera critics were quick to point out that the film contained only snippets of the great works—"operatic lollipops," as one of them put it—those singers recognized the visceral quality that Lanza brought to the music. Much as the purist might have objected, Lanza made the music exciting, larger-than-life and yes, very sexy. Pavarotti regularly tells of how, after seeing *The Great Caruso*, he would stand in front of the mirror and try to emulate Lanza's top-of-the-voice singing style and mannerisms. Carreras literally became an opera singer on the strength of the picture and Domingo cited *The Great Caruso* as having the single most defining impact on his decision to turn toward the classical stage. Richard Leech was just as moved:

> Football, and other such "vital" activities, rarely leave time for the typical American teenager to find his way to the world of opera, or anything close for that matter. However, when I first saw Mario Lanza on television, at the age of about fourteen, that all started to change for me. I now believe that when I stumbled across "The Great Caruso" I had found in Mario Lanza not only inspiration, but the kind of career role model that each of us seeks in our early years. It should be said that I was also blessed by falling into the hands of the best teachers I could have had, but I'm not sure that I ever would have pursued opera at all without that wonderfully romantic picture in my head of what an opera singer is, and that glorious sound in my ear of what the tenor voice can be.[12]

The Great Caruso may not have been high art but its influence has reached far beyond anything its young star could ever have envisioned during his lifetime. However, Mario Lanza, without whom *The Great Caruso* would not have been possible, let alone successful, pocketed a mere $55,000 for his efforts. With the tenor's ever-increasing power at the box-office, that "golden contract" with MGM was starting to look less than the sum of its parts.

With "Be My Love" topping the music charts across the globe and *The Great Caruso* proving a similar draw in movie theaters everywhere, Mario Lanza was without question the most famous tenor in show business. He was also the most famous *singer* of grand opera in the world, a subtle distinction that many critics failed to recognize when they gleefully pointed out his vocal shortcomings on his classical recordings. It was left to Callinicos to state what should have been more obvious at the time: "When you do a role on stage, you have to work at it so thoroughly, so much, and you have to look into every moment and every word you sing. Having done it on stage, you can then recall the feelings when you record it. Now, Mario didn't have that experience . . . that background. . . . That's why [he] was so great and why I admire any operatic recordings that he did."[13]

With Lanza in an expansive mood and *The Great Caruso* set to break box-office attendance records around the world, Weiler negotiated a contract with D'Arcy Advertising, Inc., for the tenor to appear in a weekly radio series, *The Mario Lanza Show*, which would be sponsored by the Coca-Cola Company. Lanza would be paid $5300 for each program, from which Weiler would take his twenty percent plus a further $500 for his duties as "producer." Given that Weiler knew little or nothing about producing a radio show, the clause should have been viewed as a suspect addition to the contract. But Lanza, who was making more money at the time than he had ever dreamed of, did not see fit to question it. The contract also called for Lanza to be responsible for overtime costs and any last-minute cancellations, all of which would add a further drain on his income.

The "Coca-Cola Show," as the series was often referred to, had the benefit of a thirty-five-piece orchestra made of some of the best session men in the business. The quota was a good ten or so less than the usual make-up for the tenor's RCA sessions but the Lanza voice was so persuasive, so overpowering, that the shortfall was not apparent to the casual listener. Ray Sinatra took charge on the conductor's rostrum, though Lanza would eventually bring Callinicos on board to work with him on the operatic and Neapolitan selections.

Joseph Di Fiore was first viola player for the series and also contributed to many of the tenor's RCA's recordings, including "Be My Love": "Lanza's voice was beautiful. . . . He was not only a singer, but also an artist. He had a natural aptitude and I don't think it had anything to do with his training. His middle and upper register were absolutely gorgeous. He never strained his voice and he never cracked on any of his top notes. Never! He was essentially a lyric tenor—he sang more like Tito Schipa than Caruso. We seldom went over time on his recordings because he would do things on a single take."[14]

Di Fiore's comment that the Lanza voice was a lyric one was essentially true at the time. In just a few short years the voice would grow considerably darker and even more powerful, a true dramatic tenor ideally suited to the opera stage. But in the early 1950s it had a lightness of tone that was appropriate for the type of material the singer was tackling then. Lanza also had an innate sense of how to control the volume he produced, depending on the occasion. The recording studio was very different to the concert hall and the singer's love affair with the microphone—how to use it to his best advantage—was known and admired by all the musicians who worked with him. His recording of "I'll Be Seeing You" is a good example of how he was able to switch from full vocal strength to sweet, lyrical softness, almost in an instant. The word "new" at the close of the song is delivered with focused power, followed in a breath by a soft mezza-voce on the pick-up line "I'll be looking at the moon" that takes the song to its conclusion. It was, in its own way, quite unique, something that no other classically trained tenor has ever been quite able to match, let alone surpass.

In all, sixty-six episodes of *The Mario Lanza Show* were broadcast between 10 June 1951 and 5 September 1952, the first seventeen on CBS and the remainder on NBC. The body of work produced by Lanza during that period—everything from opera to pop to Neapolitan songs to show tunes to classics from The Great American Songbook—was unparalleled. All performances were pre-recorded at the Radio Recorder Studio in Los Angeles, with an applause track added in for the actual broadcast.

The format of the weekly program featured four selections from the tenor, two from his guest, and two orchestral interludes from Sinatra. No male singer other than Lanza was ever featured on the series, and the tenor never sang a duet with a guest on the show. Canadian songstress Gisele MacKenzie was the weekly regular, though Rosemary Clooney, Kitty Kallen, Ginny Sims, and several other popular vocalists of the day stepped in from time to time when MacKenzie was unavailable.

Given that none of Mario Lanza's recordings for the Coca-Cola series were ever intended for commercial release the standard of performance achieved by the tenor during that two-season series was astonishing. There is a moment in every great artist's career when the gods bless his talent, a moment when everything he touches is sheer perfection. Frank Sinatra's time came in the late 1950s when, working with Nelson Riddle, Billy May, and Gordon Jenkins, he recorded a collection of popular masterpieces for Capitol Records in Hollywood. For Lanza, his golden years in the studio undoubtedly came at the time of the Coca-Cola Show sessions. Moving with consummate ease between Cole Porter and Giuseppe Verdi the one week, Victor Herbert and Luigi Denza the next, Lanza produced a body of glorious, dazzling performances that made *The Mario Lanza Show* the most eagerly anticipated radio program in America. The range and diversity of singing styles produced each week would have intimidated the most seasoned professional, but to Lanza it was just good music, all worthy of his fullest commitment.

Lanza was constantly criticized in his career for his failure to commit full-time to the classical stage. But listening to the effortless and multi-faceted singing produced each week for *The Mario Lanza Show*, it is not hard to see why he remained in that state of musical suspension. No other singer—before or since Mario Lanza—was able to handle that degree of crossover with such consummate ease. For the most part, the popular selections came off best, the tight schedule often resulting in a slightly rushed performance of the operatic arias. But there were gems there, too, including a deeply moving "Lamento di Federico" from Cilea's *L'Arlesiana,* an exquisite "Cielo e mar!" from *La Gioconda* and, as always, a thrilling "Vesti la giubba" from *I Pagliacci*. With the more popular fare, he proved consistently why he was selling more records at the time than Frank Sinatra.

His take on Porter's "What Is This Thing Called Love?" is a model of refined diction, polished phrasing, and gorgeous tones. "Valencia," "Day In, Day Out," "Love Is the Sweetest Thing," and "La Danza," to name just a handful of classic Lanza performances, literally explode with the sort of joy so synonymous with his singing. And his tasteful reading of such classics as Noel Coward's "I'll See You Again" and Oley Speaks' "Sylvia" offered a sharp rebuttal to those who felt that the tenor was only comfortable singing at the top of his admittedly magnificent lungs. Virtually the entire American Songbook was covered on the series, though curiously Lanza never got to sing any of George Gershwin's peerless ballads—brother Ira's lyrics to Jerome Kern's "Long Ago and Far

Away" being the closest he came to it. Ray Sinatra contributed a new song for the series, "A Kiss," which Lanza sang better than its composer could ever have imagined, and his exhilarating and deeply passionate performance of "When You're in Love" reportedly moved the song's lyricist, singer Frankie Laine, to tears.

Lanza's program of songs invariably called for him to deliver some of those famous top notes to his audience and he seldom disappointed. *The Mario Lanza Show* opened and closed each week with "Be My Love" and his dazzling high C at the end never failed to thrill. There were times, admittedly, when he was asked to hit notes that when heard today seem rather tasteless—an absurd and wildly overwrought finish to "The Desert Song" being an example—but those occasions remained the exception rather than the rule. At the conclusion of *The Mario Lanza Show* the tenor signed off by wishing his listeners "the very best of everything in life always." At that golden moment in his career, that just about summed up all that he himself represented.

Mario Lanza's recordings for the Coca-Cola series would eventually provide a treasure trove of peerless recordings for RCA, the full extent of which has not been exhausted to this day. The sessions were always approached with the utmost care and the recording sound quality captured throughout the two seasons was superb, some of the very best in the tenor's career. When listened to today, transferred to compact disc by RCA from the original masters, the performances from the Coca-Cola series offer ample evidence of a great talent at the very peak of its interpretive and vocal powers.

On 27 June 1951 Lanza was also presented with a gold disc from RCA Victor for sales in excess of one million copies for his hit single "Be My Love." Lanza's parents attended the ceremony, along with conductor Ray Sinatra and columnist Hedda Hopper. Hopper was there at Lanza's invitation and the expense of rival gossip columnist Louella Parsons. The studio chiefs, who had wanted both women photographed with their bankable star, were less than pleased. Lanza was simply repaying a favor to Hopper, but Parsons felt snubbed, and the singer seldom received a positive word from her in her newspaper column after that. Given the complete absence of any real talent from either woman, it is remarkable to consider the influence Hedda Hopper and Louella Parsons exerted over the studios in those days. By 1951 their power was starting to wane, but even then neither was to be underestimated.

A decade earlier, Parsons had used all her wiles to try and persuade the producers of *Citizen Kane* to destroy all prints of Orson Welles' masterpiece before its world premiere. The film was reputedly based on the life of Parsons' employer, William Randolph Hearst, and whatever Hearst asked for he usually got. Luckily for the sake of cinema history he failed, but it was not from any lack of effort by Ms. Parsons. Hopper was no saint either, more famous for her colorful hats that for any real contribution she made to show business history, but she was generally more sympathetic to the tenor and his problems than her colleagues: "Hedda Hopper was one of Mario's dear friends. . . . She was married to a baritone, DeWolf Hopper. Mario knew him as the 'whisky baritone' and he'd have all his shots of whisky before he sang. Of the press, Hedda Hopper was probably Mario's champion. He could do no wrong with Hedda."[15]

Lanza surprised a lot of people in Hollywood later when he singled out three people who played significant roles in his rise to stardom. His comments were made at the Photoplay Magazine Gold Medal Award Dinner held at the Coconut Grove Room in the Ambassador Hotel in Los Angeles. Terry Robinson was there and recalled the impact his friend's words had on at least one other great singer present that night.

> One of the greatest awards in Hollywood at that time was the Photoplay Magazine Award given to the best actor and the best actor and voted by the fans—the people who buy the tickets and go to the movies. . . . Mario won it in the male category, Doris Day in the female. When Mario went up and received his award, he thanked three people that helped him with his career. He thanked the writer, Hedda Hopper, his producer Joe Pasternak. . . . and then he thanked someone who was having trouble at that time with his own career. He was seated right near us and when Mario mentioned his name—Frank Sinatra—I think he almost fell off his chair! Mario had never forgotten how nice Frank was to him when he was starting out. Frank was dumbfounded and very moved by the gesture.[16]

A glance at Mario Lanza's recording schedule for the years 1951 and 1952 reveals a singer being pulled in every direction imaginable. In addition to his radio program, he was also kept busy recording for RCA and MGM. It was through working with the film studio that the impending storm clouds began to gather. Production delays on *The Student Prince* had prompted MGM to push ahead with another vehicle for their money-making star. Titled *Because You're Mine*, the project had Lanza as a famous opera star who gets drafted into the army, falls in love with his sergeant's sister, and sings a lot; not much of an advance, in other words, from *That Midnight Kiss*.

Lanza sat in Pasternak's office as the storyline was explained to him and couldn't believe what he was hearing. It was clear to everyone that this was merely a filler for the studio, a chance to keep the cash flow rolling in while *The Student Prince* was being readied. To Lanza, it was not good enough. He had expected a classy follow-up to *The Great Caruso* and instead he was being offered Caruso in the army! Pasternak did his best to placate him, assuring him that Brodszky and Cahn were already on board working on a great new song for the production. But the tenor was having none of it and stormed out of the producer's office calling the project "junk" and vowing to have nothing to do with it.

Dore Schary lost no time in reminding him of his contractual obligations. If he failed to report to the set of *Because You're Mine*, Lanza would be suspended. In the weeks that followed, fuming at being dictated to by Schary and to a lesser extent by Pasternak, Lanza retreated to his own private comfort zone. He overate prodigiously, piling on the pounds and ignoring Terry Robinson's pleas for control. By the time filming was set to commence on *Because You're Mine* in May 1951, Lanza topped the scales at an impressive 250 pounds, and the results were especially evident on the screen. It was his unique way of showing his defiance at being compelled to make the picture, but as filming progressed he began to lose weight. By the time the picture had completed its shoot on 9 February 1952 Lanza was a remarkable 91 pounds lighter. Given that movies are shot out of sequence, *Because You're Mine* opens with a slimmed-down Lanza singing an aria from *Cavalleria Rusticana*. Later in the picture, in scenes captured at the beginning of the nine-month shoot, he looks huge.

In all Lanza lost twenty-five days due to "illness," and his contract was suspended twice during filming. Director Alexander Hall did his best to keep the peace on the set but the problems were compounded by the tenor's coolness toward his costar, soprano Doretta Morrow. A cousin of singer Vic Damone, Morrow had been recruited by MGM from her successful Broadway appearance in *The King and I*, but her acting skills on the screen left a lot to be desired. She was also a very heavy smoker, which her costar found distasteful. Lanza himself enjoyed the occasional cigarette but he was always mindful of the damage it could do to his voice. *Because You're Mine* was Doretta Morrow's only film; tragically she would succumb to cancer at age forty-one in 1968. Lanza's other costars in the picture included James Whitmore, veteran actress Spring Byington, and Eduard Franz, who had also worked with Lanza on *The Great Caruso*.

The saving grace of *Because You're Mine*, as with all of Mario Lanza's pictures, was the singing. Script problems notwithstanding, Lanza was in exceptionally fine voice for the recording sessions, the first of which took place on 12 July 1951 with Johnny Green conducting. Ironically, the first song recorded that day, "All the Things You Are," did not make it to the final cut. Lanza would record Jerome Kern's lovely ballad several times in his career but never better than this take for MGM. The recording languished in the studio vaults for forty-seven years until Turner Entertainment in conjunction with Rhino Records released it in 1998 on a compact-disc compilation called *Be My Love: Mario Lanza's Greatest Performances at MGM*. It was worth the wait. Historians interested in understanding why Lanza remained trapped between classical and popular musical forms would do well to track down this recording.

The opera content in *Because You're Mine* was especially light. Lanza only got to sing two complete arias— "Addio alla madre" from *Cavalleria Rusticana* and "O paradiso" from *L'Africana*—and a duet "Addio, addio" from *Rigoletto*, with soprano Peggy Bonini providing the off-screen vocals for her on-screen counterpart Paula Corday. Lanza's deeply felt performance of Albert Hay Malotte's "The Lord's Prayer," added to the production at the tenor's insistence, was a particular standout. And his explosive performance of "Granada" featured near the close of the film showed why he was still the most exciting tenor in the world.

Brodszky and Cahn reunited for the title song, which was gorgeously sung by the tenor. His version for RCA recorded a year later would give him his third million-selling single. The song was also nominated for an Academy Award the following year but lost out to the theme from *High Noon*, "Do Not Forsake Me, Oh My Darling." Lanza also saw to it that two of his musical associates made contributions to the film: Irving Aaronson with the "The Song Angels Sing," adapted as was Aaronson's

wont from another composer's music—in this instance Brahms—and
Ray Sinatra, who contributed the lyrics to "Lee-Ah-Loo." Pleasant
songs all, each of them enhanced by Mario Lanza's complete commitment to the music and his dazzling vocal prowess.

On 6 August 1951, while *Because You're Mine* was struggling through
its disjointed shooting schedule, *Time* magazine honored the new
singing sensation by putting Lanza on their cover. Under the heading
"Million Dollar Voice," the Lanza career was profiled by Pulitzer
Prize–winning sports writer Jim Murray, a friend of the tenor. The sub-
heading gave a clue to what awaited the reader inside: "Would Caruso
fracture 'em in Scranton?" Murray, who was not credited on the article,
took a surprisingly harsh and deeply cynical look at the singer's lifestyle:
"Lanza's idea of dieting is to pile chicken legs, half-pound chunks of rare
steaks and a mound of barbecue kidneys on his plate, devour them and
then heap on a second helping." Murray even took a particularly mean-
spirited swipe at Lanza's vocal capabilities: "MGM's expert sound technicians, who now do virtually no tampering with Lanza's voice, can do
wonders with their electronic gadgets."[17] In lieu of a photograph, *Time's*
cover featured an illustration of Lanza's face, with an impish Caruso
peering over his shoulder—a not-so-subtle reminder to the music purist
just who the real master was. The artwork was created by Boris
Chaliapin, son of the great Russian bass. Terry Robinson recalled the
effect the article had on the tenor: "Sam Weiler took over the interview
with Jim Murray and Weiler cut everyone out of the story except himself. When the magazine came out, we realized the story wasn't good for
Mario but I blame Sam Weiler for that, more than Jim Murray. Mario
didn't worry about it. He quoted Walter Winchell when he said that as
long as they mention your name and spell it correctly, don't worry about
what they say about you. That was [Mario's] outlook."[18]

Lanza was also kept busy recording for RCA. On 28 September
1951 the tenor and Ray Sinatra joined forces with the Jeff Alexander
Choir at Republic Studios for a selection of Christmas carols. One of
the songs completed at the session was "Guardian Angels" with lyrics
by Harpo Marx. Terry Robinson as usual was on hand when Lanza and
Marx met to discuss the recording.

Mario had a lawyer named Larry Beilenson whose wife Gerda used to
write song lyrics. She had come up with a lullaby called "Guardian

Angels" and Mario loved it, though he couldn't believe that Harpo Marx had written the music. Mario rehearsed the song with Costa and when the Beilenson's told Marx about it, Harpo said he'd like to meet Mario. When we went over to his house, I rang the bell and a little bald man came to the door—looked like a house-man or a guy who had a shoe store. I introduced Mario and myself and told the little man that we were here to see Mr. Marx. He laughed and said "I am Mr. Marx!" Mario and I started breaking up. I think we had expected Harpo to come out wearing the wig and honking the horn! The song eventually became the one Mario would sing the children to sleep every night.[19]

Proof that the filming of *Because You're Mine* was not a complete battleground all of the time came in January 1952, when Betty and the two children surprised the now slim tenor with a birthday party on the set. Photos taken on the day belied the tensions that had preceded it, with Lanza looking happy, handsome, and completely relaxed. Terry Robinson was hired for a fight sequence in the picture, and Lanza's parents Tony and Maria had a walk-on part in a scene at a train station. Maria was even given a line to speak, in which she asks for her famous son's autograph.

But the most poignant moment in the nine-month shoot took place off camera. It came on the day a young girl visited the set, a ten-year-old girl named Raphaela who was dying of Hodgkin's disease. Her story gave the lie to claims that Mario Lanza at that time was an ego-inflated out-of-control superstar. It was a story that began with a phone call to the tenor's home in Beverly Hills, a call that was answered by Terry Robinson: "Mario was a major star and I would screen his calls. We were watching TV one evening and I took a call long-distance for Mario Lanza. It was from a nun in a hospital in New Jersey and she told me this story about a young girl, a fan of Mr. Lanza's, who was dying of leukemia. She was only 10 years old and it was her dying wish to speak to Mario. She was a young girl named Raphaela Fasano who was terminally ill of Hodgkin's disease and the hospital did not expect her to live. Mario took the call and started to talk to her."[20]

Raphaela greatest wish was to hear her idol sing her favorite song, "The Tina-Lina," especially for her. No one really thought that the world's most famous tenor could be contacted by simply picking up the phone and making a call, but Josephine Fasano, Raphaela's mother, felt it was at least worth a try. Her efforts paid off more than she could ever have imagined. Soon after their conversation Lanza decided that singing "The Tina-Lina" over the telephone to the ailing child was not good enough and arrangements were made to have Raphaela flown with her mother and a private nurse to California, with all expenses paid by the tenor. Newsreel cameras were on hand as the child arrived by plane from the East Coast, and for the remainder of her stay in Hollywood Raphaela Fasano was treated like a movie star. A visit to the set of *Because You're Mine*, photographs taken with celebrities James Stewart, Ricardo Montalban, Lana Turner, and Jimmy Durante, parties and games with the Lanza children and her picture in the newspapers—everything was done to make the child feel happy, loved, and important. On his radio show broadcast of 22 October 1951, Lanza dedicated the opening number, "The Tina-Lina," to his special friend.

In all, Raphaela spent five magical days with Lanza and his family before returning to New Jersey. Thereafter hardly a Friday night would pass without a phone call to the Fasano home from Hollywood, sometimes to just chat, other times to sing. The calls from Mario Lanza to the Fasano home continued until 30 January 1953, when the child's father informed the distraught tenor that Raphaela had passed away quietly the day before. Raphaela Fasano was laid to rest at Holy Cross Cemetery in North Arlington, New Jersey. Enclosed in the casket with her remains was a sterling silver immaculate conception medal, a gift from Mario Lanza to his young friend.

The Fasano family has never forgotten the tenor's heartfelt generosity toward the little girl. Decades after Mario Lanza's own passing, when family and friends gather each year at the Mario Lanza Ball in Philadelphia to honor the great singer, Josephine Fasano can invariably be seen among the crowd, her presence offering dignified testament to one man's kindness and generosity of spirit.

Because You're Mine finally stumbled to its fractured conclusion on the MGM lot on 8 February 1952. To Lanza's amazement, it was chosen for Britain's Royal Command Film Performance later that year, though this had probably more to do with the tenor's success in *The Great Caruso* than any sincere belief in the quality of the new picture. The premiere was scheduled for 27 October but Lanza did not attend, the first time in the event's history that the star of the picture was not present for the screening. Some viewed it as a snub to Her Majesty, but

Lanza sent his sincere apologies, explaining that his wife was pregnant with their third child and he would not leave her side. He would get his chance to make amends to Her Majesty five years later at another, more personal command performance.

Notwithstanding the on-set wars, *Because You're Mine* proved a gold mine at the box-office, Lanza was soon topping the charts again with the film's title song, and the money kept rolling in. The picture's reviews were generally complimentary, though the tenor's wild weight swings during the production were noted: "Lanza slimmer than in *Caruso*. Sometimes seems heavier. Reminder of long delay in making filming while Lanza made weight. Terrific Lanza singing. Lanza really lets his voice give out [on 'Granada']."[21] "Mario sings with all the vigor and expression that have made him one of the most popular phenomena of the modern musical screen."[22]

Joe Pasternak believed that now, with preparations for *The Student Prince* underway, all would be well once again with his truculent star. He was wrong. Unbeknownst to Pasternak, Schary, Callinicos, or Terry Robinson—unbeknownst perhaps to the singer himself—a line had been crossed between Mario Lanza and the management at MGM, a bend in the road from which there would be no turning back. Far from being on track again, the simmering feud between star and studio was soon to erupt in a manner that would shake Mario Lanza's fabulous career to its very foundations.

CHAPTER EIGHT

The Student Prince

After the endless succession of headaches encountered on the set of *Because You're Mine*, Pasternak went out of his way to ensure a stress-free ride on *The Student Prince*, surrounding his difficult star with some of the best musicians in the business. George Stoll was selected as the picture's musical director, Maurice dePackh would arrange and orchestrate the individual selections, and at Lanza's request, Callinicos was engaged to conduct the MGM Studio Orchestra for the tenor's recordings. In an effort to further diminish the likelihood of any on-set shenanigans, Pasternak signed Ann Blyth, the singer's costar from *The Great Caruso*, to the new production. Curtis Bernhardt would be the film's director, and some of the studio's finest supporting actors were also bought on board. Edmund Gwenn, best known for his portrayal of Santa Claus in *Miracle on 47th Street*, was chosen to play the prince's teacher; S. Z. "Cuddles" Sakall, the actor so delightful in *Christmas in Connecticut*, would be the inn-keeper; and John Williams would provide sterling back-up as the stuffy Lutz.

Lanza loved the role of the rebellious Prince Karl Franz, who briefly defies his royal calling to fall deeply in love with a servant girl, Kathy. And at the outset everything augured well for a trouble-free production. Screenwriters William Ludwig and Sonya Levien returned to pen the script, though their efforts this time were far less litigious. Still, in typical Hollywood fashion, MGM could not leave well enough alone and it was decided that Nicholas Brodszky would be hired to augment the Romberg/Dorothy Donnelly score with three new songs: "Summertime in Heidelberg," "Beloved," and "I'll Walk with God." Brodszky's partner on this occasion would be Paul Francis Webster, a gifted lyricist and eventual multi–Academy Award winner for such songs as "Secret Love," "Love Is a Many Splendored Thing," and "The Shadow of Your

Smile." The three new songs were hardly improvements on the Romberg originals—though "Summertime in Heidelberg" has a striking quality of its own—and "Beloved" and "I'll Walk with God" in particular would have the purists up in arms.

Lovers of the Romberg score were further incensed when Webster was engaged to "soften" some of Dorothy Donnelly's lyrics. Thus, on the "Serenade," "could my heart but still its beating" became "could I hear this song forever." On "Golden Days," "how we laughed with a gaiety that had no sting" became "how we laughed with a joy that only love can bring," and so on. The changes were small but telling and one can only speculate why the studio felt it necessary to tamper with the original score.

For a time Lanza genuinely believed *The Student Prince* would be his greatest movie: "If they thought I fractured 'em in *Caruso*, wait'll they see this one" he told Callinicos. In preparation for the recordings, Lanza and Costa rehearsed two hours every day for three weeks. Even by his own general high standard, it was soon apparent that Lanza was producing some of the best singing of his career. The first recording for the soundtrack was made at MGM on 18 June 1952, and it was a memorable one.

Many songs would be closely associated with Mario Lanza throughout his career, but to some none capture the Lanza mystique more forcefully than his recording of "I'll Walk with God." His accompanist for the recording was organist Wesley Tourtelot, who had provided the backing for Lanza's memorable rendition of "The Lord's Prayer" for the *Because You're Mine* soundtrack the previous year. The new song was certainly not the highpoint of Nicholas Brodszky or Paul Francis Webster's careers. Webster's lyrics had a pedestrian quality to them "I'll walk with God, from this day on. His helping hand, I'll lean upon," while Brodszky's melody had a stop-start rhythm that in lesser hands than Lanza's might not have worked at all. But it was what Lanza did with the song on that summer's day in 1952 that showed why he was without doubt the most exciting and charismatic tenor in the world at that time. Mario Lanza transformed the banal into the magical, and all in one single perfect take. Terry Robinson drove his friend to the studio for the recording and recalled a brief stop on the way.

Mario had me park the car at the Church of the Good Shepherd on Santa Monica Boulevard where he went once in a while. He asked me to wait at the back and went to the altar himself where he made the sign of the cross and prayed for a moment. We drove to the studio in silence and when we got to the studio he made the recording, "I'll Walk With God," with an organist [Wesley Tourtelot] in one take. He sang that song in a way that nobody in the world could ever sing it. Many years later I was called to try to help Paul Francis Webster, who had suffered a stroke. Webster had written the words to "I'll Walk With God" and he had more Oscars in his house than any I've ever seen. I asked him about the song and he pointed to the Oscars for all the songs he'd helped write. He told me that his biggest income came from "I'll Walk With God," sung by Mario Lanza.[1]

On 24 June 1952 Lanza reported for rehearsals on the set of *The Student Prince*. It proved to be a short working day. In his discussions with director Bernhardt, the tenor was asked to hold back in his approach to the title role. This, after all, was the story of a stiff, upper-class Prussian prince who autocratic manner is gradually softened by his love for a poor servant girl. It was not the story of a singing truck driver or a larger-than-life singing star from the back streets of Naples. More restraint was called for from the tenor if the picture was to work at all. Lanza, as Callinicos observed, reacted as though he had been gored and promptly walked off the set.

In the weeks that followed Lanza stayed away, refusing to return unless Bernhardt was replaced. Pasternak—with a firm nod of approval from Dore Schary—declined. Curtis Bernhardt had done nothing wrong, and with the battles from the set of *Because You're Mine* still fresh in everyone's mind, Pasternak and Schary were reluctant to make any concessions to their temperamental singing star. Perhaps if everyone had realized the impasse that was about to follow, more efforts would have been made to resolve that initial dispute, but no one was in any mood at that time to compromise.

With the help of Terry Robinson, Lanza had shed most of his excess weight in preparation for filming *The Student Prince*, but in the weeks that followed he gradually began piling the pounds back on. Several attempts were made to get the singer back to the film set, all to no avail, and Lanza's contract was suspended on 14 July 1952. Finally, in an attempt to break the impasse, Terry Robinson drove Tony and Maria Cocozza to Schary's office, where they met with Pasternak and Loew's representatives Eddie Mannix, Ben Thau, and Nick Schenck. With production of *The Student Prince* at a complete standstill, everyone agreed that something had to be done to get Lanza back to work. Lanza was a big star, but he was not bigger than the studio. The next move was up to him.

Following a hurried family conference, Lanza agreed he would return to the set, though the first priority was to complete the soundtrack recordings. On 29 July 1952 Lanza and Callinicos reunited at the MGM studios for three songs, one of which would set the final seal on the future of *The Student Prince* debacle. Lanza began the session with a peerless performance of the "Serenade," one of his conductor's favorite recordings. Like most of the body of work recorded from the Romberg score, it was completed in a single take. Lanza's restraint and control on this beautiful song was quite remarkable. Every word, every phrase was carefully judged and judiciously placed as the romantic melody soared to its glorious conclusion. This was not Mario Lanza singing but a heartfelt plea from the prince, Karl Franz, to the servant girl Kathy.

Ann Blyth also joined the tenor for an equally lovely "Summertime in Heidelberg," but something very curious also occurred in the studio that day. Sandwiched in between these two numbers Lanza sang one of the other new songs written for the production, "Beloved." In a peerless recording session, the likes of which he would never surpass, Mario made one small vocal miscalculation that would eventually lead to the final shutdown of the *Student Prince* production.

Long since buried in the MGM vaults, Mario Lanza's July 1952 recording of "Beloved" finally saw the light of day in 1998, when it was included on the Turner/Rhino compact disc *Be My Love: Mario Lanza's Greatest Performances at MGM*. It makes for a fascinating listening experience. All the vocal poise of Karl Franz is abandoned for what the tenor recognized was a passionate declaration of undying love. He felt that even Webster's lyric demanded that caution be thrown to the wind: "If this be madness, then call it madness. I only know I'll never rest till you are mine." It wasn't that Mario Lanza sang "Beloved" badly—few singers today could even begin to compete with his intense performance here—it was that he sang it *as* Mario Lanza. It jarred. It was different. It was out of place. It was *not* the student prince.

Terry Robinson, who was there with Lanza in the studio that day, remains a fierce defender of the tenor's approach to the song. This, after all, was a man telling a woman he loves her passionately: "You are my life, my love, my all!" But there was another way that Mario Lanza could have sung the song—another way he *would* sing the song that would eventually find its way to the soundtrack of the film. But not, alas, before disaster had struck.

The remaining sessions for *The Student Prince* unquestionably resulted in the single greatest body of work ever produced by Mario Lanza in the recording studio. Everything from the plaintive "Golden Days" to the richly romantic "Deep in My Heart, Dear" to the rousing "Drink, Drink, Drink" was stamped with the Lanza voice to such a degree that the score remains indelibly linked to him to this day.

The real problems began when Lanza reported back for rehearsals on the MGM lot. Listening to the playback of "Beloved," director Curtis Bernhardt had the audacity—as Lanza saw it—to suggest that perhaps a less passionate approach was called for here, a little less Lanza and a little more Karl Franz. Terry Robinson watched the confrontation from the sidelines: "Curt Bernhardt, who always carried a little baton, didn't like Mario's recording of 'Beloved' because it was too emotional and he said that to Mario. What Mario wanted Curt to say was 'My God, I never heard anything like that!' Instead, he asked Mario to do another take, and Mario said 'You sing it! There's no Prussian who can sing with the heart of an Italian. I'm gonna make love to this woman tonight. This is what I'm telling her in the song, Goddammit!' And he stormed out."[2]

Lanza was more than prepared to accept criticism of his acting, but his *singing*? Even by MGM's overbearing and authoritative standards this was something new. In an attempt to restore some sanity to events that were quickly spiraling out of control, Dore Schary made arrangements for Lanza to consult with psychiatrist Dr. Augustus Rose at the UCLA Medical Center in Los Angeles. One wonders if the irony of Lanza being sent to a psychiatrist by the very company that had caused so much of his rage was not lost on the troubled singer. In any event, he agreed to go, and Terry Robinson drove his friend to the meeting.

Dr. Rose had helped Judy Garland and other troubled stars that were going through tough times, and the studio wanted Mario to have this consultation with him. I waited outside while he talked with Mario so I don't know everything that went on in the consulting room, but I heard Dr. Rose use the word "megalomania." He said Mario was suffering from megalomania. That was his diagnosis. But Mario didn't take offense. On the drive home afterwards he told me that he and Dr. Rose spent a lot of the time talking about opera. Rose was very knowledgeable in that area. But Mario had heard a lot of things said about him over the years and this was just one more.[3]

Some of the company he kept at the time did not help Lanza's troubled state of mind. Actor-singer John Carroll had a ranch in the Hollywood Hills, and Lanza spent much of his time there drinking and complaining of his treatment by MGM. Carroll had had his own run-ins with the studio and provided a sympathetic ear, but the excessive drinking sprees were not helping either man to get his professional life in order.

Despite the very best attempts of family and friends to get him to return to work, Lanza continued to stay away from the MGM soundstage. On 4 September 1952, production of *The Student Prince* was officially cancelled. Lanza had been paid $8333.32 by MGM for *The Student Prince* and the studio did not have one scene in the can to show for it. Lew Wasserman of MCA met with Schary to try and resolve the dispute but nothing came of it. Finally, with a lawsuit hanging over his head, Lanza sat down with Schary in his office on 14 September to try and iron out their difficulties. The meeting did not last long. Terry Robinson, sitting in the outer office with Schary's secretary Richard Handley, heard the shouting begin almost immediately. Schary had kept a list of all the tenor's misdeeds and accused him of failing to maintain the studio's image of how a star should look and behave. Lanza's replies were all but unprintable. Later, pale and shaking in the car on the drive home, Lanza confided to Robinson that he would not be returning to the set of *The Student Prince*.

On 19 September 1952 MGM filed suit against its box-office star in the U.S. District Court seeking $695,888 in special damages (money actually lost on the production) and $4.5 million in general damages to cover prospective losses to MGM through the cancellation of the picture. The company also sought to reinforce that clause in the tenor's contract that prevented him from singing in concert, making recordings, or singing on the radio for the fifteen month duration of his contract, or until the dispute was settled. The court saw no reason to deny their claim.

On 21 September Lanza responded to the studio's lawsuit in a letter to Ben Thau at Loew's, Inc., claiming that he had not in any way been guilty of any breach of the terms and conditions of the contract. Furthermore, he was "ready, willing, and able" to honor all the terms of his contract and to return to the set of *The Student Prince* as requested. Assuring them of his best intentions for a speedy resumption of work, Lanza signed off by writing his signature in letters almost six inches high. In its own curious way, the florid signature gave much insight into the tenor's troubled state of mind at that time. In truth he had no intention of ever making the picture, at least not while Schary and Bernhardt were still on board.

The difficulties were further compounded when Lanza had an unexpected parting of the ways with Sam Weiler. Financial reports from MarSam had indicated the tenor's finances were not as healthy as they should be. Weiler had made a number of bad investments. Given the huge sums of money he had been pocketing from his client's career, Lanza was in no mood to forgive. By the time the singer's letter of 21 September was sent to Loew's, Weiler had been replaced by Fred Matsuo. The next time Lanza and Weiler would meet would be in court.

One pleasant interlude took place during this troubled time. George London had mentioned to Lanza that Jussi Björling would like to meet with him next time he was in Los Angeles. Björling had actually tried out for the role of the great Caruso in the late 1940s before Lanza had locked down the part, and he greatly admired Lanza's singing. The feeling was mutual. Lanza had never forgotten that evening in 1940 when Björling had thrilled his audience at the Met with a stunning performance as Manrico in *Il Trovatore*. Their subsequent get-together in Beverly Hills was actually a reunion, though the Swedish tenor could be excused for not remembering the brash young man who had shaken his hand fourteen years earlier. Accompanied by Terry Robinson and an executive from RCA, Björling and Lanza spent a relaxed afternoon regaling each other with colorful stories from the diversified worlds of grand opera and Hollywood. The memories were shared over a bottle of Chivas Regal scotch, and by the time Björling took his leave both tenors were pleasantly intoxicated. Björling, if anything, had a worse drinking problem that Lanza and would tragically suffer a fatal heart attack at age forty-eight in 1960, one year after Lanza's own passing.

In the end, despite all the promises and all the reassurances, Mario Lanza chose not to return to MGM and *The Student Prince*. The one bright spot in the dark months that followed came on 12 December, when Terry Robinson drove Lanza to the hospital to see his first-born son—and the Lanza's third December baby. Betty joked that her husband was always talking about the writer Damon Runyon, which was how Damon Anthony Lanza came to have his name.

The Lanza's were now living at 500 Bel Air Road. In January 1953, the owners of their previous accommodation at 810 North Whittier sued for $17,000 in damages, claiming missing items and holding the singer responsible for an illegally erected eight-foot fence and the installation of exterior wiring without the owner's permission. The matter, which received much negative publicity for Lanza in the papers, was eventually resolved when the tenor paid more than $9,000 in full settlement of the claim. Terry Robinson had his own explanation for why the singer was often sued for damage to properties: "Every house they rented the Lanzas got sued because Betty would cover the pool or a fishpond to protect the kids. She would knock holes and put gates on the stairways so the kids wouldn't fall down. Every piece of furniture had rubber around it so the children wouldn't hurt themselves. Betty was a mechanic. She could fix anything. Mario couldn't fix a thing, even put trains together for the kids, and neither could I."[4]

Mario Lanza had now been officially unemployed for four months, with no offers of work he could accept, and no end in sight to his dispute with MGM. Weiler's mismanagement of his finances was the hard icing on a very stale cake. To make matters worse, the IRS had also presented him with a bill for back-taxes in excess of $200,000. In just one short year, Mario Lanza had gone from being the most sought-after and employable singer in to the world to someone who could not get paid for singing for his supper, even if he had wanted to.

RCA did find one way around the dispute with MGM. Although Lanza was prevented from making any new recordings, there was still a vast pool of glorious material sitting in the vaults at the Radio Recorder Studio in Los Angeles, recordings that had been made for *The Mario Lanza Show* and that could, with a little doctoring, be issued on disc by RCA. That source, as has been noted, provided a wealth of future record material that still continues to produce "new" Mario Lanza recordings to this day.

In fairness to MGM, they viewed the lawsuit primarily as a means to get their star back to work. He was the one who walked away, and something had to be done to bring him to his senses. What Schary, Pasternak, Schenk, Thau and all the suits at Loew's failed to fully appreciate, however, was the depth of Mario Lanza's rage against their authority and what he perceived as their complete lack of appreciation for his talent. The standoff remained deadlock until 10 April 1953, when MGM finally conceded defeat and terminated its contract with the tenor. The following month Lanza agreed to the company using his peerless recordings for a new production of *The Student Prince*, one that would now be made without him. To the very end Joe Pasternak had entertained the belief that Lanza would return to the set, and at one point there was even speculation that Pasternak's earlier discovery, Deanna Durbin, might be lured out of retirement to join him for the picture. It was not to be.

As part of the settlement, Lanza agreed to record "Beloved" the way Bernhardt had felt the song should have been sung in the first place. On 20 May 1953 the tenor and Callinicos returned to the MGM studios for one last recording. The session was completed in one hour and forty minutes and produced one of Lanza's very finest recordings, superior in every way to the earlier version. The singer's control was masterful, with the all the pathos firmly kept in check. To this writer at least, Mario Lanza's 1953 recording of "Beloved" captures the very essence of the man as a truly great romantic singer. No matter how good the tenor's operatic recordings were—and most of them were excellent—all of them could be compared favorably or otherwise with those of his peers in the classical world. With a performance like "Beloved" he stood alone. No other popular tenor ever brought such intensity, such extreme commitment and depth of feeling to songs like this. "Beloved" may have inadvertently led to a major confrontation on the set of *The Student Prince*, but in a perverse way it was almost worth it for the quality of performance Lanza brought to the remake that day in 1953.

The Student Prince went before the cameras later that year with the young British actor Edmund Purdom playing the role of Prince Karl Franz. Pasternak, with an eye on the huge profits *The Jolson Story* had brought in seven years earlier, knew that an actor miming to another man's voice would work if the songs and the singer were good enough. For *The Student Prince* they were. The film has a lush, rich feel to it, with all the great MGM production values brought to bear on it, though there was little that could be done to improve the hackneyed storyline. Purdom, who had been discovered by MGM in Laurence Olivier's touring production of *Anthony and Cleopatra*, certainly acquitted himself well in the title role. Ann Blyth's singing matched her acting skills, but for some reason she became a blonde for her role as Kathy. Much of the film's charm came from its supporting cast of Edmund Gwenn, "Cuddles" Sakall, and John Williams, and even viewed in today's more cynical climate the picture is still very easy to sit through. What eventually lifted it way above the norm was the missing star, billed in the credits as "The Singing Voice of Mario Lanza."

Years later, Purdom recalled the experience of working to the great recordings: "His voice was a simply fabulous voice to act to. It was an absolutely tremendous experience. I used to have the playback on the set going absolutely flat out. It was enough to make you sweat, just listening to the voice, particularly at a very high level."[5] Purdom would later marry actress Linda Christian, who was then wed to Lanza's good friend Tyrone Power.

The final, sad irony of the saga of *The Student Prince* came with the film's eventual choice of director. With all the delays incurred on the project, Curtis Bernhardt had moved on to another production, leaving the *Prince* to be completed by Richard Thorpe, the man who had work so amicably with Mario Lanza on *The Great Caruso*. Lanza reportedly never saw the film, believing that the public would never accept another actor lip-synching to his singing voice. When the picture proved only a modest success at the box-office the following year, the tenor felt fully vindicated.

Mario Lanza was now free to do whatever he wanted. Sign a contract with another movie company. Make more recordings. Go on tour. Even return to the opera house. But something had happened to him after the yearlong battle over *The Student Prince*—something that had attacked his confidence and was continuing to gnaw away at his psyche. First MGM, then Weiler, and now the IRS bleeding him for money—everyone was turning against him. The logical thing to do, of course, was to get into shape and go back to work, but logic played little part in Mario Lanza's troubled mind in those early months of 1953.

Callinicos did manage to drag him back to the recording studio on 17 June, when the two joined forces at Republic Studios to record a song Costa had written for Lanza called "You Are My Love." Lanza had been putting off recording it for some time, but at last he agreed to it and the date was set. "You Are My Love" was a pleasant song with a simple lyric by Paul Francis Webster: "You are my love, you're the sun in my sky, you're the love song that I will remember." Lanza's performance was a good one, with little indication of the singer's troubled state of mind coming across in the two takes he made that day. Three other songs were also recorded at the session, "If You Were Mine" and "Call Me Fool," two typically overheated 1950s ballads, and "Song of India." It was on the last that Lanza created another peerless recording. Working to a fabulous lyric by Johnny Mercer, Lanza transformed the Rimsky-Korsakov melody into something quite extraordinary. Singer Mel Tormé in his memoir recalled hearing the song on the car radio one day and being deeply affected by the tenor's performance and Mercer's beautiful words: "Then I hear the song that only India can sing, softer than the plumage on a black raven's wing." Through the magic of his voice and his deep interpretative skills, Lanza brought all the drama, all the passion, and all the color of India to that recording. It remains one of the very best he ever did. Remarkably, more than two years would pass before the great voice was successfully captured in a recording studio again.

Lanza kept Callinicos on a coaching retainer but the singer did little work in the months that followed, choosing instead to overeat, drink to excess, and rage at the injustices he had felt had befallen him. The fact that he could have turned everything around by simply going back to work did not seem to occur to him. Lanza was so ensconced in his feelings of persecution and insecurity that he became a virtual recluse in his Bel Air home. Few outside his family besides Callinicos and Terry saw him in those days. In just one short year the most famous tenor in the world had managed to fall off the face of the planet.

Lanza's depression grew so intense at one point that it almost cost him his life and that of Terry Robinson:

> Mario's favorite car was a Cadillac and he wanted to take it out for a drive one day. Mario usually didn't like to drive but he was really in a downer so we went out on the road. . . . Mulholland Drive, where it's narrow to the top and then there's an awful drop back down. So we're driving and he's complaining about everything going wrong in his life, and I noticed

he was driving faster and faster. I tried to calm him down but he kept driving faster and there were no seat belts in those days. Mario said "Are you afraid? If we go off this cliff your name will live forever. Mario Lanza and his best friend killed in a car crash!" I told him sure, I was frightened and I begged him to slow down. Eventually he pulled over and when I got out to take over the wheel I saw that the front left tire was losing air fast. If that tire had blown when he was driving like that we would have died. But there was one funny side to the whole thing, though I didn't see it at the time. Mario and I were both nonmechanical and it took us almost an hour to figure out how to change the tire. When I drove home that night my hands were shaking. That was the scariest time of my life with Mario.[6]

The one thing that Mario Lanza could have done and *should* have done at that time was to make that long-awaited return to the opera house. Thanks to the Coca-Cola recordings, royalties were still pouring in from RCA and indeed his biggest selling album of all time was still to come. What was needed now, what Callinicos and Robinson desperately tried to have him do, was for Lanza to refocus and get back in shape, mentally and physically. With the proper commitment and approach, Lanza could have readied himself in six months for an appearance on the classical stage, though it would have to be at one of the lesser opera houses in the United States. Rudolf Bing was now the general manager of the Metropolitan Opera Company, an autocratic dictator who had nothing but contempt for classical artists who sold their talent to Hollywood. In Bing's eyes, Lanza was little more than a glorified pop singer. *The Great Caruso* notwithstanding, Lanza would be lucky to audition for a part in the chorus. The similarities between Bing's iron hand at the Met and Dore Schary's vicelike rule at MGM were not lost on Mario Lanza.

One man who was staking out a fine career at the Metropolitan Opera House was George London, who came to visit. He was shocked at what he saw. Mario Lanza was thirty-two years old, singing better than ever—when he chose to—and behaving like a man whose life was all but over. In later years, Lanza would listen to London's recordings endlessly, thrilled that his friend had achieved such success on the opera stage. But to Callinicos, Lanza's pride was always tinged with regret, a deep-rooted sadness that he himself had not followed the same course. London did what he could in 1953 to encourage his friend to reclaim his classical career, but Lanza could not be reached. Film, radio, television, and concert offers came in almost daily but Lanza continued to ignore them all, chained, as Costa observed, by inner compulsions that were incomprehensible to those around him.

Lanza's business affairs resurfaced briefly in the public eye on 25 August when, though his attorney Robert Kopp, he filed suit at the Santa Monica Superior Court against Sam and Selma Weiler for negligent handling of the singer's finances. Lanza cited four reasons for his claim, which sought payment of $255,863.37 in damages: (1) Weiler had made investments with his own money, hanging on to them if they turned out well, but paying himself back out of Lanza's bank account on grounds he made the investments for Lanza if they lost money; (2) he drew commissions for himself from Lanza's special bank account, and then collected again from other accounts in which Lanza had funds; (3) he paid off expenses of his own interests on the premise that they were Lanza's expenses, with checks on Lanza's account; and (4) he paid himself bigger commissions that he had coming under the succession of contracts he had with the tenor. For good measure, the tenor also offered a bizarre reason for his failure to appear before the cameras on *The Student Prince*. According to a statement made by Lanza, the singer's attorney, Milton A. Rudin, had stalled production on the picture to shut off his income until he had found a way to remove Sam Weiler from the payroll. Lanza's claim against Weiler was compelling but few, if any, believed his excuse for the problems surrounding *The Student Prince*.

Weiler counter-sued with a demand for outstanding payments he claimed were due to him. The dispute was eventually settled with Weiler walking away with five percent of the tenor's royalties for the remainder of his life. That five percent manifested itself into substantial sums of money in the decades that followed, but to Sam Weiler it was not enough. Remarkably, he sued the Lanza estate unsuccessfully for additional sums on a number of occasions over the years and even stooped at one point to selling copies of the Coca-Cola shows before being held in check by a lawsuit. Decades after Mario Lanza had passed on, Sam Weiler would continue to receive his five percent royalty payments from RCA, a staggeringly handsome pay-off for his initial investment in the singer's career.

The final indignity to a miserable year came on 28 December 1953 when Lanza and Callinicos traveled to Warner Bros. Studios to record selections from *The Student Prince*. In keeping with RCA's practice of having the tenor re-record music from his MGM films, arrangements were put in place for Lanza to make a complete set of new recordings from the Romberg score, this for an RCA Red Seal release. The songs chosen for the session that day would represent both sides of Lanza's artistry: the softer, mezza-voce approach to "Summertime in Heidelberg" and the full-voiced tenor of "I'll Walk with God." In place of Ann Blyth, who was contracted to another label, RCA engaged the services of Gale Sherwood, who was serving at the time as a latter-day singing partner to Nelson Eddy. In addition to a duet with Lanza on "Heidelberg," Sherwood would record her own solo, the popular "Come Boys!" Henri René was one of two A&R representatives in charge of the session, while Manie Sacks took charge of the overall production.

The studio was booked from eight to eleven o'clock and all that was accomplished as far as the eventual *Student Prince* album was concerned was one recording. The RCA recording logs show one take of each song from Lanza, one of the introduction from Callinicos, and one solo from Gale Sherwood. Only the orchestral overture from Callinicos made it to the final release. Lanza had been drinking heavily again and his vocal tones were distressingly poor. Costa remarked later that he couldn't even begin to compare it to the beautiful sounds his friend had created for the MGM soundtrack. It was the first time that the great voice had failed him in the recording studio, and Lanza felt more humiliated than ever.

In the end, RCA through Manie Sacks negotiated with MGM for the use of the original, peerless soundtrack recordings to *The Student Prince*. By then Gale Sherwood had moved on to other work, but Sacks had recently signed a young soprano named Elizabeth Doubleday to the company's RCA label. Doubleday, who like Lanza hailed from Philadelphia, had studied with Rosa Ponselle and Sacks had been looking for a suitable project for her. She was eventually brought in to overdub her voice on two selections: "Summertime in Heidelberg" and "Deep in My Heart, Dear." In another piece of studio trickery, the RCA engineers repeated a section of Lanza's soundtrack performance of "Deep in My Heart, Dear" twice—at the beginning of the song and again at the close after Doubleday's vocal had used as a bridge in the middle. It was seamlessly done, however, and the tenor's voice was so compelling that hardly anyone noticed the deception.

Elizabeth Doubleday never made another successful recording for RCA, but she did return to the matter of her contribution to *The Student Prince* several decades later. In the mid-1990s, Doubleday sued RCA for additional royalties she felt were due to her. To RCA's surprise, she won her action though the settlement was not too substantial.

The Student Prince became the first direct movie soundtrack recording by Mario Lanza to be released by RCA. It also became one of the first soundtrack recordings in history to sell over one million copies, and it remains to this day the finest of all Lanza's albums. One has only to listen to "Golden Days," "I'll Walk with God," "Serenade," or "Drink, Drink, Drink"—virtually any track from the album—to understand why Mario Lanza at that time was the most beloved tenor in the world.

The Student Prince remains Mario Lanza's best-selling album and has never been out of circulation since it was first issued in 1954. Interestingly, although the RCA recording is in mono, the original sessions were captured in three-track stereo. Three songs in this format were finally issued on compact disc on the 1998 Turner/Rhino *Be My Love: Mario Lanza's Greatest Performances at MGM* and revealed a remarkable improvement in sound quality. Sadly, the Turner/Rhino disc was later withdrawn due to threatened litigation by BMG, who own the rights to Lanza's recordings on disc. It is to be hoped that the complete three-track stereo Lanza sessions from 1952 will be issued in their entirety before much more time has passed. The quality of the tenor's performances deserves nothing less.

Mario Lanza now faced a new year with no steady work on hand, no plans to return to the concert stage, let alone the opera house, and the sobering realization that his once fabulous voice had been found wanting in the recording studio. His only income came from record royalties and, while that would sustain him for a time, the moment had clearly come to put his life in order again. Having that knowledge and being able to do something about it, though, were two very different things. Through stark necessity, 1954 would see his return to center stage but it would not be in the way that he, or anyone else for that matter, quite imagined it at that time.

CHAPTER NINE

The Long Road Back

The hope that Mario Lanza might redirect his talents back to the classical stage resurfaced briefly at the beginning of 1954. In February, following a discussion with the tenor, Callinicos paid a visit to his friends Irving and Alexander Broude, music publishers who were based in New York. Costa had suggested that the tenor might like to work with some of the lesser-known arias from seldom-performed operas like Cilea's *Gloria*, Leoncavallo's *Zaza*, and Mascagni's *Iris*. The operas themselves might have fallen out of favor but there was still a wealth of good material in them that someone with Lanza's vocal skills could reintroduce to the public. In all Costa collected thirty-five tenor solo arias, and for a time the new music seemed to rejuvenate the singer. Every day, from ten to twelve o'clock each morning, the two would work diligently to the point where even Costa began to think that his friend had beaten his depression. Once again he was wrong. After a few months, Lanza put aside the scores and drifted back to his old ways.

The difficulties in the Lanza household were brought into sharp focus because Betty was expecting again. This time it would be a May baby. Whatever problems Lanza had with his own psyche—and there were many—he was never less than a loving and devoted father. He worshipped his children to distraction and would serenade them to sleep with gentle renditions of some of their favorite songs, Harpo Marx's "Guardian Angels" being a particular favorite. A new addition to the household thrilled him but it also served to remind him that something had to be done to kick-start his career again.

At the end of February, the IRS filed claim against the tenor in the amount of $169,153.00 for back taxes. Betty, in her own severe depression with a difficult pregnancy, took to her bed. In time, Betty Lanza developed an unhealthy reliance on pills and sedatives of every nature, often turning to them for relief from her husband's turbulent lifestyle. The lien on her husband's earnings also resulted in the inevitable staff lay-offs in the household, the final indignity as far as she was concerned. She was wrong. Worse was to come.

Lanza's problems were further compounded by that fact that he was still without proper management. As the months rolled by it soon became evident that the singer's recording royalties alone would not suffice to keep all the expenses at bay. Without telling her husband, Betty Lanza had Terry Robinson take one of her fur coats to Al Teitelbaum, self-styled "furrier to the stars" who had a business at 414 North Rodeo Drive in Beverly Hills. The Lanzas and the Teitelbaums had known each other on and off for a number of years, and Lanza bought many of his wife's best pieces at the furrier's shop. Now it was time to see if Teitelbaum would return the favor by buying back some of the merchandise.

News of Mario Lanza's fall from grace was everywhere in the media those days, but even so Teitelbaum was shocked. Robinson explained that everything had been downhill since Lanza had parted with Weiler. He didn't trust anyone and he did not seem to know how to get his career moving again. Maybe Al could help? Teitelbaum agreed to do what he could, but the call would have to come from Lanza himself.

Several days later the two men met, discussed the singer's difficulties, and speculated on where and how his career should move from here. Before he left the house that afternoon Al Teitelbaum agreed over a handshake to become Mario Lanza's new manager. Why or how anyone thought that a Beverly Hills furrier would be an appropriate person to handle the career of the most famous—and to some the most infamous—tenor in the world is not clear. But to Teitelbaum's credit he lost no time in getting to work.

The first thing that was taken care of was the contract, which was signed on 1 May 1954. Teitelbaum immediately became the beneficiary of a perpetual ten percent of all earnings generated by Mario Lanza, though remarkably the contract did not call for the furrier to actually find any work for his new client. Teitelbaum immediately brought attorney Greg Bautzer on board, in return for which Bautzer's firm, Bautzer and Grant, would receive a perpetual right to five percent of the tenor's gross income. That word "perpetual" also figured in Teitelbaum's choice of tax attorney J. Everett Blum, who settled for a perpetual right to two and a half percent of the singer's income. Like Teitelbaum, his contract did not actually guarantee any services to the tenor. Last to join the new Lanza team was business administrator Myrt Blum, Jack Benny's brother-in-law, who jumped on board for a guaranteed five percent of Mario Lanza's income. When all was said and done, and with his settlement with Sam Weiler thrown into the equation, Lanza was accountable for a staggering thirty-five percent plus of his gross income in perpetuity to people he hardly even knew. Had Mario Lanza realized the full impact of Al Teitelbaum's managerial skills he might never have bothered to work again, but the Lanza of 1954 was in no mental or physical state to quarrel with anything or anyone who appeared have his best interests at heart.

Lanza also took the time to renegotiate his contract with RCA, though he rejected out of hand a guarantee of $1 million for one hundred recordings. Some questioned whether it was a smart move. Lanza hadn't recorded anything in a year and RCA opted to release his recordings on their Black Seal label, the net result of which was smaller royalty checks. The release of the Coca-Cola recordings on disc helped, but even that was of little immediate benefit to the singer. In a casual moment, Lanza had signed over the rights to the Coke Shows to the Teitelbaums for value received, a situation that would take decades to resolve before the rightful ownership of the recordings reverted back to the singer's children. Lanza was a very great singer but his business sense was practically nonexistent. Still, to his adoring public at least, the great Lanza voice was hitting the record stores again through the Coke Show recordings and *The Student Prince* soundtrack LP.

On 19 May 1954, Terry Robinson and Mario Lanza repeated their drive-to-the-hospital ritual for the last time when they went to greet the singer's newborn son. Lanza and Betty briefly toyed with the idea of calling him Mario Lanza Jr., but Robinson wisely counseled that the pressure of having such a name might be considerable. As he grew older the questions leveled at him would be inevitable: "Do you have your father's voice? Can you sing?" and so on. In the end, wiser heads prevailed and the newest member addition to the Lanza family was named Marc. In a pattern that repeated itself one last time, Lanza merged his business dealings with his private life when he invited Al Teitelbaum and his wife Sylvia to be the child's godparents. Both willingly accepted.

The following day MGM held a press showing of *The Student Prince* and a month later the film was released to the public. Reviews were mixed, with most of the praise going to Lanza's singing, and the picture did not fare well at the box-office. Costume dramas set in fairytale kingdoms had lost most of their appeal by 1954, and although Lanza claimed that picture died because no one would accept his singing voice coming from another actor's mouth, the real truth of the film's failure was to be found somewhere in between.

Lanza was also briefly considered for the title role in Paramount Pictures' planned retelling of another old operetta chestnut, Rudolf Friml's *The Vagabond King*. Kathryn Grayson had already signed on to the production but her former costar was in no physical or mental condition in early 1954 to undertake such a project. In the end the role of *The Vagabond King* went to the Maltese tenor Oreste Kirkop, who had a good strong singing voice but little on-screen presence. The picture quickly faded from view and Kathryn Grayson retired from films soon after.

What brought Mario Lanza back to the public eye was an appearance on Chrysler Motors' new entertainment series *The Shower of Stars*, which was scheduled to make its television debut on 30 September 1954. Through negotiations handled by Teitelbaum, Chrysler agreed to pay the tenor $40,000 for an appearance on the season premiere, plus a bonus of two new cars. Lanza's initial delight at the huge pay deal—a very considerable sum in those days for what would be a relatively brief appearance—soon turned to dismay when he was informed that the money would be used to offset his tax arrears. He was in no position to quarrel, however, and by August he had begun rehearsing again with Costa.

The format of the show, which would be broadcast live on CBS, called for the tenor to sing three songs of his own choosing and appear in a comedy sketch with comedian Fred Clark. Two fading show business luminaries, the husband-and-wife team of Betty Grable and Harry James, would join him on the program. Lanza hated the idea of appearing on television, which at the time was looked down upon by most of the major stars in Hollywood, but he had finally run out of options. He had to start making money again and the offer from Chrysler Chairman L. L. Colbert could not be ignored.

In preparation for the appearance, Lanza checked himself in to the Las Encinas Sanitarium in Pasadena, ostensibly to lose weight. In fact, he had been drinking far too heavily and had even resorted to taking the drug Antabuse to help curb his addiction. The sanitarium was a popular retreat for stars who needed to dry out between pictures and Lanza found some comfort in seeing Spencer Tracy strolling the grounds during his stay.

The rehearsals with Callinicos that followed went well, and in truth the singer was in excellent voice. But if his drinking had brought under control, the tenor's weight was still too high. As the date of the broadcast approached, his inner fears began to take hold. What if he was unable to sing on the night? What if the fabulous top notes were found wanting? What if he missed a cue and couldn't start over? In his troubled state of mind, he began to see himself as an object of ridicule in the eyes of the countless millions who would tune in to see if he still had what it took to be a great singer. His weight didn't help either. Topping the scales at well over 220 pounds, this was the heaviest he had ever appeared in public. True, there had been wild fluctuations in weight on the set of *Because You're Mine,* but back then he had at least looked fit. After two years of inactivity, two years of excessive bingeing on food and alcohol, he looked the worse for wear. Clearly, it was time to panic.

Lanza would later point out that some of the acts on the *Shower of Stars* prerecorded their selections but it was a lame excuse, as the other contributions had been newly prepared for the broadcast. The problem with Lanza's contribution was how he went about his own peculiar brand of deception. Instead of preparing some new material in the studio with Costa, the tenor opted to mime to previously recorded selections, all of them made at a time when his spirits and his voice were more at one with his career: "Marechiare," "Vesti la giubba," and "Be My Love." Because the singer was scheduled to perform on the television show without a chorus, a recording of his signature tune with orchestra only had to be located. That problem at least was solved when a cut from the Coke Show broadcasts was pulled in time for the broadcast. The problems that followed would not be so easily dealt with.

For two weeks before the show was set to air, Lanza and Costa worked meticulously every day to master the miming. Callinicos was secretly appalled that his friend would stoop to such unnecessary trickery, but there was little he could do about it. Nothing he could say or do would convince Lanza to show the world that the great and truly prodigious voice was still intact. Lanza would appear live on *The Shower of Stars* but his voice would not.

Lanza did fairly well on the night miming to the old recordings, but one really has to wonder if he ever truly believed he would get away with the trickery. For one thing, all his costars and the technicians on the set knew what was going on. It would surely be only a matter of time before it became common knowledge in the media. As it transpired, the deception never got past the broadcast. At a reception following the show in the Beverly Hills Hotel, Lanza was surrounded by well-wisher's, including Hedda Hopper sporting one of her ubiquitous hats, Nicholas Brodszky, Al and Sylvia Teitelbaum, Betty Lanza, looking radiant in an elegant gown, and Terry Robinson. The problems started when columnist James Bacon asked Lanza why he opted to mime to four-year-old recordings. Lanza panicked and promptly denied it, claiming that he had made the recordings a few days before the show. CBS unwisely entered the fray by siding with the singer but the lie was soon found out and the media, understandably, were merciless. Columnist Sheila Graham, who by then was vying with her colleague Louella Parsons to see which of them could be more condescending toward the tenor, headed her column with a particularly telling caption: "Mario Collects 40 G's Pay Without a Song." Jack Gould, television critic of the *New York Times*, was even more to the point when he referred to the debacle as "Zombie TV."

The publicity was just as devastating for CBS, whose own credibility had now been called into question. The following day, CBS President J. L. Volkenburg issued a statement that Lanza's doctor had warned it was impossible for him to sing. Not wanting to forego the tenor's much-anticipated appearance, CBS agreed to allow him to perform as he had. Lanza, his humiliation complete, owned up to the fiasco soon after. He was not prepared to disappear with a fight, however. He had to prove he could still sing. Four days after his disastrous appearance on *The Shower of Stars*, Lanza arranged for a brief recital in his Bel Air home. Among the list of invitees were James Bacon, Louella Parsons,

Hedda Hopper, Sheila Graham, noted music critic Max de Schauensee, and several other journalists. To add to the occasion, Lanza arranged for Giacomo Spadoni to accompany him on the piano. Spadoni, shock of white hair, French beret, and neatly trimmed and waxed mustache, made for an impressive and intimidating figure. Lanza felt that the old man brought an air of class to the proceedings, something that was not in evidence on the *Shower of Stars* performance.

The recital consisted of "Be My Love," "Vesti la giubba," and the great and demanding *Bohème* aria "Che gelida manina." Two of the songs called for high Cs and with the tenor's guests seated a few feet from him, no one would be fooled if he didn't deliver. Sammy Cahn's oft-quoted remark about how scary it was to hear the great Lanza voice at close range must have been subconsciously echoed by everyone in the room that day. He sang, as Callinicos recalled, "better than any of those reporters, columnists, soothsayers and essayists had ever heard anyone sing." They applauded Lanza to the echo and followed it up with glowing reports in their columns in the days that followed. But while Lanza had proven to the journalists he still could sing, he still had to convince his public. Six days later, CBS and Chrysler announced that Lanza would return to a new *Shower of Stars* program on October 28. This time the man and his magnificent voice would appear live and again for the same salary and the same perks.

Lanza's pride would not permit him to repeat the scandal of his first appearance on live television, and on the afternoon of the second broadcast, he rehearsed one of the two numbers chosen for the show. "Someday" from *The Vagabond King* was well suited to the tenor's lyrical style and he had sung it successfully on one of the Coke Shows three years earlier. Nothing, though, would ever compare to his singing of the song on 28 October 1954. Both performances were captured for posterity, the rehearsal take in sound only and the live version on film; both are stunning. Giacomo Spadoni was credited with taking charge of the orchestra that evening, and the old maestro is seen shaking hands with Lanza immediately following the performance. With Betty standing in the wings offering support, Lanza also sang a powerful, deeply felt "E lucevan le stelle" from *Tosca*, which earned him a rave review from Max de Schauensee. The great voice was clearly in better shape than ever and, to Lanza's adoring public, the only mystery that remained was why he had chosen to mime on the first program.

Lanza kept de Schauensee's review in a scrapbook and gave away the two Chrysler cars to business associates. Having proven to his critics and now to the world that he could still sing, he felt he had made his point. If Teitelbaum could negotiate a new movie deal, fine. If not, he would rest on his laurels, such as they were, until something befitting his talents turned up. No one even dared to mention the opera house. Director Leo McCarey did want the singer to appear in a musical version of *Marco Polo*, reportedly to costar Ann Blyth and Orson Welles. Hedda Hopper grandly proclaimed the bizarre concept as having "the finest script I have ever read"[1] but no studio shared McCarey's vision and the project never got off the ground.

The tenor also had an interesting encounter with a famous Hollywood eccentric at that time. Lanza was informed through attorney Greg Bautzer that Howard Hughes had expressed an interest in having the tenor star in a new film *Serenade* based on the popular James M. Cain novel. Like most of Cain's work, Warner Bros. owned the rights to the story. It's unlikely that the studio viewed the moody plotline as the basis for a Mario Lanza musical. But Hughes saw the possibilities of transforming it into a compelling drama for Lanza and was willing to negotiate with Warner Bros. if the tenor committed to the project.

Hughes' sense of paranoia was evident even then: he arranged for Lanza to meet him at a photography shop on Melrose Avenue in West Hollywood at three o'clock in the morning. Terry Robinson drove him to the appointment: "Mario was waived into the building by one of Hughes' bodyguards and I was told to wait in the car. The meeting went on for over 3 hours and I fell asleep. On the drive home afterwards Mario told me Howard was a great talker and he really wanted to make movies with him. There was even talk about a big musical set in Texas."[2]

Discussions with the reclusive billionaire dragged on for months. Hughes would call Lanza regularly and regale him for hours with tales of woe about some of his troubled business dealings. After a while, even Lanza grew weary of the calls: "That son of a bitch has got me worrying about *his* money!"[3] The matter finally came to a head when Louella Parsons stopped by Al Teitelbaum's store on Rodeo Drive and repeated a rumor that the real reason for the delays in starting *Serenade* was because Lanza was having vocal problems. Teitelbaum was furious and called Bautzer with a now-or-never ultimatum: either

Hughes locks in the deal or Lanza walks. Bautzer assured him an agreement would be reached, but nothing ever came of it. *Serenade* would be made but not with Howard Hughes on board.

The tide in Lanza's affairs finally began to turn at the end of 1954. On 21 December the perfect Christmas present for the entire Lanza household arrived courtesy of Jack Warner. Anxious to makes amends for his failure to see beyond the burly opera singer who stood in his office a decade earlier, Warner officially announced that Mario Lanza would star in the film version of James M. Cain's novel *Serenade*. Through terms negotiated with Teitelbaum, the tenor signed on to the production for a salary of $150,000 plus a percentage of the profits. Warner also left open the option for a second film if *Serenade* and his working relationship with the tenor proved a success.

Serenade was certainly an unusual project for a Mario Lanza musical. Cain specialized in plot lines that explored the seamier side of life, laying the groundwork for some of the most acclaimed *film noir* movies ever to be released by Jack Warner's studio. Billy Wilder's masterpiece *Double Indemnity* came first in 1944. The Joan Crawford melodrama *Mildred Piece*, which coincidentally had garnered an Academy Award supporting actress nod for Lanza's former costar Ann Blyth, followed a year later, and Cain's turgid tale of lust and murder *The Postman Always Rings Twice* capped off a winning trio in 1946. The source would have looked stranger still had anyone taken the time to study the plot of *Serenade* more closely, with its strong homosexual storyline. The book had even been banned in several European countries. Not surprisingly, that aspect of the original novel was the first to go as screenwriters Ivan Goff and Ben Roberts, who eventually took over from Warner's original scribe John Twist, struggled to turn it into more suitable family fare.

Most important, as far as Mario Lanza was concerned, was the heavy operatic content that Warner had agreed to allow him to sing in the picture. The tenor's years in the wilderness had virtually destroyed his reputation as a singer of grand opera. Four pop songs—one of which admittedly was the splendid "Song of India"—was all he had to show for his studio time and no operatic recording of any substance had even been attempted since the Coke Shows ended. Miss the second Chrysler Show and you missed everything classical Lanza had to show for himself in the intervening years—and one solitary aria was not much to have missed. The cynic might have pointed out that the method of salvation was at Lanza's command all along, but at least he was getting back to work, and at thirty-four he was still young enough to make all the right moves.

While *Serenade* was being readied, the Lanzas uprooted once again and moved to rented accommodation at 481 Merito Street in Palm Springs, a house owned by cowboy star Rex Bell. Photographs of Bell and his wife, the former Hollywood "It" girl Clara Bow, adorned the home, much to the delight of Lanza, who found the old-time movie star memorabilia fascinating. The Lanzas also had their eye on a new home in Bel Air, but with payment still pending on the Warner Bros. deal, funds to pay for it were in short supply. The opportunity to buy the house presented itself when promoter Sammy Lewis approached Al Teitelbaum with an offer for Lanza to sing at the opening of the New Frontier Hotel in Las Vegas: "Lewis said, 'What would it take to get Mario to do the show in the New Frontier?' I knew that the highest price that anybody got was Sinatra, who was getting $25,000 a week, so I said, 'Well $50,000.' And I thought that would be the end of the conversation. And he said, 'Okay, you got it.' He wanted to tie Mario up for something like six weeks but we settled on two weeks at $50,000 a week."[4]

It was a good start to the New Year. As Callinicos remarked, not even the Mario Lanza of 1951 could laugh off that kind of an offer. Lanza was less than thrilled at the prospect of performing at a gambling casino, but for someone who had been unemployed for so long, the money offered was dazzling. After his retinue of agents and representatives had taken their share, to say nothing of the ongoing lien from the IRS, he would see only a fraction of that sum. As always, however, Lanza chose only to look at the bigger picture.

The Las Vegas deal for a 4 April opening was accepted and in the weeks that followed, Lanza set to work like a man possessed. This time he would show them all. This time he would be slim, handsome, at the very top of his game. This time he would remind everyone just who the greatest tenor in the world was. With Terry Robinson looking over his shoulder, Lanza watched what he ate and surrendered his overweight body once again to a regimen of boxing, weightlifting, jogging, tennis, and swimming. Gradually, after weeks of punishment, the weight fell off and the singer looked and sounded better than he had in years. Ray Sinatra and his wife, Prima, joined the tenor in Palm Springs, and the two musicians worked over the selections for the Vegas date.

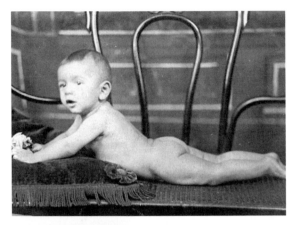

Mario Lanza as an infant.
Courtesy Terry Robinson
Collection.

Mario at one-and-a-half years old.
Courtesy Terry Robinson Collection.

Ladies' man: eighteen-year-old
Freddy Cocozza and his admirers on
the beach at Wildwood, New Jersey,
summer 1939. The lady in the fore-
front is Freddy's aunt, Hilda Lanza.
Courtesy Terry Robinson Collection.

On stage in *The Merry Wives of Windsor*, Berkshire
Music Center, Massachusetts, 7 August 1942. Lanza
is on the extreme left of the picture. Courtesy British
Mario Lanza Society.

Mario and Betty Lanza on their wedding day, 13 April 1945. Courtesy Terry
Robinson Collection.

Mario and Betty with members of the Hicks family on stage
at Chicago's Old Band Shell, 6 July 1946. The young girl in
the check suit is the tenor's niece, Dolores. Ten years later as
Dolores Hart she would give Elvis Presley his first romantic
on-screen kiss in the film *Loving You*. Courtesy Reverend
Mother Dolores Hart.

A tenor with attitude: the Bel Canto Trio at rehearsal. Left to right: Josef Blatt, pianist, Frances Yeend, soprano, George London, bass-baritone, and Lanza, circa 1947. Courtesy Terry Robinson Collection.

With Betty backstage at the Municipal Auditorium, New Orleans, for his professional operatic debut as Pinkerton in a New Orleans Opera House Association production of *Madama Butterfly*, 10 April 1948. Courtesy Terry Robinson Collection.

Elgin Watch *Holiday Star Time* radio show, 25 November 1948. Included left to right are: Dean Martin and Jerry Lewis, André Previn, Ken Carpenter, Don Ameche, Red Skelton, Frances Langford, Jack Benny, Lanza, Gary Moore, and Jimmy Durante. Courtesy Terry Robinson Collection.

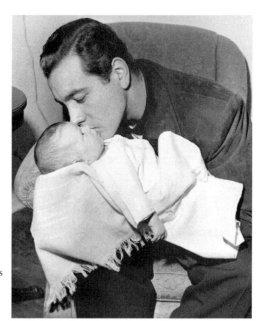

Proud father: Lanza welcomes the arrival of his first born, daughter Colleen. Courtesy Terry Robinson Collection.

The tenor and his favorite musical collaborator, accompanist and conductor Constantine Callinicos, at Lanza's first recording session for RCA, Manhattan Center, New York, 5 May 1949. Courtesy Buddy Mantia Collection.

Triumphant homecoming: Lanza and his mother join in Philadelphia's Labor Day Parade, 1949. Courtesy Terry Robinson Collection.

Outside 636 Christian Street, Philadelphia, 29 August 1949. Left to right: Antonio Cocozza, Maria Lanza Cocozza, Ellisa (Elisena) Lanza, Mario and Betty Lanza, and Salvatore Lanza. Courtesy Terry Robinson Collection.

A kiss at midnight: publicity portrait with Kathryn Grayson for *That Midnight Kiss.* Courtesy Terry Robinson Collection.

With MGM studio chief, Louis B. Mayer. Courtesy Terry Robinson Collection.

With Howard Keel on the set of
The Toast of New Orleans, 1950.
Courtesy Terry Robinson
Collection.

With Tyrone Power in Honolulu, March 1950.
Courtesy Terry Robinson Collection.

Lanza and Peter Herman Adler
discuss musical points on the
recording soundstage for *The
Great Caruso*, 23 August 1950.
Courtesy Buddy Mantia
Collection.

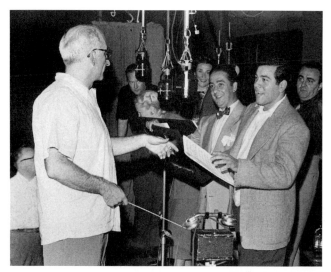

Recording session for *The Great Caruso*: Lanza, Peter Herman Adler, Giuseppe Valdengo, Nicola Moscona, Blanche Thebom, Dorothy Kirsten, and Gilbert Russell, 23 August 1950. Courtesy Buddy Mantia Collection.

Caruso redivivus! Lanza serenades Dorothy Kirsten in the *La Bohème* sequence from *The Great Caruso*. Courtesy Stephen Cutler Collection.

With Constantine Callinicos on stage at the Philadelphia Academy of Music, 13 March 1951. Courtesy Terry Robinson Collection.

Lanza and Gisele MacKenzie strike a
publicity pose for *The Mario Lanza
Show,* circa 1951. Courtesy Terry
Robinson Collection.

Perfect harmony: Left
to right, Sam Weiler,
Lanza, Joe Pasternak,
Ray Sinatra, and Irving
Aaronson (seated at
piano), 14 December
1951. Courtesy Terry
Robinson Collection.

Mario and Betty join costar
Doretta Morrow and director
Alexander Hall on the set of
Because You're Mine. Courtesy
Terry Robinson Collection.

Party at the Lanza home with Raphaela Fasano and columnist Hedda Hopper. Courtesy Terry Robinson Collection.

Lanza with his closest friend Terry Robinson. Courtesy Terry Robinson Collection.

With Sarita Monteil and director Anthony Mann on the set of *Serenade*, 1955. Courtesy Terry Robinson Collection.

Lanza and soprano Licia Albanese at the recording session for the *Otello* duet for *Serenade*, 22 November 1955. Courtesy BMG, New York.

Soprano Renata Tebaldi visits Lanza on the set of *Serenade*, December 1955. Courtesy Terry Robinson Collection.

With actress Lillian Molieri in a *Tosca* sequence outtake from *Serenade*. Courtesy Terry Robinson Collection.

The Lanza family on the Warner Bros. back lot, 1955. Left to right: Marc, Betty, Damon, Ellisa, Mario, and Colleen. Courtesy Terry Robinson Collection.

Autographing an album for British fan Joan Kesingland during a break in filming *Seven Hills of Rome*, summer 1957. Courtesy Terry Robinson Collection.

Filming *Seven Hills of Rome* with costar Marisa Allasio, 1957. Courtesy Stephen Cutler Collection.

Nightclub sequence from *Seven Hills of Rome*. Courtesy Terry Robinson Collection.

A serenade for the fans, Victoria Station, London, 14 November 1957. The lady with the glasses is Elsie Sword (née Kiss), who was in charge of Lanza's British fan club at that time. Courtesy Terry Robinson Collection.

Greeting Her Majesty, Queen Elizabeth II, at the *Royal Variety Performance*, London Palladium, 16 November 1957. Courtesy Terry Robinson Collection.

Tenor in recital: Lanza at the Royal Albert Hall, London, 16 January 1958. Courtesy Terry Robinson Collection.

Lanza resumes touring after a bout of illness, England, 1958. Courtesy John Rice Collection.

Singing in the rain, Lanza style, from *For the First Time*, 1958. Courtesy Terry Robinson Collection.

Lanza and his four children on board the SS *Napoli* during filming of *For the First Time*, 1958. Courtesy Terry Robinson Collection.

Otello death scene from *For the First Time*, 1958. Courtesy Terry Robinson Collection.

Funeral in Rome. The hearse arrives at the Church of the Immaculate Heart of Mary, 10 October 1959. Courtesy John Rice Collection.

Dr. Silvestri assists a distraught Betty Lanza into the church, with two of her children by her side. Courtesy John Rice Collection.

Mario Lanza publicity portrait, circa 1950. Courtesy Michelle Short Collection.

Screenwriter Ben Hecht dropped in for a brief visit and ended up staying a week. Like so many before him, Hecht was interested in writing an original screenplay for Lanza. The writer is probably best remembered today for his collaboration with Charles MacArthur on *The Front Page*, but he boasted an impressive number of screenplays in his own right, including the classic screwball comedy *Nothing Sacred* and *Notorious*, an elegant exercise in suspense for Hitchcock. Hecht eventually presented the tenor with an original work he cowrote with Gottfried Reinhardt called *Granada*. The script was delivered to Lanza on 17 May 1959 and was under consideration by the tenor for a future project, but by then it was too late.

Another member of the Lanza entourage in Palm Springs was Ray Heindorf, Jack Warner's choice for musical director on *Serenade*. Heindorf, who already had two Academy Awards under his belt, including his scoring for the James Cagney favorite *Yankee Doodle Dandy*, developed an immediate rapport with Lanza and respected his talent enormously. However, given the picture's extensive operatic content and Heindorf's lack of experience in that field, Lanza decided he would prepare for the classical selections with Giacomo Spadoni, with Heindorf taking care of the orchestrations.

Before anything was recorded or filmed for *Serenade*, Lanza had to fulfill his engagement at the New Frontier Hotel's Venus Room. Several days before the scheduled performance, Terry Robinson preceded the Lanza entourage to Las Vegas to set up a press conference. Palm Springs had been sweltering in 100-degree plus temperatures but Robinson was surprised to find the gambling Mecca unseasonably cool and overcast. By the time the Lanza entourage arrived at the train station on 31 March, the weather had turned from cool to cold. For more than an hour, Lanza and his family were subjected to a barrage of questions from journalists and photographers and by the time the family made it to the hotel, everyone was in a bad mood. To make matters worse, the hotel was completely booked out and the Lanza quarters were found to be too small for their unexpected nine-person contingency, which included Al and Sylvia Teitelbaum, three nurses, and a private hairdresser. The singer and his wife ended up sleeping with the baby, while the rest of the party made do with couches and folding beds. It was not an auspicious start to what was supposed to be a high-class visit, and things soon went from bad to worse.

The next morning Lanza complained of a "red throat," his term for when the voice was not feeling up to par. He blamed it on the extended interview at the station, though at first even Teitelbaum was skeptical: "My experience with Mario was that almost every time we did a recording he would always tell me his throat bothered him, 'I don't know if I can make it tonight' and so forth. So, I paid relatively little attention to it at first. But when the doctor said it, then that changed everything . . . then I knew it was for real. Mario was terribly upset. He was very upset because he could see the same thing happening that happened with the *Shower of Stars* . . . everybody's going to blame him."[5]

Las Vegas was the gambling capital of the world and bets were already starting to move that Lanza would not appear as scheduled at the New Frontier. Jack Entratter, who ran the nearby Sands Hotel—famous for its Sinatra Rat Pack parties in the decade that followed—offered odds of three-to-one that Lanza wouldn't show. Those unlucky enough to accept his bet would soon come to regret it.

On the afternoon of the concert Ben Hecht and Nicholas Brodszky stopped by and found the singer looking morose. Anxious to protect his voice, Lanza had remained in his suite and refused to attend rehearsals. The tension in the room was unmistakable and in an effort to lighten the mood, Hecht invited Lanza to join him at his suite at the Sands Hotel. The offer of a private apartment, a comforting ear, and an open bar was too good to pass up and with his throat still sore, the tenor opted to "treat" it with a selection of the finest bottles of champagne that Hecht and the Sands could offer him. By the time Al Teitelbaum arrived to prepare him for the evening performance, Lanza was past the point of no return.

On the way back to his hotel, Lanza offered assurances that he would be fine in a couple of hours. Sure, the voice was not what it should be and sure, he might have to tackle a few less demanding numbers, but that wasn't his fault. Let him rest, take it slow for a bit, and he would win over his audience, high C or no high C. Teitelbaum could hardly believe what he was seeing and hearing. In a few hours Lanza was scheduled to give a stellar performance in front of a sold-out audience, many of who had traveled from all parts of the country just to see and hear him sing. And here he was, on the cusp of a new beginning, ready to throw it all away.

Matters did not improve when the two arrived back at the New Frontier. One look at her husband told Betty Lanza that the gala evening was not going to take place. Her rage was understandable and excusable but it was also the wrong approach to take with Mario Lanza. Teitelbaum did what he could to calm the waters and encouraged Betty to take the children out for a walk while her husband rested. When she had left, Lanza, craving peace, took some of her Seconal pills and slipped into oblivion.

Downstairs in the hotel guests and journalist were already starting to arrive for the evening's entertainment. Sammy Lewis had arranged to fly in more than a hundred members of the press for the tenor's appearance on opening night and the excitement in the Venus Room that evening was palpable. As soon as he saw the look on Teitelbaum's face, Lewis knew that disaster was just hours away. A stomach pump and an oxygen mask were rushed to the tenor's suite but despite the best attempts of everyone, nothing could rouse the sleeping singer. He was gone and would not return until the effect of the pills had worn off.

As soon as it was apparent that Lanza would not appear, frantic efforts were made to find an eleventh hour replacement. Jimmy Durante, a great entertainer from the old school, heard of Lanza's plight and immediately offered to help. So too did Ray Bolger and singer Mindy Carson. It was no use. Durante walked on stage and made a brief announcement to a stunned audience of more than five hundred people that "Mario is a very sick boy. They have him in an oxygen tent, and he's unconscious."[6] No one believed him and the boos and catcalls that followed his short speech echoed long and loud into the night. Sammy Lewis took the stage and announced that drinks and meals were on the house, but the crowd would not be appeased. Coming so soon after the *Shower of Stars* fiasco, everyone in the New Frontier Hotel that night believed that Mario Lanza was well and truly finished as an entertainer—a spent-force done in by his own unpredictable and unruly behavior, with all his credibility gone.

Ironically it was probably Louella Parsons who best summed up everyone's feelings toward Mario Lanza at that time: "He suffers from an overwhelming, clutching terror that he may get up to sing and nothing will come out."[7] In a rare and quiet moment of introspection, Lanza had once confided to Terry Robinson: "God gave me a voice. It's in this throat. I'm its keeper, so I have to protect it. With you—you have a voice. With me—well, the voice has me."[8] After the incident in Las Vegas, it was clear to everyone that the voice was slowly destroying the man.

The following morning Lanza awoke to find his contract with the New Frontier had been cancelled. Singer Billy Daniels would take over the remainder of his bookings in Venus Room. Daniels was no star substitute for Mario Lanza, but at least he would show up and perform. Further indignity was heaped on the chastened tenor when the management of the hotel presented him with his bill and an order to vacate the suite. At the train station the following day, newsreel cameras captured a slim and relaxed looking singer who, faced with an onslaught of questions, pointed to his throat and tried to explain away the problem as a simple case of laryngitis. He fooled no one, and the sad end to another sorry chapter in the life of Mario Lanza came to a close as the disheartened singer headed back to Los Angeles with his family.

CHAPTER TEN

Serenade

In anticipation of what everyone believed would be a successful and highly lucrative appearance in Las Vegas, the Lanzas had placed a down payment on a new home at 355 St. Cloud in Bel Air. Now, with the Vegas trip actually having cost Lanza money, to say nothing of his reputation, concerns were raised that Jack Warner might try to pull out of filming *Serenade*, a situation that would have left Lanza in a precarious financial situation. But Warner, though clearly concerned at what happened, stood his ground and the grateful singer assured him that he would be on his best behavior throughout the shoot.

While arrangements were being made for the tenor to start recording the songs and arias chosen for the film, Lanza and Terry Robinson took a break and drove along the scenic Pacific Coast Highway. They eventually arrived in Tijuana, Mexico, where Lanza, in his usual disguise of dark glasses and a hat, strolled through the dusty town and took in the sights. They ended up in a small cantina where over a lunch of tacos, enchiladas, and beer, the singer noticed a young Mexican with a guitar. As the boy began to play "Granada," Lanza started to hum along, eventually throwing aside the dark glasses and the hat and pouring his heart into a full-voiced rendition of Augustin Lara's classic song. He was recognized immediately. Within moments the place was jammed and Lanza continued to entertain the crowd for another half an hour. Before he left, he asked Robinson for all the money they were carrying, $300, and handed it to the young guitarist.

Robinson never forgot that day. A man who had turned his back on a $100,000 engagement in Las Vegas was now singing for free in a lowly cantina in Mexico. The difference this time was that Mario Lanza was performing for his own people on his own terms. No amount of money could ever substitute for that. But money was needed a short time later when the New Frontier Hotel filed suit for just under $125,000 seeking payment for expenses incurred through the singer's disastrous nonappearance at their venue. The case was eventually settled for $13,900.

On 28 June 1955, Lanza reported for duty at the Warner Bros. studio in Burbank to begin recordings for *Serenade*. Only one song was captured that day but it was an old favorite and one that brought out the very best in the tenor: "La Danza." It would also be the first complete song that Lanza would sing in the picture. The tenor was accompanied on the recording by accordionist Dominic Frontière, who went on to enjoy a successful career as a composer for films and television, notably for the science fiction series *The Outer Limits* and *The Invaders*. In view of the extended layoff, Lanza was anxious to prove to a skeptical world that the big voice was bigger than ever. Indeed it had darkened considerably in the intervening years.

The operatic selections chosen for *Serenade* were by far the most demanding in a Lanza picture, with the singer tackling particularly challenging excerpts from *Der Rosenkavalier* and *Otello*. Some of the performance such as "Nessun dorma" would have benefited from a more thoughtful approach but for a man who hadn't sung anything of real substance in years, Lanza more than proved he had not lost his touch. His deeply felt rendition of "Lamento di Federico" reportedly moved the first-chair violinist to tears, and the voice was heard to impressive effect on the Strauss aria "Di rigori armato" and the lovely "Amor ti vieta" from *Fedora*. Equally fine were two excerpts from *Tosca* and *La Bohème,* though as a result of the film's eventual running time of more than two hours, both sadly never made it to the final print. Lanza also produced a spirited "O soave fanciulla" with soprano Jean Fenn, and what the recording lacked in subtlety it more than made up for in lung power.

The most demanding selection was a fourteen-minute excerpt from Verdi's *Otello*, which the tenor initially recorded with soprano Gloria Boh on 19 July 1955. It is doubtful that Lanza could have convincingly pulled off this piece three years earlier but the darker quality of the voice in 1955 ideally suited the part and he gave it his all. The problem was Ms. Boh. Her vocal interpretation of the distraught Desdemona was far too anemic, one that did not improve on a second recording two days later. But Lanza's take on the Otello monologue that follows the duet was superb, one of the best pieces of operatic singing he had ever done. That would be kept in the can for now while another soprano was sought for a retake of the duet.

Nicholas Brodszky and Sammy Cahn reunited for the last time on a Lanza musical with three new songs, two of which made it into the picture: the title track "Serenade" and "My Destiny"; the third song, also called "Serenade," was not used. None of the three new numbers added up to very much, though as always with Brodszky's work they were certainly melodic. Lanza's overall approach to the songs didn't help much either, with a delivery that at times was more than a little exaggerated. Indeed, if the soundtrack recordings to *Serenade* had a problem at all, it's that the singing tended to stem from an overabundance of fortissimo. Lanza was always at his most compelling when he managed to combine the sweet with the powerful—never more in evidence than on *The Student Prince* recordings—but the *Serenade* sessions prompted the tenor to head for the high Cs. Things did quiet down, beautifully, with a very sensitive reading of Schubert's "Ave Maria," and the one gentle take of the title song sung in a Mexican sequence showed how much more could have been accomplished had Lanza turned down the volume a bit. Still, if he had set out to prove the voice was stronger and more secure than ever, few could argue that he achieved his goal.

Warner assigned director Anthony Mann to helm the picture with Spanish actress Sarita Montiel, who later became Mann's wife, providing the romantic interest. Joan Fontaine played her rival for the tenor's affections and Vincent Price had no trouble stealing every scene he was in. At Lanza's insistence actor Vince Edwards, later to find fame as television's Dr. Ben Casey, was also added to the cast. Anthony Mann was arguably the best director to ever work on a Mario Lanza film, and there were few disagreements between the two men for most of the shoot. Mann had recently completed the hugely successful *Glenn Miller Story* with James Stewart, though he was probably more at home in the great outdoors, working with Stewart on a number of excellent westerns like *Winchester 73* and *The Man from Laramie*. Regardless of the genre, he knew how to bring out the best in his actors.

To many, *Serenade* shows Lanza's acting skills, such as they were, at their very best. To others, his performance is mannered and uncomfortable, though the overheated script by Goff and Roberts undoubtedly had much to answer for here. Lanza plays a poor vineyard worker, Damon Vincenti (a name change in honor of his son from the originally scripted "John Sharpe"), who is discovered singing by socialite Joan Fontaine. With a speed that only the scribes in Hollywood can conjure up, he becomes an overnight star but soon fall's victim to Fontaine's scheming ways. Sick in mind and body, Vincenti walks offstage during a performance of *Otello*, throws away his career, and loses himself and his voice in Mexico. Enter true love in the form of the very shapely Ms. Montiel, who nurses him back to health and gives him back his will to sing again. The scene in a Mexican church where the tenor regains his voice by singing "Ave Maria" is only saved from complete disaster by Lanza's sincere and deeply felt performance.

On 7 July 1955 Lanza reported for filming on *Serenade*, and no problems were reported on the set. By September, the company had moved to the town of San Miguel de Allende for the Mexican shoot. The "Ave Maria" sequence was filmed on 16 September at the church of Templo de San Felipe Neri, with Lanza miming to a recording made the month before. He repeated the performance a few days later for the local villagers, this time singing live at another church, La Parroquia, which was the largest house of worship in San Miguel. The shoot attracted a huge audience of onlookers every day, and the singer felt compelled to pay tribute to the people and the town with a brief recital.

Back in Hollywood Lanza prepared for one of the standout sequences in the picture, the scene where Damon Vincenti sings part of the passionate Act III duet from *Otello*. By this time too, Lanza had settled on his Desdemona. Shortly after noon on 22 November 1955, Lanza, Ray Heindorf, and the great Italian soprano Licia Albanese gathered at the Warner Bros. studios to record Verdi's magnificent duet "Dio ti giocondi." The closing monologue, "Dio mi potevi scagliar" would be used from the recording Lanza had made in July.

Without question, Albanese was the most acclaimed soprano Lanza had sung with. Born in Bari in southern Italy, Albanese made her first appearance on stage as Cio-Cio-San, the role in *Madama Butterfly* that would become synonymous with her name. She was also the woman who had sung a peerless Mimi to Jan Peerce's Rodolfo with the NBC Symphony Orchestra under the baton of the great Toscanini. Lanza knew there would be no time for vocal hesitation and no excuses if any mistakes were made.

The session that day proved once again what Mario Lanza's critics often tended to overlook. Before he was a movie star, before he had even considered singing in a Las Vegas hotel, Lanza had prepared first and foremost for the classical stage. Albanese recognized that the moment he began to sing, and she was enthralled:

> The quality of a voice like Mario's belongs to God . . . he had the sweetness of Gigli and the power of Caruso. He never had to repeat anything in our session. I was the one who asked to repeat because he was so good. He used his arms when he sang, to express great feeling, and he never forced the voice. Never! I get so angry today when people say it was a small voice. No! No! No! His high C was so effortless. It was so easy for him . . . so golden, so beautiful. He had a fear of the stage and I had a fear of the microphone, but he taught me so much. My heart broke when he died. Mario was coached by [Giacomo] Spadoni for our picture and he could have been the greatest opera singer. He put so much feeling into his words. There is no feeling now—only notes![1]

Lanza's fear of the stage, expressed in a candid moment to Albanese, addressed a deeper issue. The tenor was always nervous before a performance, a not uncommon experience, but his fear of singing before a live audience had more to do with the opera house than the concert platform. The opera meant interacting with his peers, answering to orchestral cues, dealing with the demands made on him from his conductor, sustaining the voice at different levels, not always of his own choosing—in short, becoming more of an artist than he was at that time. Albanese tried hard to convince him to return to the classical stage but to no avail. More work was still to be done, more studies completed before he would prove his real worth in the opera house.

Albanese knew it was an excuse, a reason to postpone what she believed was the inevitable, but she also recognized the greatness of the voice. If Lanza could sing as well as that in her presence, having virtually no operatic experience to fall back on, anything was possible. All it would take was a decision to move in a different direction, a decision that would mean change and a considerable personal sacrifice. A decision that Lanza, as yet, was not prepared to make.

Licia Albanese wasn't the only great soprano to make an appearance on the *Serenade* set. In December 1955 Renata Tebaldi stopped by to say hello and was given the grand tour. She appeared particularly taken with her famous Hollywood counterpart, as Terry Robinson recalled, "Tebaldi was one of Maria Cocozza's favorite singers and when Mario heard she was on the Warner Bros. lot he invited her onto the set. Mario didn't smoke very much—just the occasional cigarette—but he smoked a cigarette that day. Maybe he was nervous meeting Tebaldi, I don't know, but I was surprised to see him smoking. They took some pictures while she was there and then they showed her a couple of scenes from the picture. She was really charmed by him. When she saw and heard him sing 'Nessun dorma' she couldn't believe it. She was quite overcome by it."[2]

Before 1955 was out, Lanza's name was again was in the headlines, but for once the story did not concern him directly. On the evening of 27 December, the singer, Terry Robinson, and a man named Arthur Walge who acted as a bodyguard and chauffeur stopped by Al Teitelbaum's store in Beverly Hills. The place was closed but the lights were on and Teitelbaum's car was parked in its usual spot. After getting no answer to their repeated knocking at the back door, the three proceeded to the front of the building where Lanza continued to try and gain entrance. They were finally admitted by employee Al Stan and taken to see Teitelbaum, who calmly announced that he had been robbed. Lanza made a quick departure before the police arrived, but District Attorney S. Ernest Rolls ordered him to testify several months later when the matter came before the courts.

In his deposition on the night of the robbery, Teitelbaum claimed that gunmen disguised in brown delivery uniforms and brandishing guns tied up fur-cutter Stan, stashing him in a closet. They then forced the store owner to open the vault where the robbers selected more than 240 of the best furs on display, valued, according to Teitelbaum, at over $240,000. Moments later, disturbed by a pounding on the back door, the thieves made off with the merchandise leaving the furrier with a few well-placed blows as an unhappy reminder of the incident.

Teitelbaum had his entire stock insured but when he made a claim for the lost revenue, the insurance company began an investigation. It quickly became obvious that the furrier's story did not hold up. According to Teitelbaum, the noise that disturbed the robbers was Lanza and his friends banging on the back door. But the delay between their account of trying to gain entrance and the time he pressed the alarm did not jell. There was simply not enough time for the thieves to make off with such a large quantity of merchandise and not be seen by Lanza and his friends hovering around the building.

Unbeknownst to the singer and most of his associates, Teitelbaum had fallen deeply into debt and had staged a robbery with two of his associates, Clifford Vanderwyst (a.k.a. Clifford Weiss) and Claude "Woody" Wilson, as part of an elaborate insurance scam. All three were indicted and Teitelbaum was eventually convicted of conspiracy to commit grand theft and filing a false and fraudulent insurance claim. Despite appeals, the conviction was upheld and Al Teitelbaum, the man who had replaced the questionable Sam Weiler in Mario Lanza's business affairs, was sentenced to one year in prison, which he eventually served in 1959. Lanza's involvement, such as it was, in the high-profile case made headlines and he appeared twice before the grand jury in February and March 1956 to testify about the incident. He continued to stand by Teitelbaum, who remained indirectly involved with the tenor's affairs until it was time to report to jail.

Serenade premiered at Radio City Music Hall on Easter 1956. Lanza did not attend the opening, though his absence had nothing to do with any displeasure with the picture. Reviews generally were good, including one from *Newsweek,* which reported: "*Serenade* serves, if nothing else, to show that Lanza is still in possession of the God-given high C."[3] The *New York Times* applauded the fact that Lanza "was never in better voice,"[4] while *Picturegoer* observed that in the "magnificent Otello aria he comes very close to being sensational."[5] *Variety* was especially generous: "After three years away from pictures, Mario Lanza returns in better voice than ever. Many will find his Schubert's 'Ave Maria' a tremendously moving experience as Lanza sings it in an old San Felipe church to the accompaniment of an organ."[6] One review that Lanza particularly cherished came in a telegram from his friend, heavyweight boxing champ Rocky Marciano, who wrote: "*Serenade* perfectly wonderful. Loved every note. You're a real champ. When you hit 'em, they stay hit."[7]

As usual, though, when it came to Lanza, it was left to *Time* magazine to lower the tone, observing that the tenor looked like a colossal ravioli set on toothpicks, his face aflame with rich living having the appearance of a giant red pepper. The review was particularly mean-spirited, more suited to a grubby tabloid review than that of a serious journal. Lanza must have surely wondered why the magazine had it in for him, but even

Time could not overlook the obvious: "The big voice is just as big as ever, Lanza can still rattle a tea cup at 20 paces with his C and with this picture he seems sure to rattle the cash registers all across the land."[8]

Time's snide comments aside, Lanza's weight did fluctuate considerably during the filming of *Serenade*. At times he looks slim and boyish, at others bloated and ill at ease. Lanza always maintained that he sang best at a heavier weight, which meant of course that he had to struggle to lose the excess pounds if he was making a film. *Serenade* was no exception. Those wild fluctuations in his waistline were a constant source of gossip in the press and depending on his mood would occasionally send the tenor into a rage. Following one unpleasant tirade, Terry Robinson had a discussion with columnist Lloyd Shearer, one of the more sympathetic scribes who wrote about the singer's lifestyle. Shearer suggested that a psychiatrist friend of his who practiced at the Payne-Whitney Clinic in New York might be able to offer some help. Robinson knew that Lanza would never be persuaded to see him at his clinic—or "nut-house" as the singer liked to call it—but his mood had been blacker than usual and something had to be done. In the end, Betty interceded and Lanza agreed to go to New York for a talk with Shearer's friend. Everyone was careful not to mention the word clinic.

A short time later, Shearer, Robinson, and "Fred Mason," an alias that Lanza liked to use, boarded an overnight flight to New York. Lanza, who hated to fly, promptly swallowed a sleeping pill while the other two stayed awake and planned their strategy. It was arranged that they would stay at the home of Kathryn Reitzle, Lanza's former secretary and someone he respected highly. The reunion was a pleasant one, but it wasn't long before the singer was complaining about how everyone was out to get him. Later that night, the three men drove into Manhattan and Lanza was spirited into the psychiatrist's private quarters for his "friendly chat." The subterfuge did not last long. Within minutes, Shearer fled from the office pausing only to advise Robinson that the tenor was mad as hell and that he, Shearer, was heading back to the West Coast; Terry was on his own.

True to form, Lanza came storming down the hallway and out into the street, cursing Robinson and refusing to have anything more to do with him. Their friendship might have ended then and there but for the fact that Robinson was carrying all the money. Pulling his friend into a taxi, the three of them—Lanza, Robinson, and the cab driver—found their way to Nathan's Restaurant on Coney Island, where they ate hot dogs and drank root beer by the ocean long into the night. Robinson later remarked that the cabbie had better luck than the psychiatrist did in bringing Lanza back to his senses. In the end, all it took was a heart-to-heart talk by each of them about their families: superstar, weight-lifter, and cab driver, all of them brought together on a winter's night by one man's troubled soul. By the morning Mario Lanza was a new man and ready to return to Hollywood and the next round of battles in his colorful and event-filled life.

In May 1956, soon after the release of *Serenade,* Lanza returned full-time to the recording studio. It was his first major session in more than three years. RCA were anxious to capitalize on the tenor's current high profile and arrangements were put in place for him to record two albums, a number of popular songs, and several Christmas carols. First up was a project that seemed ideally suited to his talents, a collection of Broadway show tunes that would be marketed under the title *Lanza on Broadway.* Lanza's conductor for the three-day session at the Warner Bros. Studios was his old friend Irving Aaronson. He was brought on board at Lanza's insistence, much as the tenor had done for Callinicos seven years earlier. This time, however, the results were far less harmonious: "Mario was drinking heavily at the time and matters were not helped by the fact that Irving Aaronson was not a great orchestra leader. He had a little band once, but Mario wanted to help Irving who badly needed the work. He felt his voice would make up for any shortcomings from Irving. Everybody close to Mario, including Betty, tried to tell him not to do the album. But he went ahead and did it and it was his worst album. I'm pretty sure Mario knew he'd make a mistake."[9]

The selections were culled from the newest Broadway hits like *My Fair Lady* and *Carousel* as well as longer established fare such as Kurt Weill's *One Touch of Venus* and Rodgers and Hart's *The Boys from Syracuse.* Lanza had sung this type of music with great success on the Coca-Cola broadcasts but all sense of taste and musical refinement deserted him on this occasion. For once, the golden tones were strained, the singing overwrought and forced, and the top notes unconvincing throughout. Everything was sung at full-voice, with little thought for any sort of vocal polish or subtlety. Indeed, a strong case could be made that Lanza's recording of "This Nearly Was Mine" is arguably the worst performance ever captured on record by a great singer. The unedited studio take reveals the tenor muttering an epithet moments before the start of the recording, followed by an equally crude summation after the take has been completed. Clearly, this was the singing of a man at war with the world and with himself.

By the third day there were signs that some sort of vocal normalcy was starting to return. Listened to in isolation, "And This Is My Beloved" has a certain operatic grandeur to it while "On the Street Where You Live," though mannered, is perfectly acceptable in its own right. Overall though, the experience of hearing *Lanza on Broadway* in its entirety is taxing in the extreme. The performances were not helped by the decision to add reverb or an echo-enhancing effect to the finished recording, though no amount of engineering trickery could compensate for the generally dismal performance by the singer on this collection. Much of the criticism leveled at Mario Lanza in later years for his bombastic approach to certain songs undoubtedly stemmed from this body of work. Surprisingly, and perhaps sadly, the collection was a huge best seller for Lanza and RCA on its initial release.

One particular track from the *Lanza on Broadway* sessions, "You'll Never Walk Alone," was featured prominently in Peter Jackson's acclaimed 1994 film *Heavenly Creatures*. The picture, which made a star of Kate Winslet, was based on a true-life incident involving two teenagers living in New Zealand in the 1950s who shared a passion for the voice of Mario Lanza. Lanza's music is sprinkled liberally throughout the movie, one that ends unexpectedly with a gruesome murder committed by the young women. As the credits roll, the tenor's dark and somber rendition of the Rodgers and Hammerstein classic brings the proceedings to an appropriately funereal close. In one of those truth-is-stranger-than-fiction footnotes, after serving time for her crime, the character portrayed on the screen by Winslet changed her named and moved abroad. She is best known today as top-selling mystery writer Anne Perry, though whether she still listens to Mario Lanza is a moot point.

Lanza on Broadway was also a favorite record of Elvis Presley, who, as Terry Robinson recalled, visited the tenor at 355 St. Cloud around this time. The meeting was arranged through Steve Sholes, Presley's first producer at RCA.

Steve Sholes brought Elvis around to the house in Bel Air one afternoon to meet Mario. Elvis had recently signed with RCA and Steve had produced his first recordings. Steve knew of Elvis' great admiration for Mario's voice. He loved his singing, especially his recording of *The*

Student Prince. It was a very brief meeting—about fifteen minutes—but Elvis was super-polite and charming. He was a real gentleman—he called me Mr. Robinson. Through that meeting I became friends with Jerry Schilling, who traveled with Elvis, and later on I introduced him to Ed Parker, who went on to become Elvis' karate instructor. All this came about through that brief meeting with Mario in his Bel Air home.[10]

Presley also worked with directors Norman Taurog and Richard Thorpe, both of whom had close associations with Lanza. In another one of those "six-degrees-of-separation" moments, Presley's films *Loving You* and *King Creole* costarred Lanza's niece Dolores Hart: "Elvis loved Mario's voice and he knew I was related to him, but in the early stages of my career I always made a point of not mentioning who my famous uncle was. I did not want to trade on Mario's famous name and I was always discreet about it. Elvis respected that. Whenever my co-stars found out who my uncle was though, they were always surprised and delighted."[11]

The impact that Lanza and Presley had on the musical establishment was almost unprecedented. Lanza's visceral, take-no-prisoners approach to grand opera energized the medium in a way not seen since the glory days of Caruso and his influence is still felt to this day, extraordinary when you consider that he wasn't a bone fide opera star. Elvis had pretty much the same effect on a world more accustomed to the easy sounds of Perry Como and Lawrence Welk. Presley could croon with the best of them, but the abiding image of him is that of a young rocker, out to break all the rules and shake the universe. Sadly, too, the circumstances of both singers' downfall were distressingly similar. With Lanza, the downward spiral manifested itself in an overdependence on food and alcohol; with Presley it was food and drugs. And for Lanza, the decline had already begun when the two artists crossed paths in Hollywood.

During the course of their work on *Serenade,* Lanza and Anthony Mann had entered into a joint venture, which they called Cloudam Productions. A number of projects were under consideration at the time including *The Golden Voice* for Warner Bros. and a dramatic musical called *Golden Boy.* Nothing ever came of them, and Mann moved on to more action-filled projects. Lanza also entered into discussions with producer Mike Todd, whose one personally produced film, *Around the World in Eighty Days,* had recently garnered him an Oscar. Todd, who was married to Elizabeth Taylor, was interested in bringing opera to the movies for his Todd-AO wide-screen process, but he was tragically killed in a plane crash before anything could be finalized. There was also some speculation that Lanza was interested in the role of Billy Bigelow in *Carousel*, the character portrayed so memorably on screen by Gordon MacRae. But Bigelow has only two big songs in the production, both admittedly classics, and *Carousel* could hardly be deemed an appropriate showcase for Lanza's special talents.

Lanza returned to the recording studio in August 1956, this time at Republic Studios and with a different conductor, Henri René who had acted as A&R manager on some of the tenor's earlier recordings including "Be My Love." The results on this occasion were astonishing. Starting with a number of popular tunes and Christmas carols, Lanza and René then began work on an album called *A Cavalcade of Show Tunes*. The title was the only cumbersome thing about the venture, one that found the singer in magnificent voice. Terry Robinson always believed that René was the best and most sympathetic conductor that Lanza ever worked with, and the results of their musical partnership certainly bore out much of that assertion. Covering songs made popular by other entertainers, including the Allan Jones favorite "The Donkey Serenade" and Nelson Eddy's "Tramp! Tramp! Tramp!" Lanza brought his own unique vocal stamp to those evergreens. Jones may have owned "The Donkey Serenade" on film, but in the recording studio the song belonged to Lanza.

For his recordings with René, Lanza was backed by the Jeff Alexander Choir, which included singers Jacqueline Allen and Marni Nixon. Allen had provided the voice of the boy soprano seen singing with Lanza in the "Ave Maria" sequence in *The Great Caruso*, while Nixon achieved fame later on substituting for the singing voices of Deborah Kerr and Audrey Hepburn in *The King and I* and *My Fair Lady*.

A Cavalcade of Show Tunes was a magnificent return to form for the tenor, the voice all but unrecognizable from the forced and sullen singing heard three months earlier on the sessions with Aaronson. This was the Lanza sound of old, the tones fresh and supple, the top notes dazzling and free. Henri René's arrangements brought new life to such old war-horses as "Love Come Back to Me," which had a jazzy, bluesy feel to it, and "Rose Marie." The tenor's soaring high B at the close of "Only a Rose" showcased the voice at the very top of its form.

While Lanza's singing was back on target, his financial affairs were not. Debts in excess of $100,000, including tax arrears, were still pending and it was clear that another movie deal was needed if he was to bring his life back into some sort of order. That offer came from an unexpected source; one that would lure the star away from his country for what he believed would be a glorious reinvention of his troubled career.

CHAPTER ELEVEN

Seven Hills of Rome

The idea for the tenor's next picture came from producer Lester Welch, who wanted Lanza for a romantic musical to be filmed in Italy. Teitelbaum would have preferred another Hollywood picture with Jack Warner but nothing was on the table. Franco De Simone Niquesa, a representative from the Italian company LeCloud-Titanus Films, visited Lanza in Hollywood and assured him of a first-class production specially catered to the tenor's unique persona. His fee, as with *Serenade*, would be $150,000. Following contract discussions with attorneys Greg Bautzer and J. Everett Blum, Lanza accepted the offer and production of *Seven Hills of Rome* rolled into place. It says a lot about the tenor's state of affairs at the time that he signed on to the project without seeing a completed script.

Under the terms of the new agreement worked out by his attorneys, Lanza's tax arrears would be paid off through his RCA royalties over a period of several years, while the advance from Titanus would help defray some of the other debts. Ironically, the new film would be cofinanced and distributed by MGM and arrangements were already being made for Georgie Stoll and Irving Aaronson to join the production. Lanza felt it was a good omen, a new beginning in the land of his forefathers where the people appreciated a true artist. Terry Robinson wasn't so sure. Lanza appeared to have gained some control of his drinking and his mood swings, but Robinson knew that it wouldn't take much to set him off again. Betty's increasing dependency on tranquilizers was a real source of concern to him, too, but even Robinson had to admit that they both seemed particularly rejuvenated at the thought of spending some time in Rome. Lanza was even beginning to make overtones about returning to the opera stage, something he hadn't spoken of in years.

While the family was packing for Italy, Lanza received word from Philadelphia that his beloved grandmother, Ellisa, was in a coma at the city's Metropolitan Hospital. She managed to make a short-term recovery and he serenaded her over the telephone, much as he had done for Raphaela Fasano several years earlier. But the respite was a brief one. Ellisa Lanza, the eighty-one-year-old matriarch of the family returned home to 636 Christian Street, where she passed away peacefully on 13 April. The tenor was heartbroken.

Two days later, Lanza made his final recordings in the United States, reuniting with Henri René and the Jeff Alexander Choir at Republic Studios for a selection of four pop tunes. Only three were recorded. The songs were unexceptional and the tenor's voice had an unusually smoky quality to it. He was also troubled by a slight agitation of phlegm in his throat, necessitating three tries to complete the final notes of "Come Dance with Me." The one that was finally chosen was less than the best of Lanza. Still, the timbre of the voice itself was solid as a rock and there is no denying the power of his top notes captured at the session. A far better choice of song to the lackluster selections chosen that day would have been "I'll Never Stop Loving You," one of the final collaborations of Nicholas Brodszky and Sammy Cahn and one that earned both men an Oscar nod. The number, sung in the film *Love Me or Leave Me* by Doris Day would have been ideally suited to the tenor but for some reason he chose not to record it. Like "Be My Love" it had a special crossover appeal and has since been recorded successfully by José Carreras and Andy Williams.

Lanza also agreed to return to the concert platform with a series of recitals that would take him throughout the major capitals of Europe. In a memo to London agent John Coast, Bill Judd, vice president of the newly named Columbia Artists Management, Inc. (CAMI) in New York, inquired if his British counterpart would like to handle the tour, adding that "if he [Lanza] sings at all, it will only be for crushingly big fees!"[1] Coast replied that he would be only too delighted to join the Lanza roller coaster. In time he would come to question that decision.

Shortly before the Lanza entourage departed for Italy in May 1957, Betty arranged to have her sons Damon and Marc baptized at the church of St. Paul the Apostle in Westwood, Los Angeles. Father Paul Maloney, who himself was about to be transferred to Rome, presided, with the Teitelbaum's acting as godparents. The Lanza's had decided to travel cross-country to New York by train, with a stopover in Chicago to say farewell to Betty's family. Antonio Cocozza and Terry Robinson stayed behind, little realizing that they would never see Mario alive again.

After a brief stopover in Chicago, the Lanzas arrived in New York, where, to RCA's surprise, the tenor declined to be interviewed by the press. After all the troubles of the past few years and the resulting bad publicity, Lanza was ambivalent about offering explanations for his departure to Europe. He chose instead to remain closeted with his family at the Waldorf-Astoria. RCA representatives Manie Sacks and Art Rush stopped by to wish him safe journey. On the evening of 16 May 1957, the day before his departure, the singer hosted a lavish party for many of his relatives including Salvatore Lanza, who had traveled from Philadelphia. Though they would see each other again in Italy, for Lanza's grandfather it was a particularly emotional farewell.

The following morning, on 17 May 1957, the Lanza family boarded the liner *Giulio Cesare* at Pier 84, West Forty-fourth Street bound for Naples, Italy. Jerry Thorpe of RCA had sent out special invitations to an onboard champagne breakfast, and glasses were raised in celebration of Mario Lanza's new beginnings in the Old World. Thirty-six years earlier, the year of Mario Lanza's birth, from that same city and on that same month, Lanza's idol Enrico Caruso had also set sail for Naples, Italy. It was another curious little parallel that linked the two tenors, for, like Caruso, Lanza would never see the United States again.

Nine days later, on 28 May 1957, the liner *Giulio Cesare* entered the Bay of Naples, where Lanza was greeted by huge banners and crowds of cheering Neapolitans welcoming him to Italy. Dressed in a dark suit and looking tired and paunchy, the tenor was clearly taken aback by the outpouring of affection. Lanza later recalled the arrival in a phone conversation with Terry Robinson: "I knew the moment I walked down the gangplank in Naples that I had left all my problems behind in Hollywood . . . that a new life faced me in Europe."[2] Following an open-air reception, arrangements were made for Lanza to pay a discreet visit to Caruso's final resting-place, and soon after the Lanzas traveled to Rome.

Despite the lien on his earnings, Lanza never settled for anything less than the very best when it came to creature comforts. Following a brief stay at the Bernini Bristol Hotel, the family was soon ensconced in a suite at the lavish and very expensive Hotel Excelsior while a more permanent residence was sought for them.

The script for *Seven Hills of Rome* was still a work in progress when filming began in June under the direction of Roy Rowland. He had a fairly thin body of work to his credit, his best known film being the cult favorite *The 5,000 Fingers of Dr. T,* a Dr. Seuss penned fantasy starring Peter Lind Hayes. Maurice "Red" Silverstein, vice president and international and eastern head of MGM was also on hand to ensure that the tenor minded his behavior on the set. Lanza's costars in the film were American B-movie actress Peggie Castle; comedian and singer-songwriter Renato Rascel, who was popular in Italy; and Marisa Allasio, who provided Lanza's love interest in the picture. Teitelbaum had tried to persuade the producers to sign David Niven and Brigitte Bardot to the production, but the studio wouldn't come up with the money. Marisa Allasio was no substitute for Bardot, though in fairness Mario Lanza films were seldom marketed on the strength of the singer's costars. Renato Rascal, an actor of very limited talents, did contribute one song to the picture that would, in time, guarantee its success at the box-office: "Arrivederci Roma." The song also provided the Italian title for the picture when it was released the following year.

After the heavy operatic content in *Serenade,* Lanza agreed to a more lightweight selection of material for *Seven Hills of Rome.* In June, the tenor and George Stoll recorded most of the music chosen for the picture at the Vatican's Auditorium Angelico Studios. Lanza was proud of the fact that he has been given permission to record there, especially as Toscanini and the NBC Orchestra had been denied similar access to the venue on an earlier occasion. Still, if the honor was prestigious, the quality of the sound engineering was only adequate. Few if any of Lanza's recordings in Italy matched the quality of engineering captured on the Coca-Cola sessions, and those were not even intended for commercial release.

Academy Award–winning composer Victor Young contributed the title song "Seven Hills of Rome," a pleasant if unmemorable number that was certainly not in the same league as his classic "Around the World." The song was Young's last. He died before the film went into production. Georgie Stoll contributed the calypso-like "There's Gonna Be a Party Tonight," while Lanza reprised "Come Dance with Me," a song he had difficulty with at his final session with Henri René two months earlier in Los Angeles. This time there were no problems, his voice sounding fresh and secure throughout the recording. It was also decided to highlight the tenor's very real abilities as a mimic. In an amusing sequence in the picture, Lanza does a convincing take-off of Perry Como, Frankie Laine, Dean Martin, and Louis Armstrong with brief snippets of some of their most famous numbers. It may not have been high art but coming so soon after the intensity of *Serenade*, no one saw fit to complain. "Lolita," a popular favorite of Caruso's, was also added to the mix. The tenor's one complete aria, "Questa o quella," paled in comparison to his superb RCA recording of seven years earlier. In fact, it was the earlier version that was used when the soundtrack album was released the following year.

The one hit song from *Seven Hills of Rome* was "Arrivederci Roma." During his stay at the Excelsior, Lanza noticed a young street singer, Luisa Di Mio, singing Neapolitan songs for pennies outside his hotel. In an inspired moment, Lanza suggested to Roy Rowland that he hire Di Mio to sing "Arrivederci Roma" on screen with him as a duet, with Bernini's fabulous fountain in the Piazza Navona providing the perfect backdrop. Rowland had his reservations about hiring the girl but knowing the singer's penchant for unruly and unpredictable mood swings, he went along with the suggestion. It turned out to be the single most memorable and charming sequence in the movie, with Lanza crooning gently while the young street singer belted out the song at the top of her young lungs. Lanza's recording of "Arrivederci Roma" eventually brought him back to the pop charts for the first time in years.

Seven Hills of Rome had an amusing little in-joke in the picture. Having been turned down for a job in a nightclub, Lanza is about to leave when the club's resident Italian tenor breaks into a painfully forced rendition of "Be My Love," complete with a strangulated attempt at the English language. Lanza winces, rightly so, and quickly moves on. Few outside the production knew that Lanza himself, in a moment of self-mockery, provided the voice of the "Italian tenor."

Lanza also saw to it that two of the characters names in the film had a personal meaning for him: his own character, Marc Revere, was named after his youngest son, while Marisa Allasio's character, Raphaela, was in honor of little Ray Fasano. The film dealt with an American television star, Lanza, on vacation in Europe who loses all his money at the gambling tables in Monte Carlo, travels to Rome to look up a relative, and meets and falls in love with the comely Ms. Allasio. Cue for lots of singing and scenic tours of the Eternal City. It was not much of an improvement on his demands for better scripts made in the days of *Because You're Mine*, but Lanza was in less of a position to be choosy in 1957.

Filming of *Seven Hills of Rome* was briefly interrupted in July 1957, when Lanza was compelled to return to Naples to attend a charity function where he would be made an honorary citizen of the city. The producers of the picture felt that the publicity would help their efforts, and Lanza reluctantly agreed to go. As an added incentive, one of Caruso's sons would be on hand to present him with a dubious tribute called the Enrico Caruso Award, one that Lanza had little interest in receiving. The function, in fact, was part political rally, one not surprisingly that had Mafia connections. Lanza knew nothing of this as he, Betty, and Al Teitelbaum took the train from Rome for his one-off appearance at the event.

It was here than Lanza was first introduced to mobster "Lucky" Luciano, one of the event's organizers. Luciano was not quite the colorful Mafia Don he had been in his heyday a decade earlier, before he was deported back to Italy from the United States. But he still held sinister sway in Mafia circles and did his best to latch onto the unfortunate tenor. Photos taken at the time show a somber looking Mario and Betty Lanza seated in the audience, while one particular shot taken of the singer performing on stage shows him clutching a microphone. For someone who never needed any amplification, it was certainly an unusual sight, symptomatic in some ways of his unhappy experience at being compelled to attend and sing at that questionable benefit. The event ironically marked the only occasion that Lanza ever sang in public in Italy. Lanza later recounted the details to Callinicos, expressing his outrage at being forced to sing at a benefit supported by ties to the Mob: "This insidious organization harassed Mario through his whole stay in Italy. He never knew what it wanted of him, or what he should do."[3]

On his return to Rome, Lanza started drinking again, causing a two-day delay in production. Al Teitelbaum, meanwhile, learned that his 1956 conviction for fraud had been upheld. On 21 July 1957, Teitelbaum terminated his services in writing as personal manager to Mario Lanza and returned to the United States to serve his one-year sentence.

The two men never saw each other again, though they remained in contact by phone. Soon after Lanza was briefly hospitalized and treated by a Dr. Pennington. The cause given to "Red" Silverstein at the time was stress, bought on by the pressure the movie and the hectic working schedule. It was clear, though, that the years of fast living were finally starting to catch up with the troubled singer.

Silverstein also arranged for Dr. Bill Cahan, the tenor's old friend from the *Winged Victory* days, to write him a letter encouraging him to stay healthy and focused for the film. Cahan visited Rome soon after and found Lanza in good spirits and determined to make good on the advice. "Red" Silverstein did more than was expected of him to keep Lanza in a positive frame of mind during the filming of *Seven Hills of Rome*. At the end of the production, he was rewarded for his efforts with an engraved watch from the singer, which read: "Thanks for a new life." And indeed, by the time filming had been completed on *Seven Hills of Rome*, Lanza had regained control of his weight and looked and sounded fantastic.

He was interviewed by Ed Sullivan for his syndicated show in October. Aside from complaining of being homesick, he took the opportunity to send his regards to *El Champion,* heavyweight boxer Rocky Marciano. Lanza and Marciano were good friends, but the suspicion remains that the dedication was more for show business appeal than any deep affection for his pugilist friend.

Accommodation for the Lanza family was eventually located at 56 Via Bruxelles in Rome's exclusive Savoia neighborhood. The home was the magnificent Villa Badoglio, which the Italian dictator Benito Mussolini had presented to Field Marshal Pietro Badoglio in gratitude for his services in a one-sided war against the Ethiopians. The Lanzas rented only the ground floor of the building, but the fifteen rooms were more than sufficient for the singer, his wife and four children, a number of servants, two dogs, a cat, and several canaries. The rent on the lavish surroundings was $1000 per month, less than the singer had been paying for his home in Beverly Hills. The Villa Badoglio was soon the center of some of Rome's most extravagant parties, where the prince of tenors held court and entertained the famous and, on occasion, the infamous.

In September, Mario and Betty made a special visit to the birthplace of the tenor's father, Antonio Cocozza. The entire village of Filignano turned out to welcome the couple. In honor of the occasion a plaque was unveiled at the former Cocozza home: "A record of the visit of Mario Lanza, messenger of the Italian bel canto, at the place where his father was born." Dozens of photographs taken during the visit show a relaxed and slim tenor, clearly delighted to be among his Italian friends and family. (The scene played itself out again more than forty years later, in August 2003, when Ellisa Lanza Bregman returned to Filignano to unveil a striking life-size memorial to her famous father.)

Back in Rome, the Lanzas spent Halloween 1957 at the Vatican, where the couple filmed a twenty-minute interview with Father James Keller, founder of The Christophers, a New York-based Christian support organization. The motto of The Christophers was a simple one: "It's better to light one candle than to curse the darkness." Father Keller felt that a talk with Mario and Betty Lanza would be suitably inspirational and the couple did their best to live up to his expectations. Throughout the interview, the Lanzas presented the perfect image of a loving and devoted couple, both of them focused on deepening the bonds of their marriage and setting the highest of standards for their children. Lanza was magnetic and charming throughout, his hands moving expressively as he described all the sacrifices his parents had made to set him on the road to stardom. Betty, graceful and composed, laughed as she described her loving support for her husband and his fabulous career. The inspirational aspect of the show was further emphasized when Lanza described his voice as a gift from God, stressing as he so often did that he was merely the keeper of the gift.

The program was interspersed with three songs tastefully sung by the tenor: "Santa Lucia," "Because You're Mine" and Schubert's "Ave Maria." His accompanist on piano was Paul Baron, who had made his name as an orchestra leader on the popular radio series *Mystery in the Air* in the United States back in the 1940s. Baron would later play a part in some of the tenor's RCA recordings, though not, sadly, to the same high standard achieved in the Vatican studio that day. *The Christopher Program* was the only occasion that Mario and Betty Lanza were interviewed in any depth on camera. Given the tragedies that were to come, the film provided an imperishable souvenir for the four children the couple would leave behind.

With the successful completion of *Seven Hills of Rome*, Lanza began preparations for his European concert tour. His interests were also being represented by Larry Kanaga, president of General Artists, who had been successful in luring him away from MCA. Constantine Callinicos at that time was conducting for the New York City Center Opera Company but he had heard reports from "Red" Silverstein of the tenor's well-being and new outlook on life. So, when the call came from Rome to accompany Lanza on the tour, Callinicos accepted. Julius Rudel, general director of City Center generously allowed him leave of absence, and in October Costa took a flight to Italy. What he found there on his arrival surprised and delighted him. Lanza, looking slim and fit, seemed like a different person, even abstaining from alcohol at dinner later that evening. In the days that followed, Lanza talked of nothing but the great things he was going to do: More films and concert tours, more recordings and, yes, a return to the opera stage. Italy was having such a good affect on him that anything was possible. For a time, Costa believed him.

On November 7, Lanza and George Stoll joined forces at Rome's Cinecittà Studios to record four songs for RCA. The tenor was in fine voice at the session, producing a robust "Younger Than Springtime" that was superior in every way to the version he had recorded the previous year with Irving Aaronson. He also revisited "The Loveliest Night of the Year," which had a new arrangement, one that was featured in *Seven Hills of Rome*. The standouts from the session were "Never Till Now," a song from the newly released Elizabeth Taylor movie *Raintree County*, a recording that highlighted Lanza's wonderful mezza-voce, and "Arrivederci Roma" sung mostly in English. It was a good day's work, and everyone was pleased with the results.

Prior to starting his European concert tour, Lanza was invited to sing for England's Queen Elizabeth and Prince Philip at the "Royal Variety Show" to be staged at the London Palladium on 16 November 1957. The show is a gala affair held each year for the British Royalty at the 2500-seat London Palladium, and all the great entertainers of the day perform at the event. Lanza felt his performance before the Queen would be the ideal way to make amends for having to cancel out on attending the Royal Command Film Performance screening of *Because You're Mine* five years earlier. Naturally he would include the film's title song as part of his brief program at the Palladium. A follow-up appearance on the popular *Sunday Night at the London Palladium* show was also booked for 22 November. Leslie Grade, the organizer for both engagements, promptly dispatched his representative Peter

Prichard to Rome to act as tour manager and attend to the singer's needs. Prichard liked Lanza the moment he met him: "He was a real star from the old school. We used to start each day at the Villa Badoglio with a bottle of champagne for breakfast. Mario loved champagne, only the finest would do, and he drank it like it was orange juice. I'd be feeling merry by mid-morning but he'd still be sober. Costa would come by for rehearsals—some Mario would do, some he wouldn't; depended on his mood. But his voice was fantastic. Such power. And he had such charisma."[4]

On 14 November, Lanza, Betty, Costa, and Peter Prichard arrived at Victoria Station from Rome aboard the Golden Arrow express. They were greeted by crowds of chanting fans, most of them young women, who proceeded to knock the delighted tenor off his feet the moment he stepped onto the platform. An obviously star-struck reporter thrust a microphone in front of the singer and asked him if he planned to sing any arias for the Queen. Lanza, at his most disarming, pointed out that it would be ungracious to Her Majesty for him to disclose his program, suggesting only that he would "leave it as a surprise."

For their ten-day stay in London, the Lanzas stayed at the luxurious Oliver Messel Suite at the Dorchester Hotel. Leslie Grade arranged a press conference. Despite Lanza's slimmed down appearance, the inevitable questions about the tenor's weight were brought up once again. He was less than pleased and as the evening wore on the singer sought solace in his favorite beverage. To Costa's dismay, the drinking continued long into the night and into the next day: "He drank alone. He drank with friends, waiters—anyone who wandered into the suite."[5] Peter Prichard was appalled, but Costa had seen it all before. The question now was whether the tenor could pull himself together in time to sing for Her Majesty.

Costa knew that the while Lanza's drinking spree had been brought on in part because of the questions about his weight, the real cause of his friend's retreat into alcoholic oblivion ran much deeper. Lanza hadn't performed on the concert stage in over six years and here he was now getting ready to sing before the Queen of England. All the irrational fears that had haunted him before the first Chrysler Show returned to plague him, and the memory of the Las Vegas fiasco was still fresh in his troubled mind. In a moment of cloudy self-pity Lanza raised a glass to Callinicos and Prichard with the toast "La vita e breve, la morte vien" (Life is brief, death is coming). Costa had heard the phrase many times before, usually when his friend was feeling sorry for himself, but the words had increasingly begun to take on an ominous significance.

On the morning of the "Royal Variety Show," Costa received a call in his hotel room from the tenor. Despite the ravages of the two-day drinking spree Lanza sounded fresh and well, assuring his friend that he would put on a good show for Her Majesty. Amazingly, he did. Arriving at the Palladium in the afternoon, Lanza and Costa ran through the three numbers they had selected for the performance: "Because You're Mine," "E lucevan le stelle," from *Tosca,* and "The Loveliest Night of the Year." Lanza, who had an abiding fear of forgetting the lyrics, asked his conductor to mouth the words to his songs so he could cue himself in if his memory lapsed during the performance. On this occasion though, his conductor's prompting did not go unnoticed. Cyril Ornadel, musical coordinator for the Royal Variety Show sat in the stalls as Lanza rehearsed and misinterpreted what he saw: "Callinicos ran the orchestrations through [while] Mario Lanza was just sitting in the stalls. When he was ready, Lanza came up on the stage and they started to run through the numbers, and we were shattered to find that every word and every bar was mouthed by his conductor. . . . It suddenly became apparent that Mario Lanza couldn't sing a note or a bar without his conductor guiding him through the sequence. But when you stopped looking at that, you just listened to this gorgeous, natural voice that was singing so beautifully."[6]

On the night of 16 November 1957, a stellar cast joined the tenor on stage. Judy Garland, in wonderful voice, moved the audience with her signature tune "Over the Rainbow,"; Britain's wartime sweetheart Vera Lynn joined comedian Arthur Askey for "If You Were the Only Girl"; and the inimitable Gracie Fields was handed the honor of singing "God Save the Queen." It was Lanza, however, who brought the house down.

Costa knew how nervous he was the moment he strolled on stage, bowed slightly to the Royal box, and turned to face his audience. Those nearest the stage noticed the microphone discreetly slide down toward the floor. There was no need for any amplification when Lanza sang. The power and the natural beauty of the voice would provide that. Writing about the performance in *Sporting Review and Show Business* several days later, the critic observed "[Lanza's] top notes almost tore the roof off. I doubt if the Palladium has ever heard a tenor of such lungpower. Lanza . . . shows he can belt out those top notes without benefit of commercial amplification."[7]

Even Cyril Ornadel was impressed "On the night of the Royal Command, which is generally known as a stuffy audience, he got royal acclaim; absolute roars, which is most unusual for there. On the following week, when you again have a different sort of audience, they tore the place up."[8] It was nothing less that a total triumph, one man's remarkable victory over his own worst demons. In the line up after the performance, Lanza shook hands with Her Majesty, who was heard to remark: "I never knew that human lungs could produce such power and volume."[9]

Bill Judd had traveled from New York for the appearance and he, John Coast, and Leslie Grade joined the crowd at a party for the tenor afterward to offer their congratulations. Coast, in particular, was overwhelmed by the performance, believing he had just heard the greatest tenor voice in the world. Only Costa knew the effort it had taken Lanza to get through the engagement.

In a photograph taken after the performance, Lanza is seen graciously shaking hands with Her Majesty. Peter Prichard offered an amusing aside on why he was standing directly behind the singer, out of the view of the cameraman: "Mario was a great ladies man and I was there to pull him back in case he decided to give Her Majesty a kiss. Mario would kiss any good looking woman on the neck if he felt like it and I had to make sure he didn't get carried away when the Queen stopped to shake his hand! You never could tell with him."[10]

Prichard's comment about Lanza being a ladies man was certainly true to a degree. Lanza's charm with women was legendary, and there is some evidence that he climbed the fence from time to time. But he was not the rampant womanizer that some colorful accounts of his life have claimed. Callinicos was questioned on this very point in a radio interview in 1974 and his reply was unequivocal: "Definitely not! He talked about women a lot but . . . I never recall his going after women in a serious way and I would know it because we were so close. I would hardly stay away for a day or so . . . so I would [not] miss some kind of an interest in another woman."[11]

Lanza and Callinicos returned to the Palladium the following Sunday, where their program was repeated to thunderous applause. Happily, the performance this time was captured on film and while the tenor does appear somewhat uncomfortable between songs, the power of his voice and his immense charisma is captured in every moment on stage. After one prolonged cheer, Lanza remarked "You're certainly terrific," at which point a voice from the audience roared back "So are you!" It was that sort of evening.

All that remained now was for Lanza and Costa to prepare for their upcoming concert tour, which was scheduled to start in the English town of Sheffield on 4 January 1958. After the tenor's success at the Palladium, John Coast was thrilled at the prospect of his charge storming triumphantly across the major capitals of Europe. Bill Judd, who had seen the other, unpredictable side of the singer's character, was not so optimistic and cautioned Coast to be on his guard against the unexpected. It turned out to be advice well given.

CHAPTER TWELVE

The Last Hurrah

In early December, Betty Lanza was hospitalized briefly complaining of stomach pains. Tests showed it to be a slight case of malnutrition. While her husband gained weight, Betty had lost it to the point where she had to seek treatment. Any illness in the family upset Lanza, and he refused to even contemplate arrangements for his forthcoming tour while his wife was ill. Luckily, her recovery was swift and the Lanzas prepared for their first Christmas in the Eternal City.

By 20 December 1957, Lanza's entire tour of Europe had been booked solid through March 1958. John Coast could hardly cope with the offers coming for more dates and more venues, and the math suggested that Lanza would be the highest paid entertainer in his field by the time tour had concluded. Lanza, though obviously delighted at the interest the concerts were garnering, did not put himself out when it came to preparing for them. For one thing, his program of songs stayed pretty much the same as it had been for the "Caruso" tour six years earlier. The voice had darkened quite a bit since then, however, and it was decided to drop "Be My Love" and "Vesti la giubba" from the list. Lanza could still hit a C note when he wanted to, but he saw no sense in pushing it. Besides, there would still be more than enough high Bs to thrill the crowds.

Costa was staying at the Pensione Santa Elisabetta on Rome's Via Veneto and shortly before Christmas he received a letter from John Coast that contained a special request: "The German managers would frankly prefer our program if it could have one more operatic aria in it. I don't want to write this to Mario because I feel it is firstly your department as his musical advisor and I think that the program he is singing will satisfy his British audiences. But the two arias in the first half of the program altogether last probably only six or seven minutes and if Mario could have one other, and longer, Italian aria . . . I think this would be a very good alteration."[1]

Costa was forthright in his reply: "I really don't know what to say regarding the extra aria for Germany. You must know that it has been a day to day and hour to hour struggle to get Mario to prepare this program. I have gone to the house many a day at 10 a.m. and waited until 7 or 8 p.m. before I could bring him to the piano to go through the program. And most of the time it has been working with a man who has been drinking beer all day or all night the night before. But to add another aria I cannot promise you although I will try my very best."[2]

And try he did, though it was to no avail. The program stayed as it was. Costa had also made a plea on his own behalf to John Coast in a letter dated 10 December 1957. In it he requested that his name appear on the front of the program next to Lanza's with the caption "Assisted by Constantine Callinicos, Pianist." The word "accompanist" was not to appear anywhere. He also requested that a short biographical sketch of his own accomplishments should be included. He concluded by saying that as he had no manager to take care of his own interests, he was depending on the kindness of the Coast agency to take care of what he viewed as his few small needs.

Lanza and Callinicos returned to England in the New Year for their first concert in Sheffield on 4 January. The Sheffield *News Review* summed up the appearance the following day: "The fabulous star of MGM musicals opened his British concert tour at City Hall, Sheffield to a capacity audience of nearly 3,000. Four weeks ago, when booking commenced, every one of the seats was snapped up in the record-breaking time of two hours. . . . the magnificent 'Stars were brightly shining' from *Tosca* produce an ovation he is not likely to forget . . . and the finale, 'La donna e mobile' was a great thrill."[3]

From Sheffield Lanza and Callinicos moved to other sell-out concerts in Glasgow, Scotland, Newcastle, and Leicester, all of which found the singer in magnificent voice. More troubling as far as Coast and CAMI were concerned was Callinicos' demand for what, by any standards, were exorbitant fees for his services. On 13 January, Coast wrote to Bill Judd in New York complaining that in addition to his $750 fee for each concert, Costa was looking for a further weekly stipend of $250. Coast pointed out that a local pianist, Geoffrey Parsons, would provide equally sound accompaniment for $85 a concert. Lanza was less than pleased when word of the considerable disparity in fees reached him, but Costa felt he had to look after his own interests. Parsons was kept on a retainer for a while, but things soon settled down and the tour continued with Callinicos at the Steinway.

On 15 January Lanza returned to London to meet Betty, who had traveled from Rome to attend his recital at the Royal Albert Hall scheduled for the following evening. RCA had made plans to record the concert, and it promised to be a memorable affair. That same evening, Lanza and his wife joined John Coast and Costa for a performance of *Tosca* at Covent Garden. American tenor Richard Tucker was making his London debut in the role of Cavaradossi and the singer's wife, Sara, joined the Lanza party in their box for the performance. Lanza, not wanting to take away from Tucker's evening, sat in the rear well out of public view, a gesture that was deeply appreciated by Sara Tucker. After the performance, everyone adjourned to the Lanza's suite at the Dorchester for a late-night supper, where the two singers talked about everything from their vocal training, religious backgrounds, ethnic roots, and family lives.

But for all the gaiety of the evening, the Tuckers felt that Lanza was not quite the carefree singer the media sometimes suggested. Sara Tucker recalled that feeling many years later to her husband's biographer, James Drake: "It was as if Mario wanted to figure out why Richard's life had gone one way, and his own life another. He was very subdued and seemed to hang on to every word Richard spoke. He seemed to want and need a friendly ear, and in Richard he found one. Richard and I both got the impression that for all his wealth and great success, Mario wasn't really happy. Something important, something very basic was missing from his life."[4]

It did not require any deep psychological analysis to guess the root cause of Lanza's melancholia that evening. He had just attended a performance of one of the great operatic masterworks staged at one of the world's great opera houses, a house that he should have been singing in. The cynic might point out that there was nothing physically stopping him from doing so. He was only thirty-six years old, in great vocal shape, and, problems with the Met and Rudolf Bing notwithstanding, would surely have been welcomed in Covent Garden had he expressed a desire to sing there. But there was one thing that was stopping him, and that was Mario Lanza himself. Until or unless he could come to terms with his own private demons and misgivings, he would remain the guest in the private box instead of the star on the opera stage.

Lanza's own night in the London spotlight came the following evening when a capacity crowd of more than 8000 people crammed the Royal Albert Hall for his recital. With three microphones prominently placed in front of the stage, the management felt compelled to make an announcement before the concert that they were there to record the Lanza voice, not to amplify it. Lanza himself entered from the artist's side of the stage—then promptly stepped back. He told Costa afterward that he was momentarily overawed by the size of the auditorium and the crowd awaiting him. He quickly regained his composure and strode out to thunderous applause. A brief remark to the audience, "Is this real?" as he surveyed his surroundings, a discreet nod to Callinicos seated at the piano, and the concert began.

Little need be said of his performance that evening as the entire recital, minus Costa's piano solos, can be heard on BMG's *Mario Lanza: Live from London* compact disc. Suffice it to say that Lanza was in glorious voice, thrilling the crowd with dazzling high Bs that brought him such thunderous applause at the close that he felt compelled to thank them back, "Wow! Thank *you!*" Conductor Richard Bonynge witnessed the star performance that night with his wife, soprano Joan Sutherland: "We were both surprised by the size of the voice. After all, one hears how film singers' voices are amplified. We were also impressed by Lanza's innate musicality. No doubt he could have had an outstanding operatic career."[5]

Lanza's performance that night marked the first time that RCA had recorded the voice in full-spectrum stereo sound, and the subsequent release of the recital on record and compact disc has proved a steady best-seller for the company ever since. Enrico Caruso's own debut at the great hall had been marred by the news that day of his father's passing, his grief further compounded by the discovery that his common-law wife, Ada Giachetti, had eloped with his chauffeur. For Lanza, there was no such tragedy that night. With a radiant Betty looking on from the audience, the singer triumphed with a thrilling performance that few who attended would ever forget.

Two nights later Lanza made a guest appearance on *Saturday Night Spectacular,* a live broadcast for ATV Television in London. The occasion marked the last time he appeared before the television cameras.

With Costa accompanying him at the piano, Lanza sang "Softly, as in a Morning Sunrise," "Marechiare," and "I'm Falling in Love with Someone." The tones were rich and bold, and the power of his top notes drew thunderous applause.

Lanza was back in recital at the Albert Hall the following afternoon, though his performance on this occasion was slightly more subdued. On a visit to actress Lana Turner's home in Hampstead the previous day, he had stumbled on some steps leading down into the garden and fallen and bruised his ribs. His performance on the ATV program was brief enough to disguise any discomfort, but by the time of the recital he was starting to feel the effects of the fall. He did his best to make fun of the incident, commenting after hitting a high B on "Lamento di Federico" that that was how he cracked his rib. It was clear though that he was in some discomfort throughout the performance.

Whatever problems Lanza had with his health and, on occasion, his management, his difficult and combative nature did not manifest itself in front of his admirers. Following his concert at The Dome in Brighton on 12 March, the singer shared his train compartment on the journey back to London with devoted fans Dora Alker, Joan Kesingland, Elsie Kiss, who also ran his fan club, and Molly Howard. The young women found him graciousness itself and remain staunch defenders of his legacy and his character to this day.

As the tour progressed, Lanza began to complain of pains in his right leg. He was quickly diagnosed with phlebitis, another offshoot of his many years or rich living and lack of exercise. It was a complaint, moreover, that would dog him for the remainder of his life. On 22 January, Lanza, Callinicos and John Coast left London by air for Germany, and the continuation of their tour that would take them to venues at Munich, Stuttgart, Hamburg and Baden-Baden. The Munich concert on 24 January at the Kongress-saal des Deutschen Museum was a great success as far as the fans were concerned. They stormed the stage after the recital, and it took all the efforts of the security men to get the singer back safely to his dressing room.

But while the audience was thrilled by the great Lanza voice, the Munich critics were less than kind to singer's performance. Lanza's fear of flying had caused him to imbibe a little more than he should have on the trip to Germany, a fact that may have resulted in a little more vocal strain than usual that night: "Munich saw and heard the much-publicized Mario Lanza last night. It also saw and heard what the Hollywood mills had made of him. There is no doubt that such vocal chords are rarely bestowed by nature . . . he has been trained like a Caruso or a Gigli but no one has told him that there is more to these immortals than air in the lungs and vocal chords in the head. His show numbers are put across with plenty of power and embellished with high notes to make them effective exhibition pieces. There was no overriding sweetness—no satisfying 'piano'—and the public raved."[6]

Three nights later Lanza performed at the Liederhalle in Stuttgart and though the man himself was feeling poorly, the voice was in top form. Writing in the Stuttgart *Zeitung* and *Nachrichten* newspapers, the music critics observed: "Undoubtedly the tenor has a beautiful lyric voice with an unmistakable timbre and sweetness all its own, and had he the perception to use his strengths more successfully for the climax, then no words would be sufficient."[7] "He brought an especially Caruso-like brilliance to the *Tosca* aria. But only in this respect did he have the voice of a great artist."[8]

The same pandemonium from the fans broke out after the Stuttgart recital and Costa in particular noticed a change in his friend's mood in the dressing room afterward. "By the time we escaped [the crowd], Mario was exhausted. It wasn't like him. Something was wrong."[9] Dr. Frederic Frühwein was summoned to his hotel the following morning and quickly diagnosed high blood pressure and inflamed phlebitis in his leg. Complete rest was immediately ordered and the remaining concerts scheduled through the end of February were shut down. Only three weeks into the tour, the cancellations had already begun, though this time it had nothing to do with the whims of a temperamental star. Lanza's sedentary lifestyle, coupled with a steady diet of rich food and excessive drinking were finally starting to take their toll, and the chastened singer returned to Rome for treatment. It was also the last time he saw Peter Prichard:

Mario had been feeling unwell and decided to return to Rome. He always liked to be paid in dollars and after his final concert in Germany he received his fee in Deutschmark, which he didn't want. It was the weekend and all the banks were closed but saying no to Mario was not something you did lightly. It was then that I remembered a telephone number I had, to be used in case of an emergency. The year before Mario had sung at an event in Naples and afterwards as a token of appreciation he was given a number to call if he ever needed anything. Anything! The inference I took from it was that a certain Italian "family" wished to show its gratitude. I must say I was pretty desperate at the time or I wouldn't have used it. But I called the number and explained the situation, received a polite reply and an assurance that the exchange would be made the following day at our hotel. The next morning I met this neatly dressed gentleman, looked like a bank manager, who handed me a brief-case containing the dollars. We shook hands, exchanged the currency and he was on his way. Debt repaid in full!

Later, Prichard saw Lanza to train station and made the mistake of telling the singer to be mindful of the fact that he was carrying thousands of dollars in cash in his pocket. "You never told Mario what to do and when I suggested that he be careful carrying all that cash, he blew up—swore at me blind and said he didn't need the money. The next thing I know the train is pulling out of the station and Mario is flinging the cash out of the window. Dollar bills flying everywhere; total chaos! I scrambled like mad and managed to retrieve most of the cash, which I sent to Rome. That was the last time I ever saw him. It was a grand old-style exit for a great superstar!"[10]

John Coast, who had traveled to Germany for the tour was deeply troubled by his friend's declining health. On his return to London he immediately penned an extraordinary and deeply felt three-page letter, which he copied to Bill Judd at CAMI in New York:

Mario, my friend, this is a very serious letter to you, written just as much from me as a human-being as from a concert agent. . . . First, let me say this. From the start I have had the highest opinion of your voice. But when listening to you in that fantastic concert in Stuttgart the other night, knowing how lousy you were feeling, and hearing you sing that opening group in a way that I know didn't please you, I nevertheless *during that same group* felt absolutely confidant and sure that yours is the greatest living Italian tenor, and also the only true *robusto* one. Mario, feeling ill though you did, even in that group your voice was not only black and warm and dead on pitch, but it was strong as a pillar from top to bottom—it showed no trace of thinning at the top or in any other register—and purely as a love of a good voice I said to myself: "This man must *not* be allowed to destroy himself; this man *must* do the many things in his career which he still can do and should do." For your voice, my dear Mario, is unique today. . . . I tell you—di Stefano, del Monaco, even Jussi—they're not in the same league with you at all. And this brings me to my second point, which is your health.

Mario that doctor in Munich is a hell of a good man. He told you last night what he told me a day before—that you might easily kill yourself within a year if you couldn't get your physical and personal problems straightened out. He said that one day you might have some sort of a clot and pass out.[11]

Coast's letter went on to implore his friend to think of a long and happy future, one however that would not come without personal sacrifice and a new sense of resolve and high purpose. Bill Judd wrote to Lanza in a similar vein a week later: "I beg you to seek and follow the best medical advice immediately so that your physical condition will soon be improved. Your family and friends count on you and depend on you. So do your world-wide public. Remember Mario, you are the 'greatest' and we all count on you in friendship as well as professionally."[12]

Lanza did little to heed the advice. Peter Prichard fell out of favor with Betty soon after and was replaced in early February by David Tennant, who came with the highest recommendation from Coast. Despite this Tennant's own stay with the Lanzas would not last very long. In a letter to Bill Judd at CAMI, Coast explained that what Lanza needed was someone who was a "cross between valet, secretary, press-officer, stooge, listener, personal manager and a few other things."[13]

On 28 February 1958, CAMI issued a press report stating that Lanza was returning to London the following Sunday, 2 March, to continue his tour. The report also stated, almost in passing, that due to his recent illness the singer would have to walk with the support of a stick. The inflammation in Lanza's leg had been brought under control but it still necessitated the use of a cane. Later, in his suite at the Dorchester, the singer posed for photographers, showing the leg heavily bandaged. The remainder of his tour through March and April was scheduled to take him through nineteen cities, with the possibility of a return to Leicester and two more concerts at the Royal Albert Hall. The bandaged leg and the walking cane should have been warning enough that the itinerary would not be honored in full.

On 3 March Coast wrote again to Bill Judd at CAMI sounding hopeful that all would be well for the forthcoming tour. Lanza had told Coast that Paul Baron and Al Panone, a film producer, were working on plans for another European movie. Moreover, he was also planning to re-record *The Student Prince* in stereo with soprano Anna Moffo. The recording would eventually take place under Baron's conducting the following year, but without the great soprano.

Coast remained concerned about the singer's health, but if the man was slowly falling apart, the voice was not. Lanza returned to the tour on 4 March with an appearance at Bristol's Colston Hall. Two nights later, following his appearance before 6,000 screaming fans at the King's Hall, Belle Vue in Manchester, the reviewer for of the local papers misinterpreted the singer's movements on stage, though there was no mistaking the impact of the singing: "He kicked around quietly now and again . . . shrugging various limbs like an athlete or a matador carelessly waiting till all was prepared for him. The singing was a surprise. Though untouched by artistic fastidiousness, Lanza has a musical sensibility, and he sang with a sense of style that though not very developed . . . was fundamentally and naturally musical, and instinctively observant of different musical expressions."[14]

The tour continued through Newcastle, Brighton, and Bradford, breaking off on 14 March to allow Lanza to return to Rome for his daughters' confirmation. A new addition to the singer's entourage was Alex Revides, a Shakespearean actor who had ingratiated himself into the singer's circle of advisors. Lanza's unerring ability to attach himself to people who had an adverse affect on his life had not deserted him. Shortly after his return to Rome, he informed John Coast that David Tennant's services were no longer required and that his duties instead would be taken over by Revides. Alex Revides had no qualifications for the role of tour manager, other than serving as an attendant to the tenor's whims and occasional mood swings, but to Lanza that was enough.

Lanza was back on the road for an appearance in Edinburgh, Scotland, on 25 March and one in Dundee on 27 March. Two days later he flew to Northern Ireland, for an appearance organized by promoter Philip Solomon at the King's Hall, Belfast, before a packed audience of 9,000. Dubliner Christy Smith was one of many who journeyed by coach from Ireland's capital for the event.

I had bought his record *Lanza on Broadway* and to tell you the truth I thought the voice was gone. But I wouldn't have missed the chance to see him for anything. Then the bus broke down on the way to the concert and we didn't get there till the intermission! The place was awful—an airport hanger, not the sort of place for someone like him at all, but there was nowhere else big enough to handle the crowds. But then he walked out on stage and began to sing. He was amazing! This was the voice I had heard in *The Great Caruso*. It filled the King's Hall and the crowd went crazy every time he hit one of those top notes. No microphone either— the notes just soared across the hall. He was surrounded by security and they had an awful job getting him off the stage afterwards. The crowd just didn't want him to leave. I'll never forget it, or him.[15]

A recital at Leicester followed two days later, and on 1 April Lanza, Costa, and John Coast traveled to Paris, where the tenor was scheduled to perform at the Paris Olympia. With the entourage staying at the celebrated George Cinq Hotel, Coast expressed concern at the rising costs in a further letter to Bill Judd. By now, all of Coast's correspondence to the New York office were lengthy, a clear indication to Judd that all was not well on the battlefront. Coast was back at the typewriter the day after the Olympia recital: "The Paris concert last night looks like becoming another 'affaire Callas.' I was forced by Mario, only five or six days from this concert, to renegotiate a quite new contract: and a concert that had been advertised as a miniature recital . . . heard just 5 songs!"[16]

A much calmer Coast wrote again to Judd on 10 April: "We escaped alive from Paris and went to Ostend where an extremely happy and successful concert was given on the 5th. . . . Mario was in very good form."[17] The recital that followed at Rotterdam's Ahoy Hal on 7 April was a less happy affair. In an echo of his first appearance with Costa in Shippensburg, Lanza appeared in a business suit and politely announced: "My suit didn't come with me, but the voice is here!"[18] As usual, the great voice thrilled the crowd but some critics were left wanting more:

Lanza did not spare the notes . . . but he also did not follow the rules of pianissimo. The longer and the louder he sang the better the audience appreciated it. And yet . . . what a beautiful instrument this is. Seldom has such lyric fortissimo been heard! But on the opposing side, if nothing of musicality and intelligence can be offered . . . if the singer is of the opinion that he has to tell jokes, drink water in front of the audience, and pull up his trousers the way he does at home, there only remains a badly behaved boy who doesn't have even the politeness to thank his accompanist Constantine Callinicos for his patience and obedience. A strange, artistically unsatisfying evening, but again. . . . what a voice![19]

A reviewer for the *Het Parool* wrote, "Mario Lanza announced that he would not need a microphone and that indeed was correct. The voice of this former piano mover jingled the coffee cups on the saucers in the far corners of the hall. In the exaggerated high registers . . . he can't be stopped. Louder, much louder: a voice like an unpolished diamond. [But] Lanza has no technique. He is only a vocal superman who is happiest singing as if he were in his bathroom."[20] Lanza's mood was not helped by the fact that the hall was poorly heated and the audience was allowed access to refreshments during the performance. After an hour the tenor had enough. With a brief "Well, that's it!"[21] he was on his way.

Revides, meanwhile, had been unable to handle the Lanza itinerary and Coast persuaded the tenor to rehire David Tennant for the rest of the tour. Philip Solomon also joined the group as a friend and confidant to Lanza. Revides still hung around, much in the way that Terry Robinson had done seven years earlier, though without the other's high moral influence. Five concerts remained on the schedule for Central Europe: Hanover, Hamburg, Kiel, Wiesbaden, and Nuremberg, after which Lanza would return for more recitals in the United Kingdom and Ireland. An appearance at the Brussells Exhibition was also planned for 28 April, which would be broadcast live on Eurovision TV, with the tour concluding at Dublin's Theater Royal two days later. Only three of these engagements were honored.

On 11 April Lanza stepped on stage at the Neidersachschalle in Hanover, where once again the tenor's absence of formal attire irritated the critic of the *Hanoverische Algemein* newspaper: "One of his managers apologized for the fact that Lanza's evening dress had not arrived because of unforeseen difficulties and would the public forgive him. Then a stockily built, broad shouldered Italianate man walked forward to acknowledge the applause of the welcoming audience. His appearance was pure American slovenliness—a lounge suit and a crooked tie, and later, he drank water in full view of his public. The whole scene reflected the circles in which the star moved, a pre-packed bundle of 'public relations' sent to Europe at just the right time, filling the gap after Gigli."

But then Lanza began to sing and all the minor transgressions were quickly forgotten: "Ever since Mario Lanza starred in *The Great Caruso,* his name has been known throughout the world. And rightly so, for there is no equal to this naturally beautiful tenor voice in the world today. The free-flowing 'bel canto' is an irresistible attraction, the unsurpassing strength flowing from the heights of falsetto to a deep, coaxing urgency . . . nothing could deprive the evening of the infatuating attraction of the voice. Indeed, the enthusiastic reception knew no bounds."[22]

Two days later Mario Lanza appeared in recital at the vast Ostseehalle auditorium in Kiel, and it was here that the great voice was heard in public for the very last time. It proved to be an unforgettable farewell. Despite the fact that he was fighting a cold, Lanza gave the performance of his life, surprising even Costa who thought he had already heard the best the singer had to offer. "He seemed that night . . . at the mammoth indoor stadium in Kiel, Germany, to be at the height of his powers as a singer. His voice, 'darker' and richer that I had heard it in years, thrilled me. Its volume and substance rivaled any male voice I had heard in my life."[23] It was an opinion echoed by music critic Dr. Kurt Klukist writing in the *Lubecher Nachricten* newspaper the following morning:

> The hall was still. It had begun. Italian arias, folk songs, Puccini, English "pop." One thing was obvious after the first few bars . . . this man, who was not allowed to be other than the product of a well-regulated publicity machine, fell naturally and significantly into the greatest role he could play . . . he really can sing. The material belonging to this wonderfully melodious tenor is a natural gift. Lanza has a "strad" in his throat and he understands how to use it. It is difficult to know what to admire the most. The faultless breathing technique, the elastic precision of his wording. The light "piano." The constantly disciplined "forte." The well-synchronized join between the registers. Lanza sings emotionally, a smoldering fluency. His delivery is not a technical exercise but an event of blessed southern sensuality. Characteristic of the singing are the famous "tears" in the voice, that small pretence learned from the sobbing of the nightingale that most Italian tenors put on, but here is a completely natural sound. When he is not singing, he seems a little nervous, perhaps the

aftermath of a serious illness. When he sings, he is fully relaxed. He pulls his tie undone, opens his collar because of the heat. Applause, and more and applause. An encore is dragged out of him—or is two? Then with a gesture of typical romantic panache, he says goodbye.[24]

From Kiel, the party moved to the Hotel Vier Jahreszeiten in Hamburg in preparation for Lanza's appearance in the city on 16 April. Everything was undone the evening before the concert following an argument and drinking spree between Lanza and Revides, one that spilled over into the early hours of the morning. The two had been discussing the merits of Verdi's *Otello*, with Lanza periodically breaking into excerpts from the great work at the top of his lungs. The impromptu "concert" drew complaints from other guests in the hotel. People usually applauded when Lanza sang, but not at three-thirty in the morning. Costa later commented to Coast that Lanza had used up enough voice in that mad argument for three concerts.

To no one's surprise, the tenor awoke the following day complaining of a raw throat. At one-fifteen Dr. Schaake from the Hamburg State Opera was called in to examine him. He sprayed Lanza's throat, gave him an injection, and told Coast he would probably be alright in time for the concert. The word "probably" was the most damning part of the assessment. At six-thirty another doctor examined Lanza and found him to be in abysmal physical shape. He advised him to stop drinking immediately and warned him of a heart condition that needed two or three month's attention. Dr. Schaake arrived soon after and confirmed everyone's worst suspicions: while the tenor might be able to get through the program that night, the effort would undoubtedly put strain on his vocal chords. For Lanza, it was enough to cancel the appearance.

Kurt Collien, the concert manager responsible for the sold-out Hamburg recital, was desperate. The hall had already begun filling up and it would fall to him to make the announcement. To Callinicos' credit, he offered to join the hapless manager on stage and try to explain what had happened. In the end it did no good. As soon as the cancellation was announced, the place erupted in boos and catcalls. As Costa later recalled: "During the *Caruso* tour I thought I had seen everything in the way of unruly, obnoxious behavior, but I had to go to Hamburg to see my first concert-hall 'lynch mob.'"[25]

The crowd spilled onto the stage and Collien and Callinicos had to be helped out of the building by a police escort. But the disturbance didn't end at the hall. A mob made their way to the singer's hotel where they booed him relentlessly in the street before the police arrived and broke them up. Coast later learned from David Tennant that Revides had been plotting with the ailing tenor to spirit him out of the country. Al Panone was already offering a $10,000 advance from his German backers for a new film. The remaining concerts would have to wait for another day.

On the morning of 17 April 1958, Lanza and Revides caught a flight back to Rome and all the tenor's remaining concert engagements along with the Eurovision TV booking were cancelled. The official announcement came in a press release from John Coast dated 20 April, citing the singer's ill health as the cause. Lanza had left behind him a raft of bad publicity, a string of broken engagements, and a number of lawsuits for breach of contract that would follow him back to Italy. In a sad echo of his fights with the IRS in America, the tenor now owed more than £2,000 in income tax arrears to the British Inland Revenue Service.

Mario Lanza had recently turned thirty-seven and no one who was around him during that final tour would have been unduly surprised to learn that he had less than eighteen months left to live.

CHAPTER THIRTEEN

The Greatest in the World

Back in Rome Lanza took it easy for a time, though he failed to inform John Coast that he was finished touring. The long and seemingly never-ending saga of the Coast letters was quickly drawing to a close when he expressed his sense of desperation to the singer on 22 April 1958: "Please write me exactly what you want me to try and do for you now. I am sorry, but neither I nor any of my colleagues can take instructions from anybody but your own self. Yesterday Paul Baron told Philip Solomon you wouldn't be singing for months: today Revides told both Phil and me that you would be prepared to sing the April 28th date and the two early May Irish dates. These contradictions, coming from your friends or film associates, only add to the confusion and do not help you."[1]

A similar letter was dispatched to Bill Judd and Lanza's New York business managers the following day:

> Please advise me: what am I to do about this man, Mario Lanza? I have now had him on my hands for nearly four months, often for 24 hours a day at a stretch, and I am truthfully almost ripe for a breakdown myself. . . . His closest associate now is this miserable Greek, Alex Revides. Since he bunked to Rome, Mario has not spoken to me, any of his German managers or even to Phil Solomon, of Ireland, whom he professed to like so well. We can only get Revides or Paul Baron on the phone, and I'm sick to death of spending $20 a time to hear the arrogant and aggressive nonsense of a man like Revides. Revides is in the picture, I believe, because he introduced Mario to Panone, and Panone promised him big money from the Deutsche Bank and Bavaria Films for his Capri picture.

Coast concluded with a warning and a heartfelt plea: "But I must warn you all that Mario is physically deteriorating to an alarming degree. He weighed about 235 lbs. in Germany, and was giving his concerts in slacks. Now, tell me, please, what am I to do? Is it still possible to save this man, whose voice is the greatest in the world, from himself and his so-called 'friends'?"[2]

Despite the nightmare scenarios Coast had been recounting to Bill Judd at CAMI all those months, he never gave up on Lanza. Hopes remained high that the singer would agree to perform in South Africa and Australia for what were then staggeringly high fees. Many years later, long after Lanza's passing, Coast would regale his colleague Frank Powis at the London agency of the times and tribulations encountered with the star during those wild and unpredictable months. But the stories of the man himself were always told with affection, and always tinged with more than a little sadness. Lanza was a troubled soul during those last years, but Coast always maintained that he was fundamentally a great guy. Just someone, sadly, who was unable to cope with the demands his fabulous career had made on him. As an agent who handled all the great tenor voices of the day—everyone from Björling to Di Stefano, Tucker to Domingo and Carreras—John Coast was adamant to the very end about one thing. Mario Lanza had the greatest natural tenor voice of them all.

The Capri picture John Coast had referred to in his letter to Bill Judd was a project ironically titled *For the First Time*, an Italian-German coproduction that would be distributed by MGM. In May 1958, Lanza signed a contract with Alexander Grueter of Corona Films in Munich against which he would receive the not-inconsiderable sum of $200,000 plus a percentage of the profits. With the debtors lining up from his tour cancellations and associated costs still rising, the film offered him a way out of his financial woes.

Before filming could commence, however, Lanza's weight had to be brought under control. He had become enamored of a new drink, Campari, and that, along with his excessive consumption of beer, was only adding to the problems. He had started taking Antabuse tablets again to try to wean himself off the alcohol, but he ended up living with both. The tablets caused a violent reaction—shortness of breath, rapid pulse, and inflamed face—while the drinking exacerbated the whole mad scenario. Dr. Guido Moricca from Rome's Valle Giulia

Clinic was summoned to the Villa Badoglio but there was not much he could do, save to warn the singer that if he kept up this lifestyle he would soon be dead.

To salvage the new film, to say nothing of its star, Alexander Grueter arranged for Lanza to spend time at the Park Sanitarium in Walchensee, in the Bavarian Alps. The sanitarium was located in a tiny village and was frequented by movie stars, politicians, and royalty when they needed medical treatment or to just get in shape. Lanza was reluctant to submit to any treatment, but he was contractually obliged to lose forty pounds before filming of *For the First Time* was scheduled to start in September. On 28 May 1958 he checked in alone but, despite the clean air and glorious picture-postcard surroundings, he was not a happy patient. For a while he fought bitterly against the strict diet and medical checks imposed on him by his doctors, Frühwein and Schreiber. Dr. Schreiber, chief medical officer at the clinic had a reputation for handling difficult patients, Richard Burton and Elizabeth Taylor among them. Keeping Lanza in check would not be a problem.

Popular legend has it that Lanza underwent weight-reducing "twilight sleep" therapy at the Bavarian clinic, a story that received much mileage in the tabloid press in the months following his tragic death. The bizarre treatment allegedly called for Lanza to be unconscious for long periods at a time and fed intravenously while the drugs took their course. In a television interview recorded several decades after the tenor's passing, Rome columnist Mike Stern talked of the singer being injected with the urine of pregnant women in an attempt to break down fat cells in his body. Lanza certainly needed to drop the pounds but he had several months to achieve his goal before filming commenced on the new picture. As with so many stories surrounding this colorful singer, the twilight sleep treatment plays more to fantasy than fact.

As the weeks passed Lanza settled in, began to lose the weight, and started to respond to the tranquility of the surroundings. By the time Callinicos joined him to rehearse the operatic selections chosen for the new picture, Lanza was referring to Walchensee as a "bit of heaven." He swam in the lake, shopped in the nearby village of Wallgau, and enjoyed the local beer—in moderation. Schreiber was concerned at the perilous state of the tenor's liver and warned him off any heavy drinking. For a time, he listened. With Costa's arrival Lanza started working on the arias chosen for the new picture. The singer's voice, rich and dark and powerful, responded well to the daily workouts and in truth he was singing better than he had in years. Betty and the children also joined him for a vacation and by the time he checked out of Walchensee on 23 August, he was starting to look like the Mario Lanza of old once again.

Shortly after their return to Italy, Lanza and Costa reported to the Rome Opera House to record the operatic material selected by the singer for the new picture. It would be the first time the two had made a successful recording together in more than five years. The musicians at the Rome Opera were curious to hear the great Hollywood voice live, though no one expected too much. Costa later described what happened after his friend began to sing:

> They all thought that Mario's voice was the kind that needed all sorts of electronic equipment to enhance it. So after each number I was getting the reaction of the musicians who were sitting close to me at the podium . . . "Maestro, we never knew that Mario could sing. We never thought that he has a voice like this!" One of these remarks came from General Director [Riccardo] Vitale who said . . . "I would like to ask you now to be a go-between and see if [Mario] would be interested in singing Cavaradossi in *Tosca* during our opening of the Rome Opera season." [Vitale] thought Mario's voice was being magnified by electronic equipment. He never knew it was such a glorious voice.[3]

Lanza's material that day covered the familiar, "Vesti la giubba," to more demanding fare such as the powerfully sung *Otello* death scene, "Niun mi tema." A Mozart excerpt from *Così Fan Tutte* produced some delicate singing and the triumphal march from *Aida*, for which the tenor was joined by the full complement of the Rome Opera House's soloists and chorus, found the great voice in mighty form. The *Pagliacci* performance alone would have assured the "Bravo!" that greeted the tenor after each recording. The reading was bold, passionate, and heartbreaking. The voice may have lost some of the suppleness that characterized it ten years before, but gone too were some of the overwrought mannerisms that occasionally marred those earlier recordings. The Lanza voice heard at the Rome Opera House was a true operatic voice, ready to take on any and every role the tenor might choose to sing. His approach to the *Otello* aria was just as impressive, and it is not difficult to understand why the part of the tormented Moor was the one Lanza wanted most to sing on stage.

Vitale's invitation to Lanza to sing Cavaradossi was certainly an intriguing one. If the singer had managed to get his weight and his drinking under control, he could undoubtedly have made it the operatic portrayal of his career. He certainly had the vocal equipment to match any *Tosca* in the world, including the great Callas who had made the role of Puccini's doomed heroine her own. But it remains open to question whether in 1958 the singer still had the discipline to prepare for such a challenge. Costa and Vitale believed he did, but as always it was up to Lanza to make the final crucial decision. Given the state of his health and financial affairs, it was a decision that would not be made any time soon.

One surprising offshoot of the Rome Opera House sessions was the number of offers that poured in to the tenor's management from other leading houses throughout Europe and South America. As word of Lanza's performance that day began to filter through from Vitale and the musicians, interest in having Lanza sing full-length roles began to take on a whole life of its own. The singer could name his choice of role, his choice of partner, his choice of conductor, and so on. Lanza was flattered by the offers but chose to ignore them and it was left to Callinicos, in particular, to make whatever excuses he saw fit. Besides, as Lanza reminded his friend, there was too much to attend to right now. Rome and La Scala would have to wait just a little while longer.

Andrew Solt's storyline for *For the First Time* had a familiar ring to it. Originally titled "Silent Melody," Lanza was typecast as Tony Costa, a temperamental tenor with a penchant for canceling engagements, usually when the audiences were actually seated for the performance. Following one embarrassing incident in Vienna, he flees to the Isle of Capri, where during an impromptu open-air performance overlooking the Bay of Naples, he sees a beautiful young woman walk by apparently impervious to his vocal charms. Intrigued by her disregard for his singing, the tenor discovers that she is deaf. Determined to make her hear again, he takes her with him on a singing tour of Europe, where all the best specialists examine her. Eventually, following an operation, Christa awakens to the sound of her beloved gently crooning the Schubert "Ave Maria."

Even Lanza had to admit it was not high art, but he was excited at the prospect of singing a varied and demanding program of popular songs and arias in the picture. As usual, the singer liked to play with the names in his films and a careful listen to the list of people being called out in a court sequence near the end of the picture reveals one "Antonio Cocozza," a gentle tribute to his father. It is not known if Lanza's own name in the film had anything to do with his regard for "Costa" Callinicos.

George Stoll was put in charge of the musical direction with additional contributions coming from Carlo Savina and Johannes Rediske and His Band. Callinicos conducted the operatic sequences. The popular fare included the title song, "Come Prima," which was one of the tenor's very best recordings in years. "O Sole Mio" received more of a laid-back reading that the singer's powerhouse RCA and Coke Show versions, but it worked well in the picture. A brief song sung in French, "O, Mon Amour" showcased the Lanza voice at its most seductive. Stoll also contributed an excruciatingly bad, pseudo rock 'n' roll number called "Pineapple Pickers," which many regard as the worst song ever recorded by Mario Lanza. Other selections included a lusty Bavarian drinking song, a flawless Schubert "Ave Maria," and a slightly lackluster "La donna e mobile" sung to accordion backing.

For the First Time was directed by the Austrian-born Rudolph Maté, who had started his career as a cameraman working on such classics as Dreyer's *The Passion of Joan of Arc,* Murneau's *Vampyr,* and Hitchcock's *Foreign Correspondent.* His career-change to director had not been as successful, though his noir drama *D.O.A.* with Edmond O'Brien is much beloved by cineastes. Maté's experience behind the camera at least ensured that *For the First Time* was pleasant to look at, with Rome, Paris, and Vienna providing colorful backdrop to the slight storyline.

Lanza's costars in the film were Zsa Zsa Gabor, who more or less played herself; portly Austrian actor Kurt Kasznar who provided some much needed humor; and a newcomer Johanna von Koczian, who was appealing as the deaf girl. Gene Ruggiero from *The Great Caruso* joined the crew as editorial supervisor, and Peter Zinner came on board as film and music editor. (Zinner later received an Oscar nomination for his work on *The Godfather.*)

Zsa Zsa Gabor was surprised at how mellow her famous costar appeared on the set, though her observations would have surely raised an eyebrow or two at the Coast and CAMI agencies in London and New York: "Before I met him, I had heard so many terrible things about him. That he's rude, that he uses foul language and everything. I must say I spent six months with him and his family in Rome and Capri, and in Berlin, Germany, and I thought he was the nicest, kindest man I ever met. He was a sweet, darling man. I adored him and his wife Betty."[4]

In November, while Lanza and the crew were filming in Germany, the tenor received some distressing news. Hans Sohnker, one of the actors from the production, recalled what happened: "On 15 November we were invited to join a cycle race at the Berliner Sportsplatz. I joined [Lanza] there just after he had learned of the death of his actor friend, Tyrone Power. Power was forty-five years old and had died of a heart attack while making the film *Solomon and Sheba*. Lanza was quite distracted. He wrote a letter of condolence immediately. A visitor walked in and asked for his autograph. He took out his pen and blotted the ink on a serviette. With an abstracted despair, heightened by several glasses of wine, he murmured, 'I won't die . . . I won't die like Tyrone.' Then he drank more."[5]

The death of Power, coming so soon after his own health warnings, hit Lanza hard, but he seemed unable or unwilling to do anything about it. Not even the sudden passing of Nicholas Brodszky at the age of fifty-three that same year could distract the tenor from his self-destructive course. To a small group of people—people like John Coast and Bill Judd, Costa, and the several doctors who treated him—it was no longer a matter of if Mario Lanza might die, but when.

For the First Time was completed on time and without incident. The soundtrack recording was eventually nominated for a Grammy Award in 1960, the only time in Lanza's recording career that he was so honored. Overall, the movie received good reviews and almost everyone agreed that Lanza was in especially good voice for the production. "One of the better screen vehicles for Mario Lanza. His delivery of 'O Sole Mio,' 'Vesti la giubba,' and the final aria from *Otello* are splendidly rendered."[6] "Mario Lanza's voice is in top form in his latest film. Not only is he in splendid voice, but he ranges from rock 'n' roll to love songs. For cinemagoers there is no weak spot in the musical content."[7]

In late November 1958 Lanza returned to Rome to record the first in a new set of long-playing albums for RCA Victor, his first for the company in four years. He had recently signed a new five-year deal with RCA, who were anxious to capture their best-selling singer in full stereophonic sound—a format that was only then coming into its own. First up was an album of Neapolitan favorites, simply titled *Mario!* Franco Ferrara was the conductor with Franco Potenza put in charge of the chorus. A young musician named Ennio Morricone was given the task of arranging several of the numbers, which included the ever-popular "Funiculì, Funiculà," "Passione," and "Voce 'E Notte," which Lanza promptly declared as his favorite recording. Morricone went on to achieve great success as the composer on such epics as *The Good, the Bad and the Ugly; Once Upon a Time in America;* and *The Untouchables.*

It was a happy collaboration all around, with the sessions producing some of the best singing of Mario Lanza's career. His vocal control on "'Na Sera 'E Maggio," "Tu Ca Nun Chiagne," and "Dicitencello Vuie" was masterful, the rich, burnished tones capturing all the pathos inherent in this type of music. And on "Passione," one of the highlights of the collection, Lanza showed why he was still such a potent force with a performance of remarkable power and sensitivity that few other singers could match, let alone surpass. RCA executives in New York were thrilled when the tapes arrived in December, and Lanza's old friend Richard Mohr promptly dispatched a telegram to the Villa Badoglio: "Just a note to tell you how excited all of us are about your forthcoming album of Neapolitan songs. You and Ferrara certainly cooperated beautifully and I have seldom heard you sing better than this. I know the record will be a success, if only on the basis of something like 'Dicitencello Vuie' or 'Passione,' although all twelve songs are beautifully done."[8]

Alan Kayes, an A&R representative from RCA in New York, visited Lanza at the Villa Badoglio around this time to discuss a number of forthcoming album projects, including the re-recording of the singer's Christmas carols for a stereo release. Kayes also brought with him a new song, "Ev'rything" that the Walt Disney Music Company wanted Lanza to record. Jack Fine from Disney followed that up by sending Lanza the music to "My Beloved," a song taken from their new animated picture *Sleeping Beauty,* but the tenor passed on both.

Ben Hecht had better luck when Lanza signed on to star in a film called *Granada,* which Hecht was cowriting with Gottfried Reinhardt.

German Producer Arthur Brauner of CCC Films was in charge of the project, with Lanza reportedly receiving an advance close to $50,000 for his signature. The storyline was odd, to say the very least, with Lanza playing a beggar in Spain who pretends to be blind and sings in the streets for money. It was a script that would surely have to deliver more than its premise, but with Ben Hecht on board anything was possible. Lanza was also interested in filming *Laugh, Clown, Laugh*, which, with its Pagliacci overtones, at least sounded like a Mario Lanza vehicle. With a new film set for release, a new recording contract that had already produced one great album, and a host of new projects looming for the coming year, Lanza treated Betty and the children to a Christmas vacation in the holiday resort of St. Moritz in Switzerland. It would be their last Christmas together.

CHAPTER FOURTEEN

Death in Rome

The final year of Mario Lanza's life was also one of his busiest. In addition to a full recording schedule with RCA, the tenor had agreed to film a one-hour television special for Pontiac Motors that would capture him and his voice at some of the city's most famous landmarks.

Titled *Mario Lanza's Rome*, the planned production would open in the Piazza Di Spagna, where Lanza would be seen singing the popular Neapolitan song "Vieni sul mar." Next up would be a medley of four songs sung by the Trevi Fountain: "Three Coins in the Fountain," "La Danza," "Giannina Mia," and "I've Got You Under My Skin." The tenor's only aria, a choice of either "E lucevan le stelle" or "Recondita Armonia" from *Tosca* would be filmed at the Trastevere. Another medley consisting of "Be My Love," "Because You're Mine," "One Alone," and "If I Loved You" would follow, this time sung at the Coliseum. *Mario Lanza's Rome* would finally conclude with Lanza at the Sistine Chapel singing "O Holy Night" backed by a boy's choir.[1] Of all the songs selected for the production, "Three Coins in the Fountain" was the only one he would never get to sing on record.

Panone was also moving ahead to film *Laugh, Clown, Laugh* with coproducer Irving Pisor. Lanza liked the script, proclaiming it the best he had read since *The Great Caruso*. Both it and *Granada* remained on the front burner. His phlebitis continued to aggravate his leg, however, and in late April, the singer was admitted to the Valle Giulia Clinic for treatment. Costa recalled him being desperately tired, his eyes receding deep into his head. In addition to the phlebitis, his physician Dr. Giuseppe Stradone, also diagnosed dangerously high blood pressure. He urged the singer to curtail his extravagant lifestyle but Lanza had heard it all before and chose once again to ignore the warning. He had a thousand and one projects to complete. There was no time now for illness. Callinicos left Rome soon after to conduct the Athens Symphony Orchestra, but Lanza asked him to keep in touch. It wasn't long before reports reached Costa in Greece of his friend walking out of recording sessions and drinking heavily again.

First up on Lanza's recording agenda were two stereo albums for RCA, both of them reworkings of some of the singer's greatest earlier performances. Callinicos had been promised control of *The Student Prince*, a recording that would revert back to Dorothy Donnelly's original lyrics, though the three Brodszky-Webster movie songs would also be included. Instead, Paul Baron was put in charge and the results captured by Lanza and Baron at Rome's Cinecittà Studios in the spring of 1959 were nothing short of disastrous. It would be unthinkable for Lanza to improve on his peerless recordings of *The Student Prince* score laid down with Costa at MGM seven years earlier, but even his harshest critics were unprepared for the poor singing produced at Cinecittà those early summer days in 1959.

His voice sounding strained and forced throughout, Lanza struggled to get through the songs he normally sang so well. Even his approach was off, his attitude sullen and unfeeling throughout with none of the sweetness that was so evident on the earlier recordings. "I'll Walk with God" was especially painful, the voice all but unrecognizable as the singer fought in vain to bring the song to the glorious conclusion it demanded. "Golden Days" was another disaster, sung this time at full voice with very dubious engineering echo added to the closing moments while the tenor sought to hang on to the last note. After the superb work with Ferrara in December, it was an astonishing turnaround, proof if proof were needed of the singer's rapidly failing health.

Matters were not helped by an increasing state of hostility between conductor and singer. Callinicos had the misfortune to be on hand for one regrettable altercation between the two, when Lanza threw a phone at Baron, missed, and hit Costa on the knee instead. It was certainly not the sort of atmosphere conducive to producing a good body of work. Baron and Lanza's second venture together, an album titled *Lanza Sings Christmas Carols* was, if anything, even worse. Again, the selections found the tenor in vocal distress with no joy in the singing at all. Both of these recordings sold well for RCA though happily the stereo *Student Prince* has yet to see the light of day on compact disc. (No such luck with *Lanza Sings Christmas Carols*, however. The compact disc adorns the Christmas racks in record stores every holiday season, vying for shelf space with the far superior *Christmas with Mario Lanza*. The latter consists of all the singer's earlier Yuletide recordings and is superb in every way—a case, clearly, of buyer beware!)

In June 1959 Lanza and Baron reunited for one last time and to everyone's delight and surprise produced a fine album. Titled *Lanza Sings Caruso Favorites*, the twelve selections found the singer in excellent vocal form. If it was not quite the charismatic Lanza heard on the sessions with Franco Ferrara, the performances were still outstanding from start to finish. Historians interested in studying the development of the Lanza voice would do well to seek out his Rome version of "Musica Proibita" with Baron and compare it to the one recorded for the Coca-Cola series seven years earlier. While the Coke version is rich in sentiment and full of the flamboyance the singer was able to give to his voice at that time, it's the Rome version that really stands up to the critical test. It's a classic performance in every way, delivered in a manner fully befitting the song's pedigree.

Lanza's committed approach to the twelve songs selected for the album certainly appealed to the purist, who found the absence of his usual flamboyant singing style most effective. Indeed, his performance on quite a few of the songs was peerless. "Senza Nisciuno," a personal favorite of Lanza's father, could hardly be bettered, and the dark timbre of the singer's voice was particularly well showcased on Tosti's lovely "Ideale" and "Pour un Baiser." Lanza also delivered a powerful reading of the song "Serenata," which had been cowritten by Caruso, easily navigating the many musical twists and turns of this seldom-recorded piece.

On its release, *Lanza Sings Caruso Favorites* was packaged with *The Best of Caruso* as part of a double album. The second record consisted of a dozen actual recordings by the great Italian himself, and RCA felt it would be a good way to compare the two voices. They were right, and the set proved a big seller for the company on its debut the following year. RCA invited Francis Robinson, assistant manager of the Metropolitan Opera House and a noted Caruso authority in his own right to pen the sleeve notes for the record. His assessment of the latter-day Lanza voice was especially generous: "It is not merely speaking good of the dead to say that he never sounded better than on this recording, made in Rome in June, a mere four months before he died."[2]

Lanza was also visited in Rome that summer by his mother Maria, his Aunt Hilda, his grandfather Salvatore Lanza, and Betty's mother, May Hicks. It had been over two years since they had seen each other last, and the reunion was an emotional one. Lanza was overjoyed to have his family in his new home and everything was done to make their stay an unforgettable one. One lavish party at the Villa Badoglio followed another, and every celebrity who was in town was invited to meet the singer's family. Reportedly, Lucky Luciano turned up at one of the gatherings. Lanza certainly never cultivated any Mob associations, but keeping some of them out of his home—in Rome, of all places—when a come-all party was in swing was not always possible.

For Salvatore Lanza in particular, staying at "Freddy's" magnificent villa was an overwhelming experience, and his grandson saw to it that the patriarch of the Lanza family was shown all the respect he deserved. A special glass of scotch awaited him every morning and at dinner no one lifted a fork until he had. Later, when Maria and her sister were set to return to America, Lanza hid his grandfather's passport. Knowing that the old man would never visit Italy again, Mario determined to keep him on for a while longer. Salvatore, to no one's surprise, raised no objections. Lanza made his mother promise to come back at Christmas with his father and Terry Robinson. Tragically, she would be returning to Rome sooner than any of them expected.

In July, Lanza's entire family crammed into a booth at the Cinecittà Studios while the tenor recorded selections for a new album of songs from Rudolf Friml's *The Vagabond King*. The session also marked the return of the faithful Callinicos to the conductor's podium. The entire album was completed in one evening, from five till eleven, and Costa later declared it "our best and most harmonious session. . . . Mario was magnificent."[3] Lanza was indeed in good voice for most of the recordings, though the sound quality captured by the engineers that night left much to be desired. It is remarkable to think that Lanza's old mono sessions at Radio Recorder Studios seven years earlier were superior in every respect to the shoddy efforts put together at Cinecittà that summer. On "Someday" the tenor is drowned in a sea of echo, while on some of the other tracks such as "The Drinking Song" and "Song of the Vagabonds" the flat sound makes for an almost unlistenable experience. Some golden Lanza moments still managed to shine through, with an especially eloquent "Nocturne" and a duet "Only a Rose" showing the voice of later years at its most compelling. Lanza's partner on some of the songs, soprano Judith Raskin, was several thousand miles away when the singer made his recording, her own contribution being dubbed in New York several months after his death.

Among the many visitors to the Villa Badoglio that summer was RCA executive George R. Marek, who was there to negotiate a number of new recordings with the tenor. Included on the list were a couple of operettas, Lehár's *The Merry Widow* and Romberg's *The Desert Song*, along with another re-recording for stereo, a selection of arias from *The Great Caruso*. Lanza also wanted to make an album of sacred songs and there was also the matter of recordings for his new picture, which RCA would also market. Most promising of all, RCA had begun to put plans in order for Lanza to record his first full-length opera, regardless of whether the tenor actually went ahead with his planned return to the classical stage.

Toward the end of July Lanza and Costa started work at Cinecittà on *The Desert Song*, but the orchestra was not up to par and little was accomplished. Two further sessions produced even less, with Lanza looking and sounding the worse for wear. The alarms started to sound in August when the tenor was rushed to the Valle Giuila suffering from double pneumonia. Dr. Frank Silvestri was on hand and did what he could to stabilize the ailing singer's condition, but it was obvious to all that time was running out. Costa visited Lanza at the clinic and found his friend looking "years older than his 38 years."[4]

Lanza was discharged in a couple of days with the usual warning to change his ways. In preparation for the new film the singer embarked yet again on a Spartan diet, allowing himself only sips of water in what Costa remembered as an unbearably hot summer in Rome. The absence of air conditioning in the Villa Badoglio made matters worse, but Lanza had to lose the weight if the production was to go ahead, and he struggled though the sweltering days as best he could. The villa was a hive of activity, with Al Panone, Irving Pisor, and publicity agent Sam Steinman on hand daily attending to the various schedules.

Work resumed on *The Desert Song* in August. Because of uncertainties about the singer's health, Costa had recorded the orchestral backing tracks ahead of time, a technique that delighted Lanza. With Betty watching from the control booth, Lanza and Callinicos would listen to the playback once in the studio. The backing track would then be repeated and the tenor would sing to it with Costa directing him through the number. On the third playback the Lanza voice would be recorded. No selection was recorded more than once.

Given Lanza's very serious health problems at that time, it is astonishing how good the singing is on the collection. In many respects *The Desert Song* is the very best of Lanza's 1959 recordings. On "One Alone" the singing is solid and golden, very much the Lanza voice of old. "Azuri's Dance," "The Riff Song," and "One Flower in Your Garden" all find the tenor at his most compelling, the voice blazing with power and passion. Even Costa had to admit that his famous friend had not lost the ability to surprise. As with *The Vagabond King,* none of the soloists or chorus heard on the finished recording were present with the tenor at the Cinecittà Studios. Judith Raskin, bass Donald Arthur, and baritone Raymond Murcell all made their contributions to the collection in New York the following year, after the singer had passed on.

On 10 September 1959, Mario Lanza and Constantine Callinicos traveled to the Cinecittà Studios for one more recording. It would be their last together. An extraordinary journey that had begun twelve and half years earlier—a lifetime given all that had transpired since then—was finally drawing to a close on that late summer day. RCA had requested one additional track for the *Christmas Carols* collection, "The Lord's Prayer," which Lanza had sung so magnificently on record in 1951. Costa would accompany him on piano for the new version with an orchestral overdub track added later in New York. It proved to be a moving and fitting farewell to a great and unparalleled recording career, "a voice at its best—after everything and in spite of everything."[5] In a 1974 interview, Costa recalled, "We went to Cinecittà and Mario sang 'The Lord's Prayer' very, very beautifully . . . I believe the best he ever sang it in his life. So the Malotte 'Lord's Prayer'—and sometimes I think about it and I get chills—was the last thing Mario ever put down on record."[6]

Callinicos was scheduled to return to the United States later that day for an engagement with the New York City Opera and following lunch at the Villa Badoglio, the entire family lined up to wish him Godspeed. He would return in six weeks, at which time the other albums would be recorded and everyone would spend a joyous Christmas in the Eternal City. Lanza's father would join them and Terry Robinson had already obtained his passport for his very first trip to Europe. Costa would be the emissary to make sure that none of them changed their mind. As his taxi drove from away from the villa, Constantine Callinicos little realized that he would never see his friend alive again.

Over the years, there has been much discussion of how Lanza never recorded with any of the great conductors of his day. No full-length opera recordings with Toscanini or Victor de Sabata; no major classical works with Eugene Ormandy or Herbert von Karajan. Constantine Callinicos was certainly not in the same musical league with any of those giants but, in his own special way, he made a unique contribution to Mario Lanza's imperishable recorded legacy. His work with the tenor on *The Student Prince* soundtrack recordings alone has guaranteed him some sort of musical immortality. What Costa brought to Lanza's career, apart from his own innate sense of musicality, was an empathy with the singer that few other conductors could match. Had Lanza's personality been different, had he the temperament and the commitment to work with a more demanding taskmaster, particularly in the operatic field, who knows what further heights he might have scaled. But Constantine Callinicos was the one musician who understood him best, the one who returned to him and stood by him through all the fantastic highs and unexpected lows of an unforgettable career. It was entirely fitting that Costa should have been there for that last recording in Rome in September 1959. No one else had earned that privilege more. Terry Robinson agreed: "Costa Callinicos was . . . talented for Mario. He knew Mario's ways of coming into a song, of breathing, and he listened to Mario and he did what Mario wanted."[7]

Lanza's final appearance in public took place at the magnificent Baths of Caracalla in late September, when he took Betty and the children to an open-air performance of Verdi's *Aida*. The third-century ruins, universally known today as the setting for the first Three Tenors Concert, provided a breathtaking backdrop for the staging of Verdi's masterpiece, and Lanza did his best to remain incognito for the duration of the opera. His disguise of dark glasses did not work, however, and he was spotted in the audience toward the end of the first act. By the time the intermission arrived, the crowds of autograph seekers surrounding him were so great that he was compelled to leave. American journalist Harry Golden was seated nearby and noticed that he looked terribly tired.

On 29 September the Lanza family hosted the last great party at the Villa Badoglio. Peter Lind Hayes, Mario's friend from the old *On the*

Beam days, and Hayes' wife, Mary Healy, were the special guests of the evening. Afterward, the two men sat down and taped a brief interview for Hayes' radio show back in the United States. Though the effects of the free-flowing champagne were evident in Lanza's speech, he sounded happy, his mood relaxed and expansive: "Pete, I'm going to stay here another three years at least. I love it here. I love the home I'm in. . . . We're making a picture called *Laugh, Clown, Laugh* and the wonderful things that have been written in the script tell me that this may be the successor to *The Great Caruso*."[8]

Lanza and his family were also interviewed by RAI (Italian National Radio) at the Villa Badoglio for a scheduled six-part series on the tenor's life and career. Speaking mostly in Italian, Lanza, Betty, and the four children laughed and talked again about spending another three years in the Eternal City. The singer's good humor gave the lie to his rapidly declining health and his final words were sadly all too prophetic. "Ciao, many good things to you . . . Good-bye to everyone."[9]

Shortly afterward Lanza was again admitted to the Valle Giulia Clinic for treatment. He had been feeling unwell and complained of pains in the left side of his chest. His phlebitis, which had been bothering him for well over a year was still acting up, the result of the singer's failure to properly curb his diet and his lifestyle. The entire fourth floor of the clinic was put at his disposal, with Lanza holding court in Room 404. During his stay, Lanza became friendly with Giancarlo Stopponi, the seventeen-year-old son of the clinic's director, who was happy to run errands back and forth to the Villa Badoglio for the famous patient. Today, Giancarlo Stopponi is the head of administration at the Valle Giulia Clinic and has only the fondest memories of the singer, his special friend who gave him a signed record and a family portrait in gratitude for all his help. And contrary to some reports that surfaced in the tabloids later, Lanza did not undergo any weight-reducing "twilight sleep" process at the clinic; he was there solely for rest and general treatment.

Lanza did not lack for attention at the Valle Giulia in those days of early October 1959. A devoted nurse, Guglielmina Anselma Mangozzi, was in constant and loving attendance. In addition to his regular physicians Dr. Silvestri and Dr. Moricca, Lanza was also examined by Professor Loredana Dalla Torre, a heart specialist, who found alarming evidence of hypertensive heart disease with arteriosclerosis. But Lanza had heard it all before and, as usual, chose once again to ignore the warnings. By some accounts he was a less than accommodating patient, anxious to leave the Valle Giulia and return to the many engagements that awaited him. During his stay at the clinic Mrs. Alfredo Panone visited Lanza to report on developments for the new picture and television special. Her visit only increased his anxiety to be rid of the hospital, but his body was slow to respond to the treatment and he had no choice but to remain where he was.

Shortly before his admission to the Valle Giulia, Lanza had agreed to sing at a NATO charity concert in Naples, an event that some claim was influenced in part by Lucky Luciano. American journalist Mike Stern, one of several visitors to the Villa Badoglio in those days, recalled the pressure put on the singer to appear at the event, the inference being that if he failed to show up there would be unpleasant consequences. In an effort to appease the organizers, Betty Lanza agreed to represent her ailing husband at the concert armed with several dozen signed copies of his latest LP. It has been suggested that Luciano, enraged by the tenor's failure to appear that evening, ordered a hit on his life but the notion seems more fitting for a Grade B movie than a real-life scenario. Even had they wanted to, there was little that Luciano or any of the Mob could to do to the tenor in the fall of 1959 that had not already been done by Mario Lanza himself. Mike Stern recalled that Betty Lanza was the belle of the ball held at the Royal Palace in Naples after the concert, but that did not stop the Mafia hit-man story from taking on a life of its own in the years immediately following the singer's death.

Lanza made a number of phone calls to his family during that last stay at the Valle Giulia. In the house on Toyopa Drive, Maria was surprised to learn that her beloved son was back in hospital. Lanza had done a good job of covering up his illness while she was staying with him in Rome, and when Terry Robinson joined in on the conversation the singer reassured them both that he was fine. Robinson's superb physique had graced the cover of the August edition of *Strength and Health,* and he was pleased to hear that his friend had it by his bedside. Lanza's final call was to Betty. He had had enough of the treatment and the tests and the needles, enough of the medical reprimands and the portents of doom and gloom. He was checking himself out and would return to her and his family the following day.

On the morning of 7 October, Giancarlo Stopponi was at the Valle Giulia Clinic running the usual chores for his father. He did not see

Lanza that day but he heard his voice coming from Room 404, singing an aria as if to test the instrument. Shortly before noon, the boy became aware of a great commotion in the building. He watched in surprise as staff and doctors hurried down to Room 404, a room that was now closed to him. The reason for the confusion soon became clear. Mario Lanza had suffered a sudden heart attack. For more than thirty minutes Dr. Moricca and his staff worked on the singer's prostrate body in an attempt to resuscitate him, but it was too late. At the age of thirty-eight, Mario Lanza, the man they had called an American Caruso, was dead, the result of an embolism in his swollen leg having traveled to his heart.

Even those who been fully aware of the extent of the tenor's failing health were stunned by the suddenness with which it all ended. At the Villa Badoglio, Betty Lanza was summoned to the phone expecting to hear her husband's voice. Instead, Dr. Frank Silvestri broke the shocking news to her. Her cry of despair was enough to send him rushing to the Villa, where the distraught widow was put under sedation. Silvestri's unusual lack of sensitivity in breaking the news of Lanza's death to his wife over the telephone can only be put down to the immense confusion felt by everyone near to Lanza in Rome that day. Everyone was in a complete state of disbelief. Salvatore Lanza wept copiously. No matter how great the warning signs, no matter how many times Lanza had been cautioned to change his ways or pay the price, no one was really prepared for the way it ended so quickly.

In Hollywood, Terry Robinson received a call in the early morning hours from his friend Larry Kagan, who had heard the shocking news on the radio. Robinson, stunned like everyone else, turned on the radio softly so as not to disturb the Cocozzas who he believed were still sleeping. Maria walked into the kitchen just as her son's voice singing "Be My Love" poured out from the radio. Even the look on Terry Robinson's face did not prepare her for what came next. Interrupting the song, an announcer solemnly proclaimed that that was the voice of the late Mario Lanza, who passed away today from a heart attack in Rome, Italy. Maria screamed and passed out. Tony Cocozza lost control completely and ran out into the street calling his son's name, "Freddy! Freddy!" Only Terry Robinson stayed calm, though he was no less devastated than everyone else who filled the house on Toyopa Drive that sad October day. Kathryn Grayson heard the unbelievable news on the radio while she was driving in Beverly Hills to shop for her daughter's birthday party later that evening. All she could manage to do was pull the car to the side of the road and sob.

Dr. Silvestri called Maria later that day and encouraged her to fly to Rome to be with her daughter-in-law and her family. Tony Cocozza was too distraught to travel. While Terry Robinson stayed behind to prepare for the funeral, Lanza's business manager Myrt Blum quickly made arrangements for soprano Elizabeth Doubleday to accompany Maria on the long and deeply sad journey back to Rome. It was an extraordinary act of kindness on Doubleday's part, and she never left Maria's side through all the dark days that followed. On the flight to Italy, people on board paid their solemn respects to Maria but there was little that anyone could say or do to ease her pain. The world was slowly coming to terms with the fact that it had lost a great tenor. She was coping with the fact that she had lost her only son. Only the thought of Betty and the four children alone now at the Villa Badoglio kept her in check.

Lanza's body had been moved to the Villa Badoglio, where it lay in an open casket for several days. It had been hurriedly and improperly embalmed, and visitors who came to pay their last respects were shocked by what they saw. Mike Stern was one of them. Along with Frank Folsom, an RCA executive, he stood transfixed at the sight of his friend, faced puffed and unshaven with what appeared to be bruises on it, his bloated stomach rising above the rim of the coffin. Cotton could be seen sticking out from his nostrils and ears, with a strip of adhesive tape plastered across his mouth. It was an appalling sight, one that moved Folsom to tears.

Betty Lanza, heavily sedated, refused to see anyone and for a time the four children were not told of their father's passing. It was left to Colleen Lanza to discover the shocking truth when she climbed through a window into the room where he father's remains lay in state. Some sort of order returned to the villa with Maria's arrival. Rumors had quickly circulated that the American tenor might be laid to rest near his idol Enrico Caruso in a Naples cemetery, but the Lanza family would have none of it. Following a funeral in Rome the body would be shipped back to the United States, first to his hometown in Philadelphia for a viewing and then on to California for the final internment.

The first of Mario Lanza's three funerals took place on 10 October 1959 at the Church of the Immaculate Heart of Mary (Basilica dell'Immacolato Cuore di Maria) in Rome's exclusive Parioli district. Thousands lined the streets as the remains were driven from the Villa Badoglio in a glass-lined carriage pulled by four black horses. Actors Robert Alda and Rossano Brazzi along with Mike Stern and Frank Folsom carried the casket into the church. Bandleader Xavier Cugat and actor Van Johnson were also in attendance that day. Betty Lanza, in a state of collapse, had to be assisted by Dr. Silvestri. The family had hoped to have the tenor's recording of "Ave Maria" played at the service but church authorities forbade it and it was left to a local baritone, Giuseppe Forgione accompanied by the Roman Polyphonic Choir, to sing that final farewell. The choice of a baritone at least was a wise one. No tenor alive could have hoped to live up to the memory of the man whose remains rested in the church that day. The celebrant was Father Paul Maloney, the same priest who had baptized the two Lanza boys in Los Angeles just three years earlier. For all his oratorical skills, there was little he could say to bring comfort to the shocked and grieving family.

While the household belongings were being packed at the Villa Badoglio, Lanza's remains were temporarily interred at Rome's Verrano Cemetery. Myrt Blum took charge of moving everyone back to the United States. It proved to be a major undertaking. Betty, traveling on to Los Angeles with the children, Maria, and her own mother, insisted on bringing a number of her servants, two dogs, and a canary. Salvatore Lanza accompanied his grandson's body to Philadelphia, where his friends were waiting to pay their final respects.

Lanza's remains arrived back in the City of Brotherly Love on 15 October, where the body was put on view at Leonetti's Funeral Parlor at 2223 S. Broad Street. By now, the signs of deterioration were visibly disturbing, and a plate glass cover was placed over the open casket. Hundreds of people started gathering outside the parlor at four o'clock, three hours before Leonetti's opened their door. By seven o'clock the crowd had grown to several thousand. At midnight, the owners made the mistake of closing the doors while more than two thousand mourners were still lining up to view the remains. Protests broke out and extra police were summoned to control the disturbance. Serious injury was averted when Salvatore Lanza stepped forward and informed the crowd that he would stay with his grandson's remains until the last mourner had passed by. Mrs. Antoinette Marzano, an old friend of the Cocozza's, suffered a fatal heart attack as she stood by the casket. By the time Leonetti's finally shut their doors at two o'clock that morning it was estimated that over 15,000 people filed past the singer's casket.

The following morning Requiem Mass was celebrated for Freddy Cocozza at his own church of St. Mary Magdalen de Pazzi and the body was flown to Los Angeles. The remains had deteriorated so badly that a member of the family was asked by the Hollywood funeral parlor to identify the singer. That grim task fell to Terry Robinson, who brought along clean clothes to replace the ones from Rome. The coffin too was beginning to look the worse for wear, and Robinson immediately ordered it replaced with a copper casket.

The final, heartbreaking farewell to Mario Lanza took place at the Blessed Sacrament Church on Sunset Boulevard on 21 October 1959, two weeks after his passing. In terms of the number of people attending, it was a quieter affair than the circus in Philadelphia but no less emotional. The service was presided over by the Reverend Harold J. Ring, S.J., and among the 1500 mourners were Zsa Zsa Gabor, Kathryn Grayson, Dolores Hart, Joe Pasternak, Irving Aaronson, and Georgie Stoll. Tony Cocozza collapsed at his son's flag-draped casket and had to be helped from the church. Maria could be heard repeating over and over "My baby, my baby, my baby." Betty Lanza did what she could to console them but by now she too had given up the fight. Dolores Hart still recalls with great sadness how the final tragedy played itself out: "Uncle Mario's final funeral took place at the Blessed Sacrament Church in Los Angeles. It was a terrible, high-tension time and I was shocked that they opened the casket for a final viewing before the service. His body had deteriorated quite badly but it was felt that fans wanted to see it one last time."[10]

Kathryn Grayson had opened her heart and her home to Betty and the four children on their arrival back in the United States. Soon after her husband's temporary interment at Calvary Mausoleum, Betty and the children moved into rented accommodation in Beverly Hills, the home of actor Fred Clark, where they were joined once again by the ever-faithful maid Johnny Mobley. But the tragedies of Betty Lanza's own sad life were not over yet. Her name surfaced again in the newspapers in November 1959 when it was suggested that her mother, May Hicks, had "kidnapped" the four children and taken them to Chicago. The children were quickly returned to Los Angeles after the incident was reported to the police. May Hicks stated that she had simply taken the children to allow her daughter time to rest, and Betty Lanza agreed that it had all be a misunderstanding.

To Terry Robinson and the Cocozza's, however, it was clear that Betty was quickly losing the will to live. Her need for tranquilizers and alcohol had increased to such an extent since her husband's death that she hardly seemed to function any more. In the course of their thirteen-year marriage, Mario and Betty Lanza had enjoyed more than their share of triumphs and disasters. His highs had been hers, his fabulous successes hers to savor too, and when the hard times came—the walk-outs and the cancellations, the drinking and the carousing—she had continued to stand by him. In the end, life for Betty Lanza without her husband was simply not worth living.

On the morning of 11 March 1960, Terry Robinson received a phone call from Johnny Mobley, who told him that Betty was locked in her bedroom and would not respond to her summons. Robinson rushed over to the house, broke the door down, and found the wife of his friend dead in her bed. She was thirty-seven. The coroner's report indicated a high intake of alcohol and Seconal tablets, but Terry Robinson had no illusions about the true cause of her passing: "Betty died of a broken heart. There was no life for her after Mario. She just couldn't go on."[11] Dolores Hart has her own special memory of a beloved aunt: "She was so beautiful with her long black hair and laughing Irish eyes. She had a laugh that wouldn't stop and I remember thinking when she died that I would never hear that wonderful laugh again."[12]

From that tragedy came one last salvation. At their home in Pacific Palisades, Tony and Maria Cocozza had been simply putting in time, going through the motions of their daily lives with little interest in the world around them. Maria had even stopped going to church, wanting no part of a God who would take her only child from her. All of that changed when Johnny Mobley arrived at the door with the four frightened children in tow. Now there was no time for herself and her sorrow. Now there was her son's family to care for. Maria saw it as a sign, a blessed and holy sign from the God she had turned her back on.

Following a quiet service attended by family and close friends, Betty Lanza was laid to rest next to her husband in Holy Cross Cemetery in Los Angeles. May Hicks filed for custody of the four children the following month but despite the court challenge, Colleen, Ellisa, Damon, and

Marc Lanza stayed with the Cocozzas and Terry Robinson at 622 Toyopa Drive, where they grew into adulthood. The arrangement worked because of Robinson. The Cocozza's were too elderly to attend to all the needs of the rambunctious children and it was left to Robinson to instill a fatherly sense of discipline and value into their daily lives. Mario Lanza could have asked for no finer friend.

In the decades that followed, many changes and a few more tragedies touched the lives of all those who knew, worked with, and loved Mario Lanza. Maria Lanza Cocozza continued to promote her son's legacy to the day she died following a stroke at age sixty-eight on 7 July 1970. Tony Cocozza survived her by five years, when he passed away peacefully on 22 May 1975 at the age of eighty-one. Constantine Callinicos returned to his musical roots in New York and remained a staunch defender of his friend's accomplishments and his legacy. Costa passed away from a heart attack in 1986. Sam Weiler continued to collect his five percent of the tenor's royalties until his death in 1995. Under the terms of Weiler's contract, the right to a royalty from the Lanza estate was automatically transferred to his heirs until the year 2026. Other business associates involved with the Lanza career still claim a piece of the pie. Al Teitelbaum, now in his eighties, lives in Oregon. In the 1970s, under the pseudonym "Matt Bernard," Teitelbaum revisited Lanza's life and times in a biography that took a mordant look at the tenor's career.

Sadly, some of the tragedy of Mario Lanza's life passed on to two of his children. Following the death of their grandparents, Damon and Marc Lanza shared the house at 622 Toyopa Drive but they lost the property after mortgaging it to acquire venture capital for a pizzeria and sports bar. The investment soured and the house was sold to discharge the debts. Marc became reclusive and his troubled lifestyle undoubtedly led to his premature death at age thirty-seven in 1991.

Colleen Lanza toyed with a singing career for a time, producing one recording "Don't Lean on Me" with Lee Hazlewood, who had worked successfully with Nancy Sinatra. "Don't Lean on Me" did not enjoy much chart success but Colleen acquitted herself well and might have achieved a lot more had she stayed in show business. Instead, in 1971 she married Alberto Caldera Jr., nephew to the President of Venezuela. The union failed soon after and, although she married again, her life was not a happy one. On 19 July 1997, while crossing a street near her home in Canoga Park, California, Colleen was struck by a car and never regained consciousness. She passed away on 4 August at age forty-eight.

The tenor's other two children do much to carry the flame of their father's legacy. Damon Lanza produces *The Lanza Legend*, a quarterly publication sent out to Lanza fans across the globe. The magazine differs from most fan club periodicals in that it draws on Mario Lanza's personal collection of photographs and memorabilia for its content. Damon, an extremely affable and engaging man, also travels the world promoting his father's legacy.

Ellisa Lanza married businessman Bobby Bregman, and the couple currently reside in Beverly Hills, not far from where Ellisa's parents held court in the glory days of the early 1950s. Their two sons, Tony and Nick, are Mario Lanza's only grandchildren. In an echo of his famous grandfather's career decision sixty years earlier, Tony Bregman, an actor and model, recently had his name legally changed to Lanza. The Bregman's show business roots remain strong. Ellisa's brother-in-law is the richly talented bandleader and conductor Buddy Bregman who, among many other fine achievements, arranged and conducted the peerless *Cole Porter* and *Rodgers and Hart Songbooks* with Ella Fitzgerald. The Bregman's uncle was Jule Styne, master song stylist of such perennials as "Time After Time" and "Three Coins in the Fountain," as well as the great Broadway shows *Gypsy* and *Funny Girl*. Ellisa Lanza Bregman remains a jewel in her father's legacy, a gracious and beautiful woman who brings honor to his memory whenever she speaks on his behalf.

Terry Robinson is the great survivor. A talented, fit, and highly articulate man in his mid-eighties, Robinson lives in West Los Angeles with his lovely and spirited wife, Silvia. To Lanza fans the world over seeking the truth behind the legend, Robinson remains the central fount of all Lanza knowledge. Ever gracious and charming, he never tires of recounting his event-filled days with the Tiger and all the colorful characters that surrounded him during those exciting, turbulent, and unforgettable times. Today, in between acting as an advisor at a top health club in Los Angeles, Robinson devotes what free time he has to painting, lecturing, and swimming. He is, in the truest sense of the meaning, a Renaissance man.

CHAPTER FIFTEEN

Singing to the Gods

Time, that great leveler, has been very kind to the memory of Mario Lanza. For a singer whose professional career on films and recordings spanned little more than a decade, his legacy is more secure than ever. In the September 1999 edition of *Opera News*, the magazine invited more than forty opera performers and experts to name the greatest voice they ever heard. Tenor Richard Leech reminded the readers that Lanza's passion was the reason he became an opera singer, while Graham Clarke chose Mario Lanza for "romance and love of singing." Plácido Domingo stated simply that seeing Lanza in *The Great Caruso* as a young boy was the primary reason he turned to the classical stage. Domingo also hosted the acclaimed Emmy-nominated documentary *Mario Lanza: The American Caruso* in 1983.

The Great Caruso made an equally indelible impression on José Carreras. Carreras, like Domingo, Leech, and Pavarotti, was introduced to the excitement of grand opera through Lanza's groundbreaking film. In 1993 the Spanish tenor recorded an album dedicated to his idol "With a Song in My Heart" and followed it up with a worldwide concert tour at which he performed songs and arias from Mario Lanza's repertoire. Richard Leech has since taken the tribute a step further. In between engagements at the world's premier opera houses, the singer and his wife, Laurie Higgins, found the time to pen a unique remembrance of Mario Lanza for the concert stage. Whenever his operatic schedule permits, Leech brings his peerless Lanza tribute to such venues as Grant Park in Chicago and Carnegie Hall in New York, interspersing the famous songs with the story of Mario Lanza's life and career. The sincerity of the homage is at once both personal and deeply moving.

> Mario was not just another pretty voice. His was a communicative spirit that, for generations now, has touched hearts and ignited imaginations. That

spirit continues to find a home in the hearts of new audiences, and you could say that the fire he started half a century ago is, quite simply, burning out of control, fueled by the passions of singers and listeners alike. Perhaps I can best express my thoughts on Mario's place in history with the words I use to end each of my Mario concerts. I say: "Although he never realized his dream of singing in the worlds greatest opera houses Mario Lanza left a unique legacy. As if frozen in time he will always be the young, vibrant, full voiced Mario that we find in his films and on his recordings. Mario Lanza will live forever . . . in the cherished memories of his fans . . . and in the careers of those he inspires." As I finish with the song "I'll Be Seeing You," the hushed silence that invariably follows is, to me, the loudest bravo, and the clearest evidence that our beloved Mario will, indeed, never ever be forgotten.[1]

Soprano Renée Fleming is another who clearly understands the power of the singer's lasting persona: "He has been a tremendous inspiration to myself and especially to my tenor colleagues. I appreciate it must have been extremely difficult for him to maintain his commercial success as well as his reputation as one of the great singers of his and any era."[2]

The Lanza voice remains a best seller for BMG/RCA, with the recent compilation *The Definitive Collection* topping Britain's Classic FM chart for weeks on end, a remarkable testament to the tenor's timeless and unparalleled crossover appeal. Lanza's recordings have made their mark in the history books, too. Four of the singer's albums reached number one in the pop charts, a feat that has never been matched by any other classical artist: *The Great Caruso* and *Mario Lanza Sings Christmas Songs* both made it to the top in 1951, *Because You're Mine* in 1952, and *The Student Prince* in 1954. *The Student Prince* stayed at the number-one position for an astonishing thirty-four weeks. The Recording Industry Association of America first established the criteria for certifying gold record awards for albums and singles in 1958. Lanza's *Student Prince* album was certified gold in 1960, one of the very first movie soundtrack albums to achieve that status. *The Great Caruso* collection received its certification in 1968, the first such album of operatic arias to achieve that distinction.

On 31 January 1996, the seventy-fifth anniversary of his birth, the singer's daughter Ellisa attended a ceremony in honor of her father in the grounds of London's Royal Albert Hall. With the blessing of the trustees, two trees were planted in Mario Lanza's name, the only occasion in the venue's long and celebrated history that an artist who performed there has been so honored.

On a more tangible level, the Mario Lanza Institute in Philadelphia is dedicated to perpetuating the singer's legacy through annual scholarships awarded in Lanza's name. Chartered in 1962 by attorney John A. Papola under the nonprofit corporation law of the Commonwealth of Pennsylvania, the Mario Lanza Institute holds auditions at the Settlement Music School at 416 Queen Street in South Philadelphia on the last Monday and Tuesday of October each year. The scholarship winners are announced at the annual Mario Lanza Ball, which is held in the city soon after the auditions. The ball, a gala affair, draws Lanza fans from across the globe, all of them gathering to pay tribute and to remember.

During its four-decade-long history, the Mario Lanza Institute has awarded hundreds of vocal scholarships to gifted and aspiring young singers. In addition to Papola, the original signers of the Articles of Incorporation for the Mario Lanza Institute were the tenor's uncle, Arnold Lanza, his friend Joseph Curreri, Nicholas Petrella, and Mildred Fisher, who hosted one of the leading Mario Lanza societies back in the 1960s. Nick Petrella successfully acted as president of the Mario Lanza Institute for several decades and was followed by Maynard Bertolet, who took the running of the organization to a new and even higher standard of excellence. At the time of writing, John Papola's widow, Mary, serves as institute's president.

Of the current crop of Lanza Scholarship winners, great hope rests with a young tenor, Frank Tenaglia, who is managed by John Durso, son of Freddy Cocozza's boyhood friend. Tenaglia's voice is big and round and bold, much like the younger Lanza, and Durso Sr. is quick to draw favorable comparison between the two singers.

The Mario Lanza Museum is housed at 712 Montrose Street, annexed to the Church of St. Mary Magdalen de Pazzi where Lanza sang as a young man. In addition to Lanza compact discs, rare recordings, and videotapes, the museum also showcases memorabilia from the tenor's career; it is a must for all Lanza devotees seeking material from off the beaten track.

The house at 636 Christian Street still stands, and on 7 November 1993 the Pennsylvania Historical and Museum Commission unveiled a state historical marker in honor of Mario Lanza outside its front door. The marker acknowledges Lanza's unique place in history as a radio, concert, and recording artist, with special mention being given to his 1951 film *The Great Caruso*.

The City of Philadelphia has also honored its famous son in a multitude of other ways. On 7 October 1961 Mayor Richardson Dilworth issued a proclamation naming 7 October Mario Lanza Memorial Day. The following year Maria Lanza Cocozza officiated at a ceremony dedicating Mario Lanza Park at Third and Queen Street in honor of her son. Mario Lanza Boulevard bears the tenor's name in Eastwick, Southwest Philadelphia. The Philadelphia Academy of Music, where Serge Koussevitzky helped launched the young Mario Lanza's career in 1942, has also honored the singer with a plaque bearing his name embedded in the sidewalk in front of the building.

In 1997, the Philadelphia Mural Arts Program of the Department of Recreation of the City of Philadelphia contracted artist Diane Keller to create a mural of Mario Lanza on a wall on 1327 S. Broad Street, at the corner of Broad and Reed. The mural was the brainchild of artistic director Jane Golden Heriza, who worked closely with Maynard Bertolet from the Mario Lanza Institute in developing the project. On its completion on 1 November 1997 the mural spanned an impressive forty-five feet in height to thirty-five feet in width. Mario Lanza himself could hardly have imagined a more high-profile tribute to his memory.

Lanza fan clubs continue to prosper the world over, with the flagship undoubtedly being the British Mario Lanza Society. Founded in 1961 by Pauline Franklin, the British Mario Lanza Society is also home to the Mario Lanza Educational Foundation. Chaired by William Earl, the foundation, like its American counterpart the Mario Lanza Institute, awards yearly music scholarships in Lanza's name. The British society, through generous contributions from its members, was also instrumental in sponsoring a new rose cultivated in the tenor's honor. Launched at the Hampton Court Flower Show on 3 July 2000, *Rosa "Mario Lanza"* is just one more in a long line of tributes to one man's extraordinary talent and enduring appeal.

Lanza's legacy is also well served on the web, with a number of sites dedicated to promoting his legacy (see *Resources: Mario Lanza Institute and Museum, Fan Clubs, and Websites*). The finest by far is hosted by Jeff Rense; the beautifully designed site has an array of links to all aspects of Lanza's career. It also offers an active discussion forum notable for its generally balanced and polite exchange of ideas, no small achievement in today's combative website chat room environment. Much of the credit here undoubtedly goes to Jeff Rense's guiding hand and sensible influence on all the visitors to his exemplary site.

On 31 January 1998, on the seventy-seventh anniversary of his birth, Lanza was honored with his own star on the Palm Springs Walk of Stars in California. The force behind the tribute was long-time Lanza devotee Tillie Hartley, whose concentrated efforts over the years helped bring it to fruition. A Mario Lanza star also graces Hollywood's Walk of Fame in Los Angeles. Another Lanza admirer, Alice C. Albro, has to date collected more than 23,000 signatures requesting the U.S. Postal Service issue a commemorative stamp in the singer's name. It is surely only a matter of time before he is so honored.

Hardly a year goes by without some rumor of an impending movie based on the tenor's life. Scenarios for telling his story on the screen tend to fall into two camps: those who would present it as a latter-day *Sound of Music*–type family fare extravaganza, or those who would seek to dwell on the darker side, complete with Mafia overtones. Both outlines do a disservice to the singer's memory. Lanza's career was difficult and complex, fraught with disasters that seemed to go hand in hand with its many triumphs. He was certainly no saint but to concentrate on his sins, nearly all of which were directed toward himself, would be to cloud the great legacy he left behind. Moreover, no producer should even consider making the project without using Lanza's own singing voice on the soundtrack. There are many wonderful singers today who can do justice to his songs, especially on the stage, but on film only one voice could adequately explain what all the fuss was about in the first place. The Lanza voice was wholly unique, one that continues to captivate listeners everywhere through his imperishable legacy of recordings for BMG/RCA. Given the primitive technical sound available to Caruso in his day, Lanza himself had no choice but to sing for his idol in *The Great Caruso*. There are no such problems with Lanza's own recorded repertoire, most of which was captured in pristine sound. Pity indeed the singer who would try to compete with so fresh and vibrant a legacy on the screen.

Lanza's loss to the world of grand opera is incalculable. Had he lived, had he regained control of his troubled psyche, had he focused once again on the classical stage, there are no limits to what he could have achieved here. It was surely his dream to sing on the stages of the world's great opera houses, and a compelling argument could be made that his neglect of this aspect of his career undoubtedly played a part in his early demise. Had Lanza embraced the demands of a full-time operatic career, with all the rigors and the discipline that came with it, his life, his health, and his sense of self-worth would have been the better for it. There were signs too before his death that he was finally starting to come to terms with where he should be taking his exceptional talent. During that last summer his old friend Peter Herman Adler visited him at the Villa Badoglio, and it wasn't long before the matter of the singer's true calling came up.

> I saw him for the last time while I was conducting at the Rome Opera. . . . He was working two hours a day with an operatic coach and intended to go back to opera, his only true love. He offered me "a part of him" if I would again take over planning for his operatic future. He was prepared to get rid of all other managers and press agents who had ruined his life and career. I agreed, but not for "a piece of him" like a boxing manager. His lovely Irish wife, Betty, brought me to the train accompanied by their four children. (Lanza was an excellent "Italian" father.) I was on my way to conduct a symphony concert in Bologna but promised all possible help if, first of all, he disciplined himself and reduced his basically impressive and excellent body. It was too late. All the excesses had taken their toll.[3]

Lanza's offer to Adler that he could have a "piece" of his career in return for prepping him for the classical stage is especially telling. For all Lanza's staggering successes—and in 1959 he was still the most famous tenor in the world—the statement suggests an inbred insecurity, a sense that he still felt he had to offer himself fully in return for whatever favors he deemed were necessary to further his career. There were plenty of takers and hangers-on in Mario Lanza's career, but Peter Herman Adler was not one of them. Adler could certainly have returned the singer to full vocal form, but given Lanza's rapidly declining health in 1959 there was no turning back. Mario Lanza never achieved the acclaim and the glory at La Scala, or Covent Garden, or the

Metropolitan Opera House that his exceptional vocal talent demanded and he forever remains a postscript—albeit a very significant one—in the history of the great operatic tenors of the twentieth century.

He also remains, conversely, the greatest romantic tenor of his age, due in no small part to his wholly unique crossover appeal. Every musical taste is catered to in the Lanza catalogue—and catered to well. His operatic recordings are all excellent and some even more so, though the lack of a complete work on disc is lamentable. His recordings for the soundtrack of *The Student Prince,* while not completely true to the Sigmund Romberg–Dorothy Donnelly score, is still the yardstick by which all *Student Prince* performances are judged. Even those who judge Lanza harshly for his occasional lack of vocal restraint could hardly find fault with this body of work. The voice, the approach, the commitment, the singing are all faultless—a testament to all that Mario Lanza stood for in his time, and all that he was.

Songs of faith particularly suited the Lanza voice, and it is regrettable that shortness of time prevented him from recording such obvious material as Franck's "Panis Angelicus," Mozart's "Ave Verum," Bizet's "Agnus Dei," Rossini's "Cujus Animam," and Handel's "Ombra mai fu." One only has to consider the time devoted to such fare as the execrable "Pineapple Pickers" to realize the full extent of the lost opportunity here. Still, Lanza managed to make an imperishable mark with the sacred material he did commit to disc. Both his Bach-Gounod and Schubert's "Ave Maria" are exemplary, the one showing the full glory of the voice, the other the soft pianissimo he was able to create so effortlessly. His reading of Henry Malotte's "The Lord's Prayer" is a classic by any standard, and it is to be fervently hoped that his final recording of this lovely song—so glowingly praised by Constantine Callinicos—is located in the BMG Italia vaults before too long. "I'll Walk with God" from *The Student Prince* soundtrack remains a deeply moving experience, one that transcends all the obvious limitations of the material. Similar compelling sincerity was brought to Harpo Marx's "Guardian Angels," Joyce Kilmer's "Trees," and Ethelbert Nevin's "The Rosary." Lanza's impeccable performance of Max Reger's lovely "The Virgin's Slumber Song" is a classic by any standard.

To many of his admirers, the true sound of the Lanza voice reverberates in his deeply felt approach to the great romantic standards of the Great American Songbook. At his frequent best, Lanza elevated the classic ballads of Porter, Kern, and Rodgers and Hart to a new high, his diction the equal and in some cases superior to even that of Sinatra. For a singer who was equally at home with the great arias of Puccini, Verdi, and their contemporaries, there can be no greater praise. Lanza brought an imperishable conviction to such great standards as "Begin the Beguine," "All the Things You Are," "Without a Song," "My Romance," and "I'll Be Seeing You"—to name just a few—that has not been equaled by any of his peers on the classical stage. Great artists like Tauber, Gigli, Domingo, and Carreras have all toyed with the popular songs of the day, but while their musicianship was never in question, their formal training always seemed to get in the way. One can never quite shake the feeling of a classical singer slumming it for the occasion. Such was not the case with Lanza. His innate sense for what was right for a song, his total understanding of the lyric and the intensity with which he delivered it went to the very heart of the work and made it a unique listening experience for his audience. His lack of experience on the classical stage may have denied him his rightful place in the operatic pantheon, but he remains the definitive crossover artist. Simply put, no one ever did it better.

For the most part, Lanza's films were a mixed bag, but his performance in *The Great Caruso* will surely stand the test of time. The enormous vitality, the expansiveness in Lanza's singing is evident every time he is on the screen. However much Hollywood tinkered with the operatic excerpts and the life of the man depicted in the movie, the essence of Caruso and the appeal of grand opera has never been captured better on film. Its impact on an entire generation of musicians is certainly not in dispute. In a memorable assessment of Louis Armstrong's role in the development of the jazz trumpet, Dizzy Gillespie once observed "No him, no me." The same can surely be said of the lasting influence Lanza's voice and his larger-than-life persona has had on the careers of so many of today's great operatic performers.

Joy is a key word in describing Lanza's singing. He loved to sing, even when his personal life was in turmoil, and that vocal enthusiasm literally leaps out of the speakers whenever his recordings are played. Many of those recordings, of course, are classics—songs that are his and his alone. Think of "Arrivederci Roma" or "Song of India" and you immediately think of Mario Lanza. Long before the Three Tenors got to grips with "Granada," the tune was synonymous with Lanza's voice.

Through his performance in *The Great Caruso* he brought new life to Guy d'Hardelot's turn-of-the-century ballad "Because," and for a time claimed the Bach-Gounod "Ave Maria" as his own. His joyous spin on Allan Jones' delightful and perfectly silly "The Donkey Serenade" came just months after he had thrilled diva Licia Albanese in the recording studio with his impassioned reading with her of the *Otello* duet "Dio ti giocondi." Crossover does not get more wide ranging than that. Lanza's great million selling songs—"Be My Love," "The Loveliest Night of the Year," and "Because You're Mine"—are as fresh today as when they were recorded, a faultless and lasting combination of good songs and a great singer.

Today, the tributes to Mario Lanza's memory continue on stage and on records, and it is surely only a matter of time before his event-filled life is told on the movie screen. Perhaps then history will repeat itself once more, with Lanza's glorious voice pouring forth from the speakers and inspiring a whole new age of musicians to carry the flame. It might not be quite the legacy he would have chosen for himself, but somehow it is not hard to imagine that he would be pleased.

On the evening of 24 July 1948, at a time when his whole fabulous career was starting to unfold, Mario Lanza strolled on stage at the Hollywood Bowl to the thunderous applause of an ecstatic audience. Resplendent in white jacket, impossibly handsome for someone who could sing the way he did, he announced that for an encore he would sing "Nessun dorma" from *Turandot*. Conductor Miklós Rózsa raised his baton and the orchestra began the introduction to Puccini's timeless masterpiece. Somewhat tentatively, the tenor began to sing. He was still at a point in his professional career where nervous insecurity dogged him with each appearance—something in truth he never really got over. But as the orchestra and the singer moved together through the aria, the glory of the voice and the soul of the artist began to take hold and the spell was cast.

Lanza's singing that night was as much for his peers as it was for his audience—a man, a tenor, singing to the gods of his own personal world who had inspired him down through the years to become one of their own. Standing there under the stars, Mario Lanza must have realized that he had become one of the blessed chosen few, an artist who would one day lay claim to some sort of musical immortality through the pure and simple magic of his voice. The gods smiled on him that night just as they did on the fabulous and unforgettable career that was so soon to follow. And if the ending was sad, if some of the glorious potential was not fulfilled, then that too was part of the story. What has survived, what continues to flourish and grow with each passing decade is the legacy and the legend of a peerless romantic tenor, a man who spun musical gold and created magic. No singer, no great artist, could surely ask for more.

DISCOGRAPHY

The Complete Film Soundtrack and Studio Recordings, 1948–1959

The greatest gift of Mario Lanza's extraordinary legacy is surely to be found in the many recordings he made for RCA, film soundtracks and associated sources; recordings, moreover, that span the widest musical spectrum imaginable. The following is a chronological listing of all Lanza's professional recordings, beginning with tracks laid down in 1948 for his first film *That Midnight Kiss* and on through to the final studio sessions for RCA in Rome, a little more than a decade later. The tenor's recorded recital from London's Royal Albert Hall in 1958 is also included, as is the entire body of work recorded for his weekly radio series *The Mario Lanza Show*, sponsored by the Coca-Cola Company. Selections featured on Lanza's television and radio appearances not sponsored by Coca-Cola are detailed elsewhere (see *Stage, Radio, and Television Appearances*).

Matrix numbers for all RCA American recordings are listed in parentheses after each title; reference numbers for RCA Italiana takes, where known, are likewise detailed. No such matrix numbers exist for *The Mario Lanza Show* recordings, all of which are listed here by date of radio broadcast. Recordings for *The Mario Lanza Show* were generally made within a week or so of the air date.

Every effort has been made to account for all alternate takes from Lanza's MGM and Warner Bros. sessions, though some complete performances may exist in the film studio vaults where at present partial takes only are suggested. In an earlier abridged version of this discography it was stated that Lanza had recorded five popular Italian songs in the summer of 1959, "Volare" among them. These selections are not included in this new listing. The songs were certainly on the tenor's recording schedule, but there is some question now as to whether he found the time to commit the material to disc. A similar question mark hangs over Lanza's final recording, "The Lord's Prayer," which continues to prove elusive. Still, Constantine Callinicos' moving account of that last studio session remains compelling. Perhaps before another decade has passed the recording will appear and the final footnote to a remarkable and unforgettable career will be put in place.

Finally, in response to many requests I have cross-referenced the individual song titles to their current availability on compact disc. Bracketed numbers refer to the compact discs on which the song is currently available; see the numbered list of discs at the end of this section. With one exception, all compact discs listed are BMG/RCA or BMG-licensed product.

1 December 1948, MGM Studios, Hollywood
Soundtrack recordings for *That Midnight Kiss*
MGM Studio Orchestra conducted by Charles Previn
    Mamma Mia, Che Vo' Sapè? (Nutile-Russo) (Giacomo Spadoni, piano)
    They Didn't Believe Me (Kern-Reynolds) (Kathryn Grayson, soprano) [11]
    I Know, I Know, I Know (Kaper-Russell)

9 December 1948, MGM Studios, Hollywood
Soundtrack recordings for *That Midnight Kiss*
MGM Studio Orchestra conducted by José Iturbi
    Aida: Celeste Aida (Verdi)
    L'Elisir d'Amore: Una furtiva lagrima (Donizetti) (José Iturbi, piano)

30 December 1948, MGM Studios, Hollywood
Soundtrack recording for *That Midnight Kiss*
MGM Studio Orchestra conducted by José Iturbi
    Love Is Music (Tchaikovsky-Charles and André Previn) (Kathryn Grayson, soprano) [11]

31 December 1948, MGM Studios, Hollywood
Soundtrack recording for *That Midnight Kiss*
MGM Studio Orchestra conducted by José Iturbi
    One Love of Mine (Tchaikovsky-Charles and André Previn) (Kathryn Grayson, soprano) (outtake)

14 January 1949, MGM Studios, Hollywood
Soundtrack recording for *That Midnight Kiss*
    L'Africana: O paradiso (Meyerbeer) (Irving Aaronson, piano) (outtake)

5 May 1949, Manhattan Center, New York
First RCA recording session
RCA Victor Orchestra; Constantine Callinicos, conductor
 Aida: Celeste Aida (Verdi) (D9RC-1728-1) [1, 4, 7, 13]
 La Bohème: Che gelida manina (Puccini) (D9RC-1729-1) [4, 13, 19, 21]
 Mamma Mia, Che Vo' Sapè? (Nutile-Russo) (D9RC-1730-1) [4, 13]
 Core'ngrato (Cardillo-Cordiferro) (D9RC-1731-1) [4, 13, 19]

23 August 1949, Republic Studios, Hollywood
RCA Victor Orchestra; Ray Sinatra, conductor
 They Didn't Believe Me (Kern-Reynolds) (D9RC-1257-1) [4, 13, 18]
 I Know, I Know, I Know (Kaper-Russell) (D9RC-1258-1) [4, 13]
 Mattinata (Leoncavallo) (D9-RC-1259-1) [1]

28 October 1949, Republic Studios, Hollywood
RCA Victor Orchestra; Ray Sinatra, conductor
 O Sole Mio (Di Capua-Capurro) (D9RC-1282-1) [1]
 Lolita (Buzzi-Peccia) (D9RC-1283-1) [7, 21]
 Granada (Lara) (D9RC-1284-1) [1, 7]
 Granada (Lara) (D9RC-1284-2) (alternate take)

5 December 1949, MGM Studios, Hollywood
Soundtrack recording for *The Toast of New Orleans*
MGM Studio Orchestra; Johnny Green, conductor
 Madama Butterfly: Act I Finale (Puccini) (Kathryn Grayson, soprano) [11]

6 December 1949, MGM Studios, Hollywood
Soundtrack recordings for *The Toast of New Orleans*
MGM Studio Orchestra; Georgie Stoll, conductor
 I'll Never Love You (Brodszky-Cahn) [11]

7 December 1949, MGM Studios, Hollywood
Soundtrack recordings for *The Toast of New Orleans*
MGM Studio Orchestra; Johnny Green, conductor, with Jacob Gimpel, piano
 Martha: M'appari (Flotow) (partial take)
 L'Africana: O paradiso (Meyerbeer)
 Carmen: La fleur que tu m'avais jetée (Bizet)

9 December 1949, MGM Studios, Hollywood
Soundtrack recordings for *The Toast of New Orleans*
MGM Studio Orchestra; Johnny Green, conductor
  La Traviata: Libiamo, libiamo, ne'lieti calici (Verdi) (Kathryn Grayson,
  soprano) [2]

15 December 1949, MGM Studios, Hollywood
Soundtrack recordings for *The Toast of New Orleans*
MGM Studio Orchestra; Georgie Stoll, conductor
  Bayou Lullaby (Brodszky-Cahn) (Kathryn Grayson, soprano)
  Be My Love (Brodszky-Cahn) (Kathryn Grayson, soprano) [11]
  Be My Love (Brodszky-Cahn) (Kathryn Grayson, soprano) (alternate version)

27 December 1949, MGM Studios, Hollywood
Soundtrack recordings for *The Toast of New Orleans*
MGM Studio Orchestra; Georgie Stoll, conductor
  The Tina-Lina (Brodszky-Cahn) [11]

28 December 1949, MGM Studios, Hollywood
Soundtrack recordings for *The Toast of New Orleans*
MGM Studio Orchestra; Georgie Stoll, conductor
  I'll Never Love You (Brodszky-Cahn) (revised take)
  Be My Love (Brodszky-Cahn) (retake, Lanza only)

25 January 1950, MGM Studios, Hollywood
Soundtrack recordings for *The Toast of New Orleans*
MGM Studio Orchestra; Georgie Stoll, conductor
  The Tina-Lina (Brodszky-Cahn) (with J. Carrol Naish and chorus)

17 February 1950, MGM Studios, Hollywood
Soundtrack recordings for *The Toast of New Orleans*
MGM Studio Orchestra; Georgie Stoll, conductor
  Boom Biddy Boom Boom (Brodszky-Cahn)

8 April 1950, Republic Studios, Hollywood
RCA Victor Orchestra; Constantine Callinicos, conductor
  L'Africana: O paradiso (Meyerbeer) (EORC-336-1) [13, 14]
  Carmen: La fleur que tu m'avais jetée (Bizet) (EORC-337-1)
  Carmen: La fleur que tu m'avais jetée (Bizet) (EORC-337-2) (alternate take)
  [7, 13, 21]
  Martha: M'appari (Flotow) (EORC-338-1) [13, 19]

11 April 1950, Republic Studios, Hollywood
RCA Victor Orchestra; Constantine Callinicos, conductor
Madama Butterfly: Stolta paura l'amor (Puccini) (EORC-339/340-1)
(Elaine Malbin, soprano) [13, 14]
Madama Butterfly: Stolta paura l'amor (Puccini) (EORC-339/340-2)
(Elaine Malbin, soprano) (partial take)
La Traviata: Libiamo, libiamo, ne'lieti calici (Verdi) (EORC-341-1)
(Elaine Malbin, soprano)
La Traviata: Libiamo, libiamo, ne'lieti calici (Verdi) (EORC-341-2)
(Elaine Malbin, soprano) (alternate take)
La Traviata: Libiamo, libiamo, ne'lieti calici (Verdi) (EORC-341-3)
(Elaine Malbin, soprano) (alternate take) [7, 13]

11 May 1950, Republic Studios, Hollywood
RCA Victor Orchestra; Constantine Callinicos, conductor
Ave Maria (Bach-Gounod) (EORC-350-1) (Eudice Shapiro, violin solo) [5]

15 May 1950, Republic Studios, Hollywood
RCA Victor Orchestra; Constantine Callinicos, conductor
L'Elisir d'Amore: Una furtiva lagrima (Donizetti) (EORC-351-1) [3]
Pagliacci: Vesti la giubba (Leoncavallo) (EORC-352-1) [1]
Pagliacci: Vesti la giubba (Leoncavallo) (EORC-352-2) (alternate take)
Pagliacci: Vesti la giubba (Leoncavallo) (EORC-352-3) (alternate take) [3, 7]
Rigoletto: Questa o quella (Puccini) (EORC-353-1) [3, 7, 19]
Rigoletto: La donna e mobile (Puccini) (EORC-353-1b) [3, 7]

18 May 1950, Republic Studios, Hollywood
RCA Victor Orchestra; Constantine Callinicos, conductor
Andrea Chenier: Un di all'azzuro spazio (Giordano) (EORC-354-1) [14]
Andrea Chenier: Come un bel di di maggio (Giordano) (EORC-355-1) [14]
Tosca: Recondita armonia (Puccini) (EORB-3645-1) [3]
Tosca: E lucevan le stelle (Puccini) (EORB-3646-1) [3]

29 May 1950, Republic Studios, Hollywood
RCA Victor Orchestra; Constantine Callinicos, conductor
O Holy Night (Adam) (EORC-357-1) [4, 21]
Cavalleria Rusticana: Addio alla madre (Mascagni) (EORC-358-1)
Cavalleria Rusticana: Addio alla madre (Mascagni) (EORC-358-2)
(alternate take) [7]

The Virgin's Slumber Song (Reger) (EORC-359-1) [5]
Rigoletto: Parmi veder le lagrime (Verdi) (EORC-360-1) [3]
Rigoletto: Parmi veder le lagrime (Verdi) (EORC-360-2) (alternate take)
La Gioconda: Cielo e mar (Ponchielli) (EORC-361-1) [3]

6 June 1950, Republic Studios, Hollywood
RCA Victor Orchestra; Constantine Callinicos, conductor
La Forza del Destino: O tu che in seno agli angeli (Verdi) (EORC-363-1) [21]
Serenade (Toselli) (EORC-364-1)
Serenade (Drigo) (EORC-365-1) [7]

27 June 1950, Republic Studios, Hollywood
RCA Victor Orchestra and the Jeff Alexander Choir; Ray Sinatra, conductor
The Tina-Lina (Brodszky-Cahn) (EORB-3685-1) [13]
Be My Love (Brodszky-Cahn) (EORB-3686-1) [1, 7, 19]

29 June 1950, Republic Studios, Hollywood
RCA Victor Orchestra and the Jeff Alexander Choir; Ray Sinatra, conductor
Toast of New Orleans (Brodszky-Cahn) (EORB-3687-1) [13]
Boom Biddy Boom Boom (Brodszky-Cahn) (EORB-3685-1) [7, 13]
The Bayou Lullaby (Brodszky-Cahn) (EORB-3693-1) [13]
I'll Never Love You (Brodszky-Cahn) (EORB-3697-1) [13]

17 July 1950, MGM Studios, Hollywood
Soundtrack recording for *The Great Caruso*
MGM Studio Orchestra; Peter Herman Adler, conductor
Pagliacci: Vesti la giubba (Leoncavallo)
Pagliacci: Vesti la giubba (Leoncavallo) (outtake) [11]

22 July 1950, MGM Studios, Hollywood
Soundtrack recording for *The Great Caruso*
MGM Studio Orchestra; Peter Herman Adler, conductor
Tosca: E lucevan le stelle (Puccini)
La Bohème: Che gelida manina (Puccini) (rejected)
La Gioconda: Cielo e mar (Ponchielli) (rejected)

7 August 1950, MGM Studios, Hollywood
Soundtrack recording for *The Great Caruso*
Mattinata (Leoncavallo) (a cappella)

Torna a Surriento (de Curtis-de Curtis) (Irving Aaronson, piano)
Torna a Surriento (de Curtis-de Curtis) (Irving Aaronson, piano) (outtake)
La Danza (Rossini) (Irving Aaronson, piano)

9 August 1950, MGM Studios, Hollywood

Soundtrack recording for *The Great Caruso*
MGM Studio Orchestra; Peter Herman Adler, conductor
  Because (d'Hardelot)
  Santa Lucia (Cottrau) (outtake)
  Marechiare (Tosti-Di Giacomo) (Irving Aaronson, piano; brief orchestral
  overdub added later)

11 August 1950, MGM Studios, Hollywood

Soundtrack recording for *The Great Caruso*
  Ave Maria (Bach-Gounod) (Jacqueline Allen, soprano, St. Luke's
  Choristers, and Wesley Tourtelotte, organ) [11]

18 August 1950, MGM Studios, Hollywood

Soundtrack recordings for *The Great Caruso*
MGM Studio Orchestra; Peter Herman Adler, conductor
  Tosca: Torture Scene (Puccini) (Giuseppe Valdengo, baritone, and Teresa
  Celli, soprano)
  Aida: O terra, addio (Verdi) (Dorothy Kirsten, soprano, and Blanche
  Thebom, mezzo-soprano)
  Andrea Chenier: Un di all'azzuro spazio (Giordano) (outtake)

19 August 1950, MGM Studios, Hollywood

Soundtrack recordings for *The Great Caruso*
MGM Studio Orchestra; Peter Herman Adler, conductor
  Il Trovatore: Ah! Che la morte ognora (Miserere) (Verdi) (Lucine Amara,
  soprano)
  Aida: Celeste Aida (Verdi) (Lanza recorded the last note to this aria again
  on 29 August 1950, which was then edited into the final print)

22 August 1950, MGM Studios, Hollywood

Soundtrack recordings for *The Great Caruso*
MGM Studio Orchestra; Peter Herman Adler, conductor

Rigoletto: Bella figlia dell'amore (Quartet) (Verdi) (Blanche Thebom, mezzo-soprano, Giuseppe Valdengo, baritone, and Olive May Beach, soprano)

Martha: Finale (Flotow) (Dorothy Kirsten, soprano, and Nicola Moscona, bass)

23 August 1950, MGM Studios, Hollywood

Soundtrack recordings for *The Great Caruso*

MGM Studio Orchestra; Peter Herman Adler, conductor

Cavalleria Rusticana: Vivo il vino spumeggiante (Brindisi) (Mascagni)
Lucia di Lammermoor: Sextet (Donizetti) (Blanche Thebom, mezzo-soprano, Dorothy Kirsten, soprano, Giuseppe Valdengo, baritone, Nicola Moscona, bass, and Gilbert Russell, tenor) [11]

26 August 1950, Republic Studios, Hollywood

RCA Victor Orchestra; Ray Sinatra, conductor

My Song, My Love (Beelby-Gerda) (EORB-3770-1) [7]
Because (d'Hardelot) (EORB-3771-1) (rejected)
I Love Thee (Grieg) (EORB-3772-1) [10]
For You Alone (Geehl-O'Reilly) (EORB-3773-1) (rejected)

28 August 1950, MGM Studios, Hollywood

Soundtrack recordings for *The Great Caruso*

MGM Studio Orchestra; Peter Herman Adler, conductor

Rigoletto: E il sol dell'anima (Verdi) (Jarmilla Novotnà, soprano) (outtake)

29 August 1950, MGM Studios, Hollywood

Soundtrack recordings for *The Great Caruso*

MGM Studio Orchestra; Peter Herman Adler, conductor

La Bohème: Che gelida manina (Puccini) (retake)
La Gioconda: Cielo e mar (Donizetti) (retake, excerpt only)
Rigoletto: La donna e mobile (Verdi)
Rigoletto: La donna e mobile (Verdi) (alternate take) [11]
Martha: M'appari (Flotow) (excerpt only)

17 October 1950, MGM Studios, Hollywood

Soundtrack recordings for *The Great Caruso*

MGM Studio Orchestra; Johnny Green, conductor

Cavalleria Rusticana: No, Turiddu, rimani (Mascagni) (Marina Koshetz, soprano)

18 December 1950, MGM Studios, Hollywood
Soundtrack recordings for *The Great Caruso*
MGM Studio Orchestra; Johnny Green, conductor
 Aida: Nume custode e vindice (Temple Scene) (Verdi) (Bob Ebright,
 tenor, and Nicola Moscona, bass)
 'A Vucchella (Tosti-D'Annunzio)

19 February 1951, Manhattan Center, New York
RCA Victor Orchestra; Constantine Callinicos, conductor
 For You Alone (Geehl-O'Reilly) (E1RB-1167-1) [10]
 Because (d'Hardelot) (E1RB-1168-1) [1, 7, 10]

23 February 1951, Manhattan Center, New York
RCA Victor Orchestra; Constantine Callinicos, conductor
 The Loveliest Night of the Year (Aaronson-Webster) (E1RB-1166-1) [1, 7]
 'A Vucchella (Tosti-D'Annunzio) (E1RB-1186-1)
 Marechiare (Tosti-Di Giacomo) (E1RB-1187-1)

10 June 1951 (Air Date), Radio Recorder Studio, Los Angeles
Selections recorded for the first broadcast of *The Mario Lanza Show*
Orchestra conducted by Ray Sinatra
 Granada (Lara) [17, 19]
 Serenade (Toselli)
 Because (d'Hardelot) [17, 19]
 Be My Love (Brodszky-Cahn)

17 June 1951 (Air Date), Radio Recorder Studio, Los Angeles
Selections recorded for *The Mario Lanza Show*
Orchestra conducted by Ray Sinatra
 Boom Biddy Boom Boom (Brodszky-Cahn)
 I Love Thee (Grieg)
 O Sole Mio (Di Capua-Capurro) [17, 19]
 The Loveliest Night of the Year (Aaronson-Webster) [17, 19]

24 June 1951 (Air Date), Radio Recorder Studio, Los Angeles
Selections recorded for *The Mario Lanza Show*
Orchestra conducted by Ray Sinatra
 My Song, My Love (Beelby-Gerda)
 Serenade (Drigo)

I'll Never Love You (Brodszky-Cahn)
Pagliacci: Vesti la giubba (Leoncavallo) [14]

1 July 1951 (Air Date), Radio Recorder Studio, Los Angeles
Selections recorded for *The Mario Lanza Show*
Orchestra conducted by Ray Sinatra
   Funiculì, Funiculà (in English) (Turco-Denza) [8]
   Mamma Mia, Che Vo' Sapè? (Nutile-Russo) [17]
   Someday (Friml-Post-Hooker) [17, 21]
   Thine Alone (Herbert) [17]

8 July 1951 (Air Date), Radio Recorder Studio, Los Angeles
Selections recorded for *The Mario Lanza Show*
Orchestra conducted by Ray Sinatra
   For You Alone (Geehl-O'Reilly)
   La Danza (Rossini) [8, 19]
   I'm Falling in Love with Someone (Herbert) [17]
   Torna a Surriento (de Curtis-de Curtis) [17, 19]

12 July 1951, MGM Studios, Hollywood
Soundtrack recordings for *Because You're Mine*
MGM Studio Orchestra; Johnny Green, conductor
   All the Things You Are (outtake) (Kern-Hammerstein II) [11]
   L'Africana: O paradiso (Meyerbeer)
   Mamma Mia, Che Vo' Sapè? (Nutile-Russo)

15 July 1951 (Air Date), Radio Recorder Studio, Los Angeles
Selections recorded for *The Mario Lanza Show*
Orchestra conducted by Ray Sinatra
   The Tina-Lina (Brodszky-Cahn)
   Lolita (Buzzi-Peccia)
   Rigoletto: La donna e mobile (Verdi) (in English) [8, 19]
   If [8]

22 July 1951 (Air Date), Radio Recorder Studio, Los Angeles
Selections recorded for *The Mario Lanza Show*
Orchestra conducted by Ray Sinatra
   The World Is Mine Tonight (Marvell-Posford) [12]

Yours Is My Heart Alone (Lehár) [7]
Oh, Nights of Splendor (Zamecnik-Kerr)
Tosca: Recondita armonia (Puccini)

29 July 1951 (Air Date), Radio Recorder Studio, Los Angeles
Selections recorded for *The Mario Lanza Show*
Orchestra conducted by Ray Sinatra
    All the Things You Are (Kern-Hammerstein II) [18]
    Long Ago and Far Away (Kern-Gershwin) [12, 18]
    The Touch of Your Hand (Kern-Harbach)
    The Song Is You (Kern-Hammerstein II) [6, 18]

2 August 1951, MGM Studios, Hollywood
Soundtrack recordings for *Because You're Mine*
    The Lord's Prayer (Malotte) (Wesley Tourtelotte, organ, Johnny Green
    conducting) [11]

5 August 1951 (Air Date), Radio Recorder Studio, Los Angeles
Selections recorded for *The Mario Lanza Show*
Orchestra conducted by Ray Sinatra
    Cosi Cosa (Washington-Kaper-Jurmann)
    Softly, as in a Morning Sunrise (Romberg-Hammerstein II)
    Diane (Rapee-Pollack) [8]

12 August 1951 (Air Date), Radio Recorder Studio, Los Angeles
Selections recorded for *The Mario Lanza Show*
Orchestra conducted by Ray Sinatra
    'A Vucchella (Tosti-D'Annunzio)
    Wanting You (Romberg-Hammerstein II) [6]
    Ave Maria (Bach-Gounod)

19 August 1951 (Air Date), Radio Recorder Studio, Los Angeles
Selections recorded for *The Mario Lanza Show*
Orchestra conducted by Ray Sinatra
    I've Got You Under My Skin (Porter) [18]
    Marechiare (Tosti-Di Giacomo)
    My Heart Stood Still (Rodgers-Hart) [17]
    L'Africana: O paradiso (Meyerbeer) [8]

26 August 1951 (Air Date), Radio Recorder Studio, Los Angeles
Selections recorded for *The Mario Lanza Show*
Orchestra conducted by Ray Sinatra
    Ah, Sweet Mystery of Life (Herbert-Young) [6]
    If You Are But a Dream (Rubenstein-Jaffe-Fulton-Bonx) [12, 17]
    Time on My Hands (Youmans-Adamson-Gordon) [12]

2 September 1951 (Air Date), Radio Recorder Studio, Los Angeles
Selections recorded for *The Mario Lanza Show*
Orchestra conducted by Ray Sinatra
    Without a Song (Youmans-Rose-Eliscu) [10, 19]
    Wonder Why (Brodszky-Cahn) [7]
    They Didn't Believe Me (Kern-Reynolds)
    The Lord's Prayer (Malotte)

9 September 1951 (Air Date), Radio Recorder Studio, Los Angeles
Selections recorded for *The Mario Lanza Show*
Orchestra conducted by Ray Sinatra
    Night and Day (Porter) [18, 19]
    The Desert Song (Romberg-Harbach-Hammerstein II)
    Tosca: E lucevan le stelle (Puccini)

16 September 1951 (Air Date), Radio Recorder Studio, Los Angeles
Selections recorded for *The Mario Lanza Show*
Orchestra conducted by Ray Sinatra
    With a Song in My Heart (Rodgers-Hart) [7]
    Mattinata (Leoncavallo)

23 September 1951 (Air Date), Radio Recorder Studio, Los Angeles
Selections recorded for *The Mario Lanza Show*
Orchestra conducted by Ray Sinatra
    Song of Songs (Lucas-Moya) [7]
    Strange Music (Grieg-Wright-Forrestal)
    The Rosary (Nevin) [10]

28 September 1951, Republic Studios, Hollywood
RCA Victor Orchestra and the Jeff Alexander Choir; Ray Sinatra, conductor
    Guardian Angels (Beilenson-Marx) (E1RB-777-1) [5, 21]

Silent Night (Mohr-Gruber) (E1RB-778-1) [5, 21]
The First Noel (Traditional) (E1RB-779-1) [5, 21]
O Come All Ye Faithful (Oakley) (E1RB-780-1) [5, 21]
Away in a Manger (Traditional-Kirkpatrick) (E1RB-7781-1) [5, 21]
O Little Town of Bethlehem (Redner-Brooks) (E1RB-782-1) [5, 21]

29 September 1951, Republic Studios, Hollywood
RCA Victor Orchestra and the Jeff Alexander Choir; Ray Sinatra, conductor
We Three Kings of Orient Are (Hopkins) (E1RB-783-1) [5, 21]
The Lord's Prayer (Malotte) (E1RB-784-1) [5, 10, 21]

19 October 1951, MGM Studios, Hollywood
Soundtrack recordings for *Because You're Mine*
MGM Studio Orchestra; Johnny Green, conductor
Lee-Ah-Loo (Lehmann-Sinatra)
All the Things You Are (Kern-Hammerstein II) (outtake)

23 October 1951, MGM Studios, Hollywood
Soundtrack recording for *Because You're Mine*
MGM Studio Orchestra; Johnny Green, conductor
The Song Angels Sing (Brahms-Aaronson-Webster)

30 October 1951, MGM Studios, Hollywood
Soundtrack recording for *Because You're Mine*
MGM Studio Orchestra; Johnny Green, conductor
Granada (Lara) [11]

1 November 1951, MGM Studios, Hollywood
Soundtrack recording for *Because You're Mine*
The Lord's Prayer (Malotte) (Wesley Tourtelotte, organ, Johnny Green
conducting) (outtake) [11]
Il Trovatore: Miserere (excerpt) (Verdi) (Irving Aaronson, piano)

10 November 1951, MGM Studios, Hollywood
Soundtrack recording for *Because You're Mine*
MGM Studio Orchestra; Johnny Green, conductor
Cavalleria Rusticana: Finale: Addio alla madre (Mascagni) (with Peggy
Bonini, soprano, and Kathryn Chapman, contralto) [11]

24 November 1951, MGM Studios, Hollywood
Soundtrack recording for *Because You're Mine*
MGM Studio Orchestra; Johnny Green, conductor
  Rigoletto: Addio, addio (Verdi) (Lanza only, Peggy Bonini soprano vocal
  recorded 28 November 1951)

1 December 1951, MGM Studios, Hollywood
Soundtrack recordings for *Because You're Mine*
MGM Studio Orchestra; Johnny Green, conductor
  Because You're Mine, Finale (Brodszky-Cahn) (Doretta Morrow, soprano) [11]
  Because You're Mine (Brodszky-Cahn) (Doretta Morrow, soprano) [11]

3 December 1951 (Air Date), Radio Recorder Studio, Los Angeles
Selections recorded for *The Mario Lanza Show*
Orchestra conducted by Ray Sinatra
  Valencia (Grey-Padilla) [12]
  Through the Years (Youmans-Heyman) [10, 17]
  Where or When (Rodgers-Hart) [18]
  None But the Lonely Heart (Tchaikovsky-David-Hoffman-Livingston) [10]

10 December 1951 (Air Date), Radio Recorder Studio, Los Angeles
Selections recorded for *The Mario Lanza Show*
Orchestra conducted by Ray Sinatra
  Ay-Ay-Ay (Freire-Perez) [17]
  Look for the Silver Lining (Kern-De Sylva) [10]
  Your Eyes Have Told Me So (Blaufuss-Kahn-Van Alstyne) [8, 18]
  Guardian Angels (Beilenson-Marx) [10]

17 December 1951 (Air Date), Radio Recorder Studio, Los Angeles
Selections recorded for *The Mario Lanza Show*
Orchestra conducted by Ray Sinatra
  Ciribiribin (James-Lawrence-Pestalozza) [7]
  Make Believe (Kern-Hammerstein II)
  Sylvia (Speaks-Scollard) [18, 21]
  You and the Night and the Music (Dietz-Schwartz) [18]

24 December 1951 (Air Date), Radio Recorder Studio, Los Angeles
Selections recorded for *The Mario Lanza Show*
Orchestra conducted by Ray Sinatra
  O Come All Ye Faithful (Oakley)

Silent Night (Mohr-Gruber)
O Little Town of Bethlehem (Redner-Brooks)
The First Noel (Traditional)

31 December 1951 (Air Date), Radio Recorder Studio, Los Angeles
Selections recorded for *The Mario Lanza Show*
Orchestra conducted by Ray Sinatra
Siboney (Lecuona-Morse)
Neapolitan Love Song (Victor Herbert) [6]
When Day Is Done (Katscher-De Sylva) [12]

7 January 1952 (Air Date), Radio Recorder Studio, Los Angeles
Selections recorded for *The Mario Lanza Show*
Orchestra conducted by Ray Sinatra
The Best Things in Life Are Free (Henderson-Brown-De Sylva) [12]
Temptation (Brown-Freed) [7]
Trees (Kilmer-Rasbach) [10]

14 January 1952 (Air Date), Radio Recorder Studio, Los Angeles
Selections recorded for *The Mario Lanza Show*
Orchestra conducted by Ray Sinatra
The Donkey Serenade (Friml-Forrest-Wright) [8]
The Thrill Is Gone (Henderson-Brown) [12]
Rigoletto: Questa o quella (Verdi)

21 January 1952 (Air Date), Radio Recorder Studio, Los Angeles
Selections recorded for *The Mario Lanza Show*
Orchestra conducted by Ray Sinatra
My Romance (Rodgers-Hart) [12, 18]
Lygia (Rózsa-Webster) [7, 21]
The Hills of Home (Fox-Calhoun)
One Night of Love (Schertzinger-Kahn) [12]

25 January 1952 (Air Date), Radio Recorder Studio, Los Angeles
Selections recorded for *The Mario Lanza Show*
Orchestra conducted by Ray Sinatra
The Night Is Young and You're So Beautiful (Rose-Kahal-Suesse) [17]
Somewhere a Voice Is Calling (Tate-Newton) [7, 10]
Roses of Picardy (Weatherley-Wood) [10, 17]
Begin the Beguine (Porter) [12, 19]

1 February 1952 (Air Date), Radio Recorder Studio, Los Angeles
Selections recorded for *The Mario Lanza Show*
Orchestra conducted by Ray Sinatra
  Lady of Spain (Reeves-Evans) [7]
  Charmaine (Rapee-Pollock)
  What Is This Thing Called Love? (Porter)
  I'll See You Again (Coward) [12, 18]

8 February 1952 (Air Date), Radio Recorder Studio, Los Angeles
Selections recorded for *The Mario Lanza Show*
Orchestra conducted by Ray Sinatra
  Romance (Leslie-Donaldson) [19]
  Tell Me That You Love Me Tonight (Bixio) [8]
  Among My Souvenirs (Leslie-Nicholls)
  L'Elisir d'Amore: Una furtiva lagrima (Donizetti)

15 February 1952 (Air Date), Radio Recorder Studio, Los Angeles
Selections recorded for *The Mario Lanza Show*
Orchestra conducted by Ray Sinatra
  I'll See You in My Dreams (Jones-Kahn) [17]
  Memories (Van Alstyne-Kahn) [6, 17]
  I Never Knew (Fiorito-Kahn) [7]
  My Buddy (Donaldson-Kahn) [10]

22 February 1952 (Air Date), Radio Recorder Studio, Los Angeles
Selections recorded for *The Mario Lanza Show*
Orchestra conducted by Ray Sinatra
  If I Loved You (Rodgers-Hammerstein II) [7, 18]
  Fools Rush In (Bloom-Mercer) [12, 18]
  Someday I'll Find You (Coward) [8, 17]
  Tell Me Tonight (Spoliansky-Eyton) [12]

7 March 1952 (Air Date), Radio Recorder Studio, Los Angeles
Selections recorded for *The Mario Lanza Show*
Orchestra conducted by Ray Sinatra
  Yesterdays (Kern-Harbach) [12]
  Day In, Day Out (Bloom-Mercer)
  Carmen: La fleur que tu m'avais jetée (Bizet) [14]

14 March 1952 (Air Date), Radio Recorder Studio, Los Angeles
Selections recorded for *The Mario Lanza Show*
Orchestra conducted by Ray Sinatra
  Danny Boy (Traditional) [6]
  A Kiss in the Dark (Herbert-De Sylva) [17]
  The Trembling of a Leaf (Lawrence-Green) [10]
  My Wild Irish Rose (Olcott) [6]

21 March 1952 (Air Date), Radio Recorder Studio, Los Angeles
Selections recorded for *The Mario Lanza Show*
Orchestra conducted by Ray Sinatra/*Constantine Callinicos
  Santa Lucia (Cottrau)* [8]
  A Little Love, a Little Kiss (Silesu-Ross) [12]
  Cavalleria Rusticana: Addio alla madre (Mascagni)* [8]

28 March 1952 (Air Date), Radio Recorder Studio, Los Angeles
Selections recorded for *The Mario Lanza Show*
Orchestra conducted by Ray Sinatra/*Constantine Callinicos
  The Moon Was Yellow (Ahlert-Leslie) [12]
  Core'ngrato (Cardillo-Cordiferro)* [8]
  Marcheta (Schertzinger) [12]
  Rigoletto: La donna e mobile (Verdi)* [14]

4 April 1952 (Air Date), Radio Recorder Studio, Los Angeles
Selections recorded for *The Mario Lanza Show*
Orchestra conducted by Ray Sinatra/*Constantine Callinicos
  April in Paris (Harburg-Duke) [12, 19]
  Fenesta Che Lucive (Genoino-Paolella-Cottrau)*
  And Here You Are (Novello-Levin) [7]
  La Bohème: Che gelida manina (Puccini)*

11 April 1952 (Air Date), Radio Recorder Studio, Los Angeles
Selections recorded for *The Mario Lanza Show*
Orchestra conducted by Ray Sinatra/*Constantine Callinicos
  Deep in My Heart, Dear (Romberg-Donnelly)
  Dicitencello Vuie (Fusco-Falvo)*
  You Are Love (Kern-Hammerstein II) [8]

18 April 1952 (Air Date), Radio Recorder Studio, Los Angeles
Selections recorded for *The Mario Lanza Show*
Orchestra conducted by Ray Sinatra/*Constantine Callinicos
  Play Gypsies, Dance Gypsies (Kalman-Smith-Brammer-Grunwald)
  Maria Marì (Di Capua-Russo)* [6]
  When You're in Love (Fischer-Laine) [12]
  La Gioconda: Cielo e mar (Ponchielli)*

25 April 1952 (Air Date), Radio Recorder Studio, Los Angeles
Selections recorded for *The Mario Lanza Show*
Orchestra conducted by Ray Sinatra/*Constantine Callinicos
  Alone Together (Schwartz-Dietz) [12]
  Non Ti Scordar Di Me (De Curtis)* [8]
  Rigoletto: Parmi veder le lagrime (Verdi)* [8]

2 May 1952 (Air Date), Radio Recorder Studio, Los Angeles
Selections recorded for *The Mario Lanza Show*
Orchestra conducted by Ray Sinatra/*Constantine Callinicos
  Beautiful Love (Gillespie-Young-King-Van Alstyne) [7, 18]
  Santa Lucia Luntana (Mario)*
  I'll Be Seeing You (Kahal-Fain) [6, 18]
  Aida: Celeste Aida (Verdi)* [14]

7 May 1952, MGM Studios, Hollywood
Soundtrack recording for *Because You're Mine*
MGM Studio Orchestra; Johnny Green, conductor
  Because You're Mine (Brodszky-Cahn) (main title and introduction,
  excerpt only)

9 May 1952 (Air Date), Radio Recorder Studio, Los Angeles
Selections recorded for *The Mario Lanza Show*
Orchestra conducted by Ray Sinatra/*Constantine Callinicos
  Love Is the Sweetest Thing (Noble) [7, 18]
  Andrea Chenier: Come un bel di di maggio (Giordano)*

16 May 1952 (Air Date), Radio Recorder Studio, Los Angeles
Selections recorded for *The Mario Lanza Show*
Orchestra conducted by Ray Sinatra/*Constantine Callinicos
  You'll Never Walk Alone (Rodgers-Hammerstein II) [8]

'Na Sera 'E Maggio (Pisano-Cioffi)* [8]
L'Arlesiana: Lamento di Federico (Cilea)* [14]

23 May 1952 (Air Date), Radio Recorder Studio, Los Angeles
Selections recorded for *The Mario Lanza Show*
Orchestra conducted by Ray Sinatra/*Constantine Callinicos
Andrea Chenier: Un di all'azzuro spazio (Giordano)*
Tu Ca Nun Chiagne (Bovio-De Curtis)* [8]
Somebody Bigger Than You and I (Lange-Heath-Burke) [10]

30 May 1952 (Air Date), Radio Recorder Studio, Los Angeles
Selections recorded for *The Mario Lanza Show*
Orchestra conducted by Ray Sinatra/*Constantine Callinicos
One Alone (Romberg-Harbach-Hammerstein II) [12, 19]
Canta Pe' Me (Bovio-De Curtis)* [8]
La Forza del Destino: O tu che in seno agli angeli (Verdi)* [8]

6 June 1952 (Air Date), Radio Recorder Studio, Los Angeles
Selections recorded for *The Mario Lanza Show*
Orchestra conducted by Ray Sinatra/*Constantine Callinicos
Besame Mucho (Velasquez-Skylar)
Senza Nisciuno (De Curtis-Barbieri)*
Fedora: Amor ti vieta (Giordano)* [14]

13 June 1952 (Air Date), Radio Recorder Studio, Los Angeles
Selections recorded for *The Mario Lanza Show*
Orchestra conducted by Ray Sinatra/*Constantine Callinicos
Parlami D'Amore Mariu (Bixio-Neri)* [17]
A Kiss (Brooks-Sinatra) [18]

18 June 1952, MGM Studios, Hollywood
Soundtrack recordings for *The Student Prince*
A Mighty Fortress (Luther) (Wesley Tourtelot, organ)
A Mighty Fortress (Luther) (Wesley Tourtelot, organ) (outtake)
I'll Walk with God (Brodszky-Webster) (Wesley Tourtelot, organ) [2, 5, 10, 19] (chorus and orchestra overdubs recorded 24 February 1954)

20 June 1952 (Air Date), Radio Recorder Studio, Los Angeles
Selections recorded for *The Mario Lanza Show*

Orchestra conducted by Constantine Callinicos
   Musica Proibita (Gastaldon) [17]
   Pagliacci: Un tal gioco (Leoncavallo) [14]

27 June 1952 (Air Date), Radio Recorder Studio, Los Angeles
Selections recorded for *The Mario Lanza Show*
Orchestra conducted by Constantine Callinicos
   La Spagnola (Dole-Di Chiara)
   La Bohème: Testa adorata (Leoncavallo) [14]

1951–1952, Radio Recorder Studio, Los Angeles
Alternate takes recorded for *The Mario Lanza Show*
Orchestra conducted by Ray Sinatra/*Constantine Callinicos
   Day In, Day Out (Bloom-Mercer)
   Deep in My Heart, Dear (Romberg-Donnelly) [8]
   The Hills of Home (Fox-Calhoun) [10]
   I'm Falling in Love with Someone (Herbert-Young)
   Look for the Silver Lining (Kern-De Sylva) [6]
   Love Is the Sweetest Thing (Noble)
   My Romance (Rodgers-Hart)
   'Na Sera 'E Maggio (Pisano-Cioffi)*
   Oh, Nights of Splendor (Zamecnik-Kerr)
   One Night of Love (Schertzinger-Kahn) [7]
   Santa Lucia Luntana (Mario)* [8]
   Serenade (*Student Prince*) (Romberg-Donnelly) [8]
   Someday I'll Find You (Coward)
   Wanting You (Romberg-Hammerstein II)
   You Are Love (Kern-Hammerstein II)
   You'll Never Walk Alone (Rodgers-Hammerstein II) [10]
   Your Eyes Have Told Me So (Blaufuss-Kahn-Van Alstyne)

24 July 1952, Republic Studios, Hollywood
RCA Victor Orchestra; Constantine Callinicos, conductor
   Lee-Ah-Loo (Lehmann-Sinatra) (E2RB-0299-1) [7]
   You Do Something to Me (Porter) (E2RB-0300-1) [17, 21]

29 July 1952, MGM Studios, Hollywood
Soundtrack recordings for *The Student Prince*

MGM Studio Orchestra; Constantine Callinicos, conductor
    Serenade (Romberg-Donnelly-Webster) [2, 6, 7, 11]
    Beloved (Brodszky-Cahn) (rejected) [11]
    Summertime in Heidelberg (Brodszky-Cahn) (Ann Blyth, soprano) [2,
    with Elizabeth Doubleday overdub]

31 July 1952, MGM Studios, Hollywood
Soundtrack recordings for *The Student Prince*
MGM Studio Orchestra; Constantine Callinicos, conductor
    What's to Be? (outtake)
    Golden Days (Romberg-Donnelly-Webster) [2, 7, 19]

1 August 1952, Republic Studios, Hollywood
RCA Victor Orchestra; Constantine Callinicos, conductor
    The Song Angels Sing (Aaronson-Webster) (E2RB-0297-1) [7]
    Because You're Mine (Brodszky-Cahn) (E2RB-0298-1)

5 August 1952, MGM Studios, Hollywood
Soundtrack recording for *The Student Prince*
MGM Studio Orchestra and chorus; Constantine Callinicos, conductor
    Drink, Drink, Drink (Romberg-Donnelly-Webster) [2, 7, 19]

7 August 1952, MGM Studios, Hollywood
Soundtrack recordings for *The Student Prince*
Chorus conducted by Constantine Callinicos
    Ergo Bibamus (Eberwein) (Constantine Callinicos, piano)
    Gaudeamus Igitur (Traditional) (outtake) [2]
    Gaudeamus Igitur (Traditional) (mezza voce version; outtake)

12 August 1952, MGM Studios, Hollywood
Soundtrack recordings for *The Student Prince*
MGM Studio Orchestra; Constantine Callinicos, conductor
    Deep in My Heart, Dear (Romberg-Donnelly-Webster) (Ann Blyth,
    soprano) [2, 7 with Elizabeth Doubleday overdub; 11 with Ann Blyth]
    Deep in My Heart, Dear (Romberg-Donnelly-Webster) (partial retake,
    with Ann Blyth, soprano)

20 May 1953, MGM Studios, Hollywood

Soundtrack recording for *The Student Prince*

MGM Studio Orchestra; Constantine Callinicos, conductor

    Beloved (Brodszky-Webster) (remake, featured in film) [2, 7, 21]

17 June 1953, Republic Studios, Hollywood

Orchestra and chorus conducted by Constantine Callinicos

    Song of India (Rimsky-Korsakov-Mercer) (E3RC-2424-1) [21]

    If You Were Mine (Merrill) (E3RC-2415-1)

    If You Were Mine (Merrill) (E3RC-2415-2) (alternate take) [7]

    Call Me Fool (Kauderer) (E3RB-3071-1) [7]

    You Are My Love (Callinicos-Webster) (E3RB-3070-1) [7, 21]

    You Are My Love (Callinicos-Webster) (E3RB-3070-2) (alternate take)

28 December 1953, Warner Bros. Studio, Hollywood

Orchestra conducted by Constantine Callinicos

    Summertime in Heidelberg (Romberg-Donnelly-Webster) (E3RC-2530-1)

    I'll Walk with God (Brodszky-Webster) (E3RC-2532-1) (recorded for RCA, both takes rejected) Orchestral introduction featured on RCA *Student Prince* soundtrack album recorded at this session. Soprano Gale Sherwood recorded "Come Boys" at this session but the track was unreleased. Ms. Sherwood was replaced on the RCA album by soprano Elizabeth Doubleday.

28 June 1955, Warner Bros. Studios, Hollywood

Soundtrack recording for *Serenade*

    La Danza (Rossini) (Dominic Frontière, accordion) [20]

30 June 1955, Warner Bros. Studios, Hollywood

Soundtrack recording for *Serenade*

    Torna a Surriento (de Curtis-de Curtis) (Jacob Gimpel, piano) [1, 20]

5 July 1955, Warner Bros. Studios, Hollywood

Soundtrack recording for *Serenade*

    La Bohème: O soave fanciulla (Puccini) (Jacob Gimpel, piano) [14, 20] (Lanza only, Jean Fenn soprano vocal recorded 23 August 1955)

7 July 1955, Warner Bros. Studios, Hollywood

Soundtrack recording for *Serenade*

    My Destiny (Brodszky-Cahn) (Jacob Gimpel, piano) (rejected)

    Serenade (Brodszky-Cahn) (Jacob Gimpel, piano) (test recording)

11 July 1955, Warner Bros. Studios, Hollywood
Soundtrack recordings for *Serenade*
 Der Rosenkavalier: Di rigori armato il seno (Strauss) (Jacob Gimpel, piano) [20]
 My Destiny (Brodszky-Cahn) (remake, with Jacob Gimpel, piano)

13 July 1955, Warner Bros. Studios, Hollywood
Soundtrack recordings for *Serenade*
Orchestra conducted by Ray Heindorf
 L'Arlesiana: Lamento di Federico (Cilea) [20]
 Fedora: Amor ti vieta (Giordano) [20]
 Tosca: Qual occhio al mondo (Puccini) (outtake)
 La Bohème: Ci lasciaremo all stagion fiori (Puccini) (Lanza vocal only, Jean Fenn soprano vocal recorded 23 August 1955) (outtake)
 Il Trovatore: Di quella pira (Verdi) [20]

15 July 1955, Warner Bros. Studios, Hollywood
Soundtrack recordings for *Serenade*
 L'Africana: O paradiso (Meyerbeer) (Jacob Gimpel, piano) [20]
 Serenade (Brodszky-Cahn) (different song than main theme, not used in film) (Jacob Gimpel, piano) [20]
 Serenade (Brodszky-Cahn) (as above, alternate take) (Jacob Gimpel, piano)

19 July 1955, Warner Bros. Studios, Hollywood
Soundtrack recordings for *Serenade*
Orchestra conducted by Ray Heindorf
 Otello: Dio ti giocondi (Gloria Boh, soprano, duet outtake) and Dio mi potevi scagliar (monologue) (Verdi) [14, 20 monologue] (Duet rejected but brief Lanza intro and complete closing monologue from this session used for soundtrack.)
 Turandot: Nessun dorma (Puccini) (rejected)

21 July 1955, Warner Bros. Studios, Hollywood
Soundtrack recordings for *Serenade*
Orchestra conducted by Ray Heindorf
 Otello: Dio ti giocondi (Verdi) (Gloria Boh, soprano; remake, rejected)
 Turandot: Nessun dorma (Puccini) (remake, featured in film) [14, 20]
 My Destiny (Brodszky-Cahn) [20]
 Serenade (Brodszky-Cahn) [1, 20]

18 August 1955, Warner Bros. Studios, Hollywood
Soundtrack recording for *Serenade*
  Ave Maria (Schubert) (Jacob Gimpel, piano) (Organ accompaniment by
  Eugene Le Pique recorded 23 August 1955 and overdubbed for film. Lanza
  also re-recorded a brief opening vocal correction on 26 October 1955 for
  RCA record release) [6, 20]

25 August 1955, Warner Bros. Studios, Hollywood
Soundtrack recordings for *Serenade*
Orchestra conducted by Ray Heindorf
  Serenade (Brodszky-Cahn)
  Serenade (Brodszky-Cahn) (alternate version)
  Serenade (Brodszky-Cahn) (remake)

26 August 1955, Warner Bros. Studios, Hollywood
Soundtrack recording for *Serenade*
  Serenade (Brodszky-Cahn) (with guitar, marimba, accordion, bass, and
  piano accompaniment)
  Note: Lanza also recorded two partial takes of "Il mio tesoro" from *Don
  Giovanni* on this date. However, they were intentionally sung badly for
  a dramatic sequence in the picture and as such are not considered part
  of this discography.

22 November 1955, Warner Bros. Studios, Hollywood
Soundtrack recording for *Serenade*
Orchestra conducted by Ray Heindorf
  Otello: Dio ti giocondi (Verdi) (Licia Albanese, soprano; duet only, see
  note for 19 July 1955) [14 complete duet, 20 excerpt only]

14 May 1956, Warner Bros. Studio, Hollywood
Lanza on Broadway, RCA recording
Orchestra conducted by Irving Aaronson (Jeff Alexander Choir overdub
added later)
  More Than You Know (Youmans-Rose-Eliscu) (G2RB-3295-2)
  Why Was I Born? (Kern-Hammerstein II) (G2RB-3296-5)
  This Nearly Was Mine (Rodgers-Hammerstein II) (G2RB-3297-2)
  Falling in Love with Love (Rodgers-Hart) (G2RB-3298-4)

15 May 1956, Warner Bros. Studio, Hollywood
Lanza on Broadway, RCA recording
Orchestra conducted by Irving Aaronson (Jeff Alexander Choir overdub added later)

So in Love (Porter) (G2RB-3299-5)

Speak Low (Weill-Nash) (G2RB-3300-3)

My Romance (Rodgers-Hart) (G2RB-3113-6)

September Song (Weill-Anderson) (G2RB-3114-6)

17 May 1956, Warner Bros. Studio, Hollywood
Lanza on Broadway, RCA recording
Orchestra conducted by Irving Aaronson (Jeff Alexander Choir overdub added later)

Younger Than Springtime (Rodgers-Hammerstein II) (G2RB-3115-4)

And This Is My Beloved (Wright-Forrest) (G2RB-3116-1) [1, 6]

On the Street Where You Live (Loewe-Lerner) (G2RB-3117-10) [18]

You'll Never Walk Alone (Rodgers-Hammerstein II) (G2RB-3118-1) [6]

10 August 1956, Republic Studios, Hollywood
Henri René and His Orchestra with the Jeff Alexander Choir

This Land (Stanley-Taylor) (G2PB-4779-5) [7]

Earthbound (Taylor-Richardson-Musel) (G2PB-4780-6)

Deck the Halls (Traditional) (G2PB-4781-4) [5]

Hark the Herald Angels Sing (Mendelssohn-Wesley) (G2PB-4782-4) [5, 21]

God Rest Ye Merry Gentlemen (Traditional) (G2PB-4786-2) [5, 21]

Joy to the World (Handel-Watts) (G2PB-4787-2) [5, 21]

15 August 1956, Republic Studios, Hollywood
Henri René and His Orchestra with the Jeff Alexander Choir

O Christmas Tree (Traditional) (G2PB-4788-6) [5, 21]

Love in a Home (De Paul-Mercer) (G2PB-4789-3) [7, 10]

Do You Wonder? (Raye-Hill) (G2PB-4790-3) [7]

I Saw Three Ships (Traditional) (G2PB-4791-1) [5, 21]

It Came Upon a Midnight Clear (Sears-Willis) (G2PB-4792-2) [5]

27 August 1956, Republic Studios, Hollywood
A Cavalcade of Show Tunes, RCA recording

Henri René and His Orchestra with the Jeff Alexander Choir
    I've Told Ev'ry Little Star (Kern-Hammerstein II) (G2RB-4824-10) [20]
    Only a Rose (Friml-Hooker) (G2RB-4825-5) [18, 20]
    Will You Remember? (Romberg-Young) (G2RB-4826-2) [7, 20]
    Yours Is My Heart Alone (Lehár) (G2RB-4827-1)

31 August 1956, Republic Studios, Hollywood
A Cavalcade of Show Tunes, RCA recording
Henri René and His Orchestra with the Jeff Alexander Choir
    Rose Marie (Friml-Stothart-Harbach-Hammerstein II) (G2RB-4832-2) [20]
    The Donkey Serenade (Friml-Stothart-Wright-Forrest) (G2RB-4833-3) [20]
    All the Things You Are (Kern-Hammerstein II) (G2RB-4834-4) [7, 20]
    Gypsy Love Song (Herbert-Smith) (G2RB-4835-4) [20]

6 September 1956, Republic Studios, Hollywood
A Cavalcade of Show Tunes, RCA recording
Henri René and His Orchestra with the Jeff Alexander Choir
    Lover Come Back to Me (Romberg-Hammerstein II) (G2RB-4828-2) [20]
    Tramp! Tramp! Tramp! (Herbert-Young) (G2RB-4829-3) [20]
    Giannina Mia (Friml-Harbach) (G2RB-4830-2) [20]
    Thine Alone (Herbert) (G2RB-4834-2) [20]
    Yours Is My Heart Alone (Lehár) (G2RB-4827-3A retake) [20]

15 April 1957, Republic Studios, Hollywood
Henri René and His Orchestra with the Jeff Alexander Choir
    A Night to Remember (Segal-Kalmanoff) (H2PB-0527-6) [7]
    Behold! (Moore-Reid) (H2PB-0528-6) [7]
    Come Dance with Me (Blake-Leibert) (H2PB-0529-6) [7]

June 1957, Auditorium Angelico and Via Margutta Studio, Rome
Soundtrack recordings for *Seven Hills of Rome*
Italian National Radio Symphony Orchestra and Chorus conducted by
George Stoll/*Silvio Clementelli
    Seven Hills of Rome (Young-Adamson)
    Seven Hills of Rome (Young-Adamson) (different version, not featured
    in film)
    There's Gonna Be a Party Tonight (Stoll)
    Lolita (Buzzi-Peccia)
    Arrivederci Roma (Garinei-Giovannini-Sigman-Rascel) (with Luisa di Mio)
    [1, 6, 19]

Come Dance with Me (Blake-Leibert)
Imitation Sequence (Excerpts from M'appari; Jezebel; Temptation; Memories
Are Made of This; When the Saints Go Marching In)
Rigoletto: Questa o quella (Verdi)*
All the Things You Are (Kern-Hammerstein II) (partial take)
Ay-Ay-Ay (Freire-Perez) (partial take)
The Loveliest Night of the Year (Aaronson-Webster) (partial take)
Lanza also recorded a partial take of "Be My Love" but not in his
natural voice. The selection was made for a joke sequence in the picture.

7 November 1957, Cinecittà Studios, Rome
Orchestra conducted by George Stoll
Never Till Now (Green-Webster) (H2PB-8042-3) [7]
Younger Than Springtime (Rodgers-Hammerstein II) (H2PB-8043-2) [7]
The Loveliest Night of the Year (Aaronson-Webster) (J2PB-0730)
Arrivederci Roma (Garinei-Giovannini-Sigman-Rascel) (Italian/
English version) (J2PB-0731)

16 January 1958, Royal Albert Hall, London
Mario Lanza Recital
Constantine Callinicos, piano
L'Arlesiana: Lamento di Federico (Cilea) [9]
L'Arianna: Lasciatemi Morire (Monteverdi) [9]
Già Il Sole Dal Gange (Scarlatti) [9]
Pietà, Signore (Stradella) [5, 9]
Tell Me O Blue, Blue Sky (Giannini-Fraser) [9]
Bonjour, Ma Belle (Behrend-Eden) [9]
The House on the Hill (Charles) [9]
Tosca: E lucevan le stelle (Puccini) [9]
Mamma Mia, Che Vo' Sapè? (Nutile-Russo) [9]
'A Vucchella (Tosti-D'Annunzio) [9]
Marechiare (Tosti-Di Giacomo) [1, 9]
Softly, as in a Morning Sunrise (Romberg-Hammerstein II) [7, 9]
I'm Falling in Love with Someone (Herbert-Young) [9]
Because You're Mine (Brodszky-Cahn) [1, 9]
Seven Hills of Rome (Young-Adamson) [9]
Rigoletto: La donna e mobile (Verdi) [9]

Late August 1958, Rome Opera House
Soundtrack recordings for *For the First Time*
Orchestra, soloists, and chorus conducted by Constantine Callinicos
  Aida: Grand March (Verdi) (JKBW-4613/4614) [4]
  Pagliacci: Vesti la giubba (Leoncavallo) (JKBW-4644) [4]
  Otello: Niun mi tema (Verdi) (JKBW-4645) [4]
  Così Fan Tutte: Trio, Act I, No. 16, Scene XII, E voi ridete (Mozart)
  (with unknown bass and baritone) (JKBW-4646)
  I Love Thee (Grieg) (JKAW-5334) [4]

September 1958, Cinecittà Studios, Rome
Soundtrack recordings for *For the First Time*
Orchestra conducted by Carlo Savina/*George Stoll
  Ave Maria (Schubert)* (with choir and organ accompaniment)
  (JKBW-4672) [4, 10, 19]
  Ave Maria (Schubert)* (alternate take, used in film)
  O Sole Mio (Di Capua-Capurro) (JKBW-4677) [4, 7]
  Come Prima (Panzeri-Ram-Taccani-DiPaola) (JKAW-4679) [4, 7]
  O Mon Amour (Assot-Monnot) (JKBW-4681) [4]
  Rigoletto: La donna e mobile (Verdi) (with accordion accompaniment)

Fall 1958, Berlin, Germany
Soundtrack recordings for *For the First Time*
Johannes Rediske and His Band
  Hofbrauhaus Song (Bette-Hauf) [4]
  Pineapple Pickers (Stoll) [4]

November–December 1958, Cinecittà Studios, Rome
Mario! RCA Living Stereo recording
Orchestra conducted by Franco Ferrara, chorus by Franco Potenza
  Funiculì, Funiculà (Turco-Denza) [1, 16]
  Dicitencello Vuie (Fusco-Falvo) [16]
  Maria Marì (Russo-Di Capua) [16]
  Voce 'E Notte (Lardini-De Curtis) [16]
  Canta Pe' Me (Bovio-De Curtis) [16]
  O Surdato 'namurato (Califano-Cannio) [16]
  Come Facette Mammeta? (Capaldo-Gambardela) [16]
  Santa Lucia Luntana (Mario) [16]

Fenesta Che Lucive (Genoino-Paolella-Cottrau) [16]
Tu Ca Nun Chiagne (Bovio-De Curtis) [16]
'Na Sera 'E Maggio (Pisano-Cioffi) [16]
Passione (Bovio-Tagliaferri-Valente) [16]

April 1959, Cinecittà Studios, Rome
The Student Prince, RCA Living Stereo recording
Orchestra conducted by Paul Baron
Chorus overdub recorded in New York, 24 September 1959

Summertime in Heidelberg (Brodszky-Webster) (Lanza only; Norma
Giusti, soprano overdub added later) (KKBW-5700)
Gaudeamus Igitur (Traditional) (KKBW-5701)
Just We Two (Romberg-Donnelly) (Lanza only; Norma Giusti, soprano
overdub added later) (KKBW-5702)
Thoughts Will Come Back to Me (Romberg-Donnelly) (KKBW-5703)
Golden Days (Romberg-Donnelly) (KKBW-5704)
I'll Walk with God (Brodszky-Webster) (KKBW-5705)
Serenade (Romberg-Donnelly) (KKBW-5706)
Beloved (Brodszky-Webster) (KKBW-5707)
Drink, Drink, Drink (Romberg-Donnelly) (KKBW-5708)
Deep in My Heart, Dear (Romberg-Donnelly) (Lanza only; Norma
Giusti, soprano overdub added later) (KKBW-5709)

May 1959, Cinecittà Studios, Rome
Lanza Sings Christmas Carols, RCA Living Stereo recording
Orchestra conducted by Paul Baron
Chorus overdub recorded in New York, 16 and 17 September 1959

We Three Kings of Orient Are (Hopkins) (KKBW-5823) [15]
O Come All Ye Faithful (Oakley) (KKBW-5824) [15]
O Little Town of Bethlehem (Brooks-Redner) (KKBW-5825) [15]
The First Noel (Traditional) (KKBW-5826) [15]
Silent Night (Mohr-Gruber) (KKBW-5827) [15]
Away in a Manger (Traditional-Kirkpatrick) (KKBW-5995) [15]
Guardian Angels (Beilenson-Marx) (KKBW-5996) [15]
Joy to the World (Handel-Watts) (KKBW-6018) [15]
Hark, the Herald Angels Sing (Mendelssohn-Wesley) (KKBW-6019) [15]
It Came Upon a Midnight Clear (Sears-Willis) (KKBW-6020) [15]
God Rest Ye Merry Gentlemen (Traditional) (KKBW-6024) [15]

O Christmas Tree (Traditional) (KKBW-6025) [15]
Deck the Halls (Traditional) (KKBW-6026) [15]
I Saw Three Ships (Traditional) (KKBW-6027) [15]

June 1959, Cinecittà Studios, Rome

Mario Lanza Sings Caruso Favorites, RCA Living Stereo recording
Orchestra conducted by Paul Baron
   Vieni Sul Mar (Anonymous) [3]
   Senza Nisciuno (De Curtis-Barbieri) [3]
   Musica Proibita (Gastaldon) [3]
   Vaghissima Sembianza (Donaudy) [3]
   Serenata (Bracco-Caruso) [3]
   Lolita (Buzzi-Peccia) [3]
   Luna D'estate (Tosti) [3]
   L'alba Separa Dalla Luce L'Ombra (Tosti-D'Annunzio) [3]
   Pour un Baiser (Tosti-Doncieux) [3]
   La Mia Canzone (Tosti-Cimmino) [3]
   Ideale (Tosti-Errico) [3]
   Santa Lucia (Cottrau) [1, 3]

July 1959, Cinecittà Studios, Rome

The Vagabond King (Friml-Post-Hooker), RCA Living Stereo recording
Orchestra conducted by Constantine Callinicos
Soloist and chorus overdubs recorded in New York, 8–10 March 1960
   Love Me Tonight (KKBW-6085) [16]
   Tomorrow (Judith Raskin, soprano) (KKBW-6088) [16]
   Drinking Song (KKBW-6089) [16]
   Nocturne (KKBW-6090) [16]
   Nocturne (reprise, not featured on disc) (KKBW-6091)
   Song of the Vagabonds (KKBW-6092) [16]
   Finale (Judith Raskin, soprano) (KKBW-6093) [16]
   Only a Rose (Judith Raskin, soprano) (KKBW-6094) [1, 16]
   Someday (Judith Raskin, soprano) (KKBW-6096) [16]

August 1959, Cinecittà Studios, Rome

The Desert Song (Romberg-Harbach-Hammerstein II), RCA Living
Stereo recording
Orchestra conducted by Constantine Callinicos

Soloists and chorus overdubs recorded in New York 1960
  Then You Will Know (Judith Raskin, soprano) (KKBW-6141) [2]
  Riff Song (KKBW-6142) [2]
  The Desert Song (Judith Raskin, soprano) (KKBW-6143) [2]
  My Margo (not featured on Living Stereo album)
  One Flower in Your Garden (Donald Arthur, bass) (KKBW-6150) [2]
  One Alone (KKBW-6151) [1, 2]
  One Alone (reprise, not featured on Living Stereo album) [7]
  Azuri's Dance (KKBW-6154) [2]
  I Want a Kiss (Judith Raskin, soprano, Raymond Murcell, baritone)
  (KKBW-6155) [2]
  One Good Boy Gone Wrong (Judith Raskin, soprano) (KKBW-6157) [2]

10 September 1959, Cinecittà Studios, Rome
Final RCA recording session
  The Lord's Prayer (Malotte) (Constantine Callinicos, piano)

Mario Lanza on Compact Disc
[1] *Mario Lanza: The Legendary Tenor* (BMG 6218-2-RC)
[2] *The Student Prince and The Desert Song* (BMG GD60048)
[3] *The Great Caruso and Lanza Sings Caruso Favorites* (BMG 60049-2-RG)
[4] *For the First Time and That Midnight Kiss* (BMG 60516-2-RG)
[5] *Christmas with Mario Lanza* (BMG 6427-2-RG)
[6] *Be My Love* (BMG 60720-2-RG)
[7] *The Mario Lanza Collection* (BMG 09026-60889-2)
[8] *Don't Forget Me* (BMG 09026-61420-2)
[9] *Mario Lanza: Live from London* (BMG 09026-61884-2)
[10] *You'll Never Walk Alone* (BMG 09026-68073-2)
[11] *Be My Love: Mario Lanza's Greatest Performances at MGM*
      (Rhino-Turner R2 72598)*
[12] *When Day Is Done* (BMG 09026-63254-2)
[13] *Mario Lanza in Hollywood: That Midnight Kiss and The Toast of*
      New Orleans (Soundies/BMG SCS 4104)
[14] *Opera Arias and Duets* (BMG 09026-63491-2)
[15] *Lanza Sings Christmas Carols* (BMG 09026-63178-2)
[16] *Mario!/The Vagabond King* (BMG 09026-68130-2)
[17] *I'll See You in My Dreams* (Jeff Rense/BMG Special Products
      DRC-12672)**

[18] *My Romance* (BMG 09026-63751-2)

[19] *Mario Lanza: The Definitive Collection* (BMG U.K. 82876-614032)

[20] *Serenade/A Cavalcade of Show Tunes* (BMG U.K. 82876-625932)

[21] *You Do Something to Me/Christmas Hymns and Carols*
(Collectables COL 7323)

* MGM soundtrack recordings

** Available online at www.mariolanza.net

THE RECORDED LEGACY

Alphabetical Listing of All Recorded Material by Mario Lanza

The following is an alphabetical listing of all recorded material by Mario Lanza that is currently available on disc or cassette. Source references are noted in parentheses after each title (CCS, Coca-Cola Show; MGM, MGM soundtrack recording; PR, private noncommercial recording; R, Radio [not Coca-Cola Show]; RCA, RCA Records; S, Stage; TV, television; WB, Warner Bros. soundtrack recording). The index is intended as a reference guide to the diverse body of music sung by Lanza during his career. Included here are performances from Lanza's non-Coca-Cola Show radio appearances (R), as well as several private recordings (PR); these selections were not repeated in the recording studio and as such are not detailed in the main discography. See *Stage, Radio, and Television Appearances* section for further information.

'A Vucchella (PR, MGM, RCA, CCS, S)
Agnus Dei (S)
Ah, Moon of My Delight (R)
Ah, Sweet Mystery of Life (CCS)
Aida: Act I, Celeste Aida (MGM, RCA, CCS)
Aida: Act I, Nume custode e vindice (Temple Scene) (MGM)
Aida: Act II, Grand march (MGM)
Aida: Act IV, O terra, addio (MGM)
All Alone (R)
All the Things You Are (CCS, MGM, RCA)
All Ye Thankful People Come (R)
Alone Together (CCS)
America the Beautiful (R)
Among My Souvenirs (CCS)
And Here You Are (CCS)
And This Is My Beloved (RCA)

Andrea Chenier: Act I, Un di all'azzuro spazio (PR, S, RCA, CCS, MGM)
Andrea Chenier: Act IV, Come un bel di di maggio (PR, RCA, CCS)
April in Paris (CCS)
Arrivederci Roma (Italian version) (MGM)
Arrivederci Roma (Italian/English version) (RCA)
Ave Maria (Bach-Gounod) (RCA, MGM, CCS)
Ave Maria (Schubert) (WB, MGM, TV)
Away in a Manger (RCA)
Ay-Ay-Ay (CCS)
Azuri's Dance (RCA)

Bayou Lullaby (MGM, RCA)
Be My Love (MGM, RCA, CCS, R)
Beautiful Love (CCS)
Because (RCA, CCS)
Because You're Mine (MGM, RCA, TV, S)
Begin the Beguine (CCS)
Behold! (RCA)
Beloved (MGM, RCA)
Besame Mucho (CCS)
Best Things in Life Are Free, The (CCS)
Blue Skies (R)
Bonjour, Ma Belle (S)
Boom Biddy Boom Boom (MGM, RCA, CCS)

Call Me Fool (RCA)
Canta Pe' Me (CCS, RCA)
Carmen: Act II, La fleur que tu m'avais jetée (PR, MGM, RCA, CCS)
Cavalleria Rusticana: Addio alla madre (PR, RCA, MGM, CCS)
Cavalleria Rusticana: No, Turiddu, rimani (MGM)
Cavalleria Rusticana: Vivo il vino spumeggiante (Brindisi) (MGM)
Charmaine (CCS)
Ciribiribin (CCS)
Come Dance with Me (RCA, MGM)
Come Facette Mammeta? (RCA)
Come Prima (MGM)
Core'ngrato (RCA, CCS)
Cosi Cosa (R, CCS)
Così Fan Tutte: Trio—Act I, No. 16, Scene XII, E voi ridete (MGM)

Danny Boy (CCS)
Day In, Day Out (CCS)
Deck the Halls (RCA)
Deep in My Heart, Dear (R, MGM, RCA)
Der Rosenkavalier: Act I, Di rigori armato il seno (WB)
Desert Song, The (CCS, RCA)
Diane (CCS)
Dicitencello Vuie (CCS, RCA)
Do You Wonder? (RCA)
Donkey Serenade, The (CCS, RCA)
Drink, Drink, Drink (MGM, RCA)
Drinking Song: *The Vagabond King* (RCA)

Earthbound (RCA)
Elisir d'Amore, L': Act II, Una furtiva lagrima (PR, S, MGM, RCA, CCS)
Ergo Bibamus (MGM)

Falling in Love with Love (RCA)
Fedora: Act II, Amor ti vieta (CCS, WB)
Fenesta Che Lucive (CCS, RCA)
First Noel, The (RCA, CCS)
Fools Rush In (CCS)
For You Alone (RCA, CCS)
Funiculì, Funiculà (CCS, RCA)

Gaudeamus Igitur (MGM, RCA)
Già Il Sole Dal Gange (S)
Giannina Mia (RCA)
God Rest Ye Merry Gentlemen (RCA)
Golden Days (R, MGM, RCA)
Granada (RCA, CCS, MGM)
Guardian Angels (RCA, CCS)
Gypsy Love Song (RCA)

Halloween Suite (S)
Hark the Herald Angel's Sing (RCA)
Hills of Home, The (CCS)
Hofbrauhaus Song (MGM)
House on the Hill, The (R, S)

I Know, I Know, I Know (MGM, R, RCA)
I Love Thee (RCA, CCS, MGM)
I Never Knew (CCS)
I Saw Three Ships (RCA)
I Want a Kiss (RCA)
Il Trovatore: Act III, Di quella pira (WB)
Il Trovatore: Act IV, Ah! Che la morte ognora (Miserere) (MGM)
I'll Be Seeing You (CCS)
I'll Never Love You (MGM, RCA, CCS)
I'll See You Again (CCS)
I'll See You in My Dreams (CCS)
I'll Walk with God (MGM, RCA)
I'm Falling in Love with Someone (PR, R, CCS, S, TV)
I've Got You Under My Skin (CCS)
I've Told Ev'ry Little Star (RCA)
Ideale (RCA)
If (CCS)
If I Loved You (CCS)
If You Are But a Dream (CCS)
If You Were Mine (RCA)
Imitation Sequence: *Seven Hills of Rome* (MGM)
It Came Upon a Midnight Clear (RCA)

Joy to the World (RCA)
Just We Two (RCA)

Kiss, A (CCS)
Kiss in the Dark, A (CCS)

La Bohème (Leoncavallo): Act III, Testa adorata (CCS)
La Bohème (Puccini): Act I, Che gelida manina (PR, RCA, MGM, CCS)
La Bohème (Puccini): Act I, O soave fanciulla (PR, S, WB)
La Bohème (Puccini): Act III, Ci lasceremo alla stagion dei fior (PR, WB)
La Bohème (Puccini): Act IV excerpt Marcello finalmente (PR)
La Danza (MGM, CCS, WB)
La Forza del Destino: Act III, O tu che in seno agli angeli (RCA, CCS)
La Gioconda: Act II, Cielo e mar! (RCA, MGM, CCS)
La Fanciulla del West: Act III, Ch'ella mi creda (PR)

La Mia Canzone (RCA)

La Spagnola (CCS)

La Traviata: Act I, Libiamo, libiamo, ne'lieti calici (MGM, RCA)

La Traviata: Act II, De' miei bollenti spiriti (PR)

La Traviata: Act IV, Parigi o cara (S)

Lady of Spain (CCS)

L'Africana: Act IV, O paradiso (MGM, RCA, CCS, WB)

L'Alba Separa Dalla Luce L'Ombra (RCA)

L'Arianna: Lasciatemi Morire (S)

L'Arlesiana: Act II, Lamento di Federico (S, RCA, CCS)

Lee-Ah-Loo (MGM, RCA)

Little Love, a Little Kiss, A (CCS)

Lolita (RCA, CCS, MGM)

Long Ago and Far Away (CCS)

Look for the Silver Lining (CCS)

Lord's Prayer, The (RCA, MGM, CCS)

Love in a Home (RCA)

Love Is Music (MGM)

Love Is the Sweetest Thing (RCA)

Love Me Tonight (RCA)

Loveliest Night of the Year, The (RCA, CCS, MGM, TV, S)

Lover Come Back to Me (RCA)

Lucia di Lammermoor: Act I, Verranno a te sull'aure (R)

Lucia di Lammermoor: Act II, Sextet (MGM)

Luna D'estate (RCA)

Lygia (CCS)

Madama Butterfly: Act I, Stolta paura l'amor (S, MGM, RCA)

Madame Sans-Gêne: Act II excerpt, Questa tua bocca, profumata e pura (PR)

Make Believe (CCS)

Mamma Mia, Che Vo' Sapè? (R, MGM, RCA, CCS, S)

Marcheta (CCS)

Marechiare (PR, RCA, CCS, S, TV)

Maria Marì (CCS, RCA)

Martha: Act III, Finale (MGM)

Martha: Act III, M'Appari (PR, MGM, RCA)

Mattinata (RCA, MGM, CCS)

Memories (CCS)

Mighty Fortress, A (MGM)
Moon Was Yellow, The (CCS)
More Than You Know (RCA)
Musica Proibita (CCS, RCA)
My Buddy (CCS)
My Destiny (WB)
My Heart Stood Still (CCS)
My Margo (RCA)
My Romance (CCS, RCA)
My Song, My Love (MGM, RCA, CCS)
My Wild Irish Rose (CCS)

'Na Sera 'E M aggio (CCS, RCA)
Neapolitan Love Song (Victor Herbert) (CCS)
Never Till Now (RCA)
Night and Day (CCS)
Night Is Young and You're So Beautiful, The (CCS)
Night to Remember, A (RCA)
Nocturne: *The Vagabond King* (RCA)
Non Ti Scordar di Me (CCS)
None But the Lonely Heart (CCS)

O Christmas Tree (RCA)
O Come All Ye Faithful (RCA, CCS)
O Holy Night (RCA)
O Little Town of Bethlehem (RCA, CCS)
O, Mon Amour (MGM)
O Sole Mio (RCA, CCS, MGM)
O Surdato 'namurato (RCA)
Oh, Nights of Splendor (CCS)
On the Street Where You Live (RCA)
One Alone (CCS, RCA)
One Flower in Your Garden (RCA)
One Good Boy Gone Wrong (RCA)
One Love of Mine (MGM)
One Night of Love (CCS)
Only a Rose (RCA)
Otello: Act I, Gia nella notte densa (Love Duet) (R)

Otello: Act I, Inaffia l'ugola (Brindisi) (R)
Otello: Act III, Dio ti giocondi (WB)
Otello: Act IV, Niun mi tema (MGM)

Pagliacci: Un tal gioco (CCS)
Pagliacci: Vesti la giubba (PR, R, S, RCA, CCS, MGM)
Parlami d'Amore Mariu (CCS)
Passione (RCA)
Pecchè? (PR)
Pietà, Signore (S)
Pineapple Pickers (MGM)
Play Gypsies, Dance Gypsies (CCS)
Pour un Baiser (RCA)
Pretty Girl Is Like a Melody, A (R)

Riff Song (RCA)
Rigoletto: Act I, Questa o quella (RCA, CCS, MGM)
Rigoletto: Act II, E il sol dell'anima; addio, addio (S, MGM)
Rigoletto: Act II, Parmi veder le lagrime (RCA, CCS)
Rigoletto: Act III, Bella figlia dell'amore (MGM)
Rigoletto: Act III, La donna e mobile (PR, MGM, RCA, CCS, S)
Romance (CCS)
Rosary, The (CCS)
Rose Marie (RCA)
Roses of Picardy (CCS)

Santa Lucia (CCS, MGM, TV, RCA)
Santa Lucia Luntana (CCS, RCA)
Senza Nisciuno (CCS, RCA)
September Song (RCA)
Serenade (Drigo) (RCA, CCS)
Serenade (Toselli) (RCA, CCS)
Serenade (WB)
Serenade (WB, different song)
Serenade: *The Student Prince* (R, CCS, MGM, RCA)
Serenata (RCA)
Seven Hills of Rome (MGM)
Siboney (CCS)

Silent Night (RCA, CCS)
So in Love (RCA)
Softly, as in a Morning Sunrise (CCS, R, S, TV)
Somebody Bigger Than You and I (CCS)
Someday (CCS, TV, RCA)
Someday I'll Find You (CCS)
Somewhere a Voice Is Calling (CCS)
Song Angels Sing, The (MGM, RCA)
Song Is You, The (CCS)
Song of India (RCA)
Song of Songs (CCS)
Song of the Vagabonds (RCA)
Speak Low (RCA)
Strange Music (CCS)
Summertime in Heidelberg (MGM, RCA)
Sylvia (CCS)

Tell Me O Blue, Blue Sky (PR, S)
Tell Me That You Love Me Tonight (CCS)
Tell Me Tonight (CCS)
Temptation (CCS)
Then You Will Know (RCA)
There's Gonna Be a Party Tonight (MGM)
They Didn't Believe Me (R, MGM, RCA, CCS)
Thine Alone (S, RCA, CCS)
This Land (RCA)
This Nearly Was Mine (RCA)
Thoughts Will Come Back to Me (RCA)
Thrill Is Gone, The (CCS)
Through the Years (CCS)
Time on My Hands (CCS)
Tina-Lina, The (MGM, RCA, CCS)
Toast of New Orleans (MGM, RCA)
Tomorrow (RCA)
Torna a Surriento (PR, CCS, WB)
Tosca: Act I, Love Duet (Mario! Mario! excluding "Qual occhio . . .") (R)
Tosca: Act I, Qual occhio al mondo (WB)
Tosca: Act I, Recondita armonia (RCA, CCS)

Tosca: Act II, Torture Scene (MGM)
Tosca: Act III, E lucevan le stelle (PR, RCA, MGM, CCS, TV, S)
Touch of Your Hand, The (CCS)
Tramp! Tramp! Tramp! (RCA)
Trees (CCS)
Trembling of a Leaf, The (CCS)
Tu Ca Nun Chiagne (CCS, RCA)
Turandot: Act III, Nessun dorma (S, WB)

Vaghissima Sembianza (RCA)
Valencia (RCA)
Vieni Sul Mar (RCA)
Virgin's Slumber Song, The (RCA)
Voce 'E Notte (RCA)

Wanting You (CCS)
We Three Kings of Orient Are (RCA)
What Is This Thing Called Love? (CCS)
What's to Be? (MGM)
When Day Is Done (CCS)
When You're in Love (CCS)
Where or When (CCS)
Why Was I Born? (RCA)
Will You Remember? (RCA)
With a Song in My Heart (CCS)
Without a Song (CCS)
Wonder Why (CCS)
World Is Mine Tonight, The (CCS)

Yesterdays (CCS)
You and the Night and the Music (CCS)
You Are Love (CCS)
You Are My Love (RCA)
You Do Something to Me (RCA)
You'll Never Walk Alone (CCS, RCA)
Younger Than Springtime (RCA)
Your Eyes Have Told Me So (CCS)
Yours Is My Heart Alone (CCS, RCA)

FILMOGRAPHY

The films of Mario Lanza span a mere decade yet their impact on a generation of musicians and opera singers, in particular, is considerable. The following is a list of the tenor's seven films, along with production details of *The Student Prince* for which his singing voice only was used. Details of the music featured in the films are listed in the *Discography*.

Lanza's first appearance on a Hollywood soundstage was in the chorus of the *Winged Victory*, directed in 1944 by George Cukor for 20th Century Fox. However, the tenor was fired from the production in the fall of that year and there is no evidence that any scenes he may have filmed ever made it to the final cut.

That Midnight Kiss (September 1949) MGM
Director: Norman Taurog
Producer: Joe Pasternak
Screenplay: Bruce Manning and Tamara Hovey
Musical director: Charles Previn
Running time: 98 minutes, Technicolor
Cast: Kathryn Grayson, José Iturbi, Ethel Barrymore, Keenan Wynn, J. Carrol Naish, Jules Munshin, Thomas Gomez, Marjorie Reynolds, Amaparo Iturbi, and "introducing" Mario Lanza

The Toast of New Orleans (September 1950) MGM
Director: Norman Taurog
Producer: Joe Pasternak
Screenplay: Sy Gomberg and George Wells
Musical directors: George Stoll and Johnny Green
Running time: 97 minutes, Technicolor
Cast: Kathryn Grayson, Mario Lanza, David Niven, J. Carrol Naish, Richard Hageman, Rita Moreno, James Mitchell
"Be My Love" from *The Toast of New Orleans* was nominated for an Academy Award in the best song category, but it lost out to "Mona Lisa."

The Great Caruso (April 1951) MGM

Director: Richard Thorpe
Producer: Joe Pasternak
Associate producer: Jesse L. Lasky
Screenplay: Sonya Levien and William Ludwig, suggested by Dorothy Caruso's biography of her husband
Musical directors: Peter Herman Adler and Johnny Green
Running time: 109 minutes, Technicolor
Cast: Mario Lanza, Ann Blyth, Dorothy Kirsten, Jarmila Novotná, Carl Benton Reid, Eduard Franz, Richard Hageman, Ludwig Donath, Alan Napier
The Great Caruso won an Academy Award for best sound recording, the Oscar going to Douglas Shearer. Peter Herman Adler and Johnny Green were nominated for scoring for a motion picture, along with Helen Rose and Gil Steele for costume and design. The awards in both of these categories lost out to *An American in Paris*.

Because You're Mine (October 1952) MGM

Director: Alexander Hall
Producer: Joe Pasternak
Screenplay: Leonard Spiegelgass and Karl Tunberg
Musical director: Johnny Green
Running time: 103 minutes, Technicolor
Cast: Mario Lanza, Doretta Morrow, James Whitmore, Paula Corday, Jeff Donnell, Spring Byington
"Because You're Mine" was nominated for an Academy Award in the best song category, but it lost out to the theme from *High Noon*.

The Student Prince (June 1954) MGM

Director: Richard Thorpe
Producer: Joe Pasternak
Screenplay: William Ludwig and Sonya Levien
Musical director: George Stoll
Running time: 107 minutes, Anscolor
Cast: Ann Blyth, Edmund Purdom, Edmund Gwenn, S. Z. Sakall, John Williams, John Erickson, Louis Calhern, and "The Singing Voice of Mario Lanza"

Serenade (April 1956) Warner Bros.

Director: Anthony Mann
Producer: Henry Blanke

Screenplay: Ivan Goff and Ben Roberts, based on the novel by James M. Cain
Musical director: Ray Heindorf
Running time: 121 minutes, Warnercolor
Cast: Mario Lanza, Joan Fontaine, Sarita Montiel, Vincent Price, Joseph Calleia, Harry Bellaver, Vince Edwards, Licia Albanese, Jean Fenn

Seven Hills of Rome (January 1958) MGM/Titanus Films
Director: Roy Rowland
Producer: Lester Welch
Screenplay: Art Cohn and Giorgio Prosperi
Musical director: George Stoll
Running time: 104 minutes, Technicolor
Cast: Mario Lanza, Renato Rascel, Marisa Allasio, Peggy Castle

For the First Time (August 1959) MGM/Corona Orion
Director: Rudolph Maté
Producer: Alexander Grueter
Screenplay: Andrew Solt
Musical director: George Stoll
Running time: 97 minutes, Technicolor
Cast: Mario Lanza, Johanna von Koczian, Kurt Kasznar, Zsa Zsa Gabor
The soundtrack recording of *For the First Time* was nominated for a Grammy award in 1960 but lost out to *Porgy and Bess*.

PERFORMANCE

Stage, Radio, and Television Appearances

By all accounts hearing Mario Lanza sing live on the concert platform was a remarkable experience. From his first appearance as a budding professional at Koussevitzky's famed Berkshire Music Center at Tanglewood in 1942 to his dramatic and triumphant farewell at the vast Ostseehalle in Kiel, West Germany, sixteen years later, Lanza never sold his audience short. His appearances on live radio and television, too, though less frequent, created just the same impact.

What follows is a chronological account of the most important moments in the tenor's stage (S), radio (R), and television (TV) career. An asterisk after a title indicates that a recording exists for that entry. The fact that only one professional opera engagement is listed serves as poignant reminder of all that was lost and all that might have been.

7 and 13 August 1942
The Merry Wives of Windsor (S)
Berkshire Music Center, Tanglewood, Massachusetts
Mario Lanza's graduation performance as Fenton in Otto Nicolai's comic opera, *The Merry Wives of Windsor*, took place on 7 August; a repeat performance with a slightly different cast was presented on 13 August. The conductor for both evenings was Boris Goldovsky. Felix Wolfes, Henry Gregor, Leonard Bernstein, and Lukas Foss assisted in the musical preparation.

Summer 1943
On the Beam (S)
His operatic career on hold during the war years, Lanza found himself in the U.S. Army looking for a way to continue his singing. He found it in this, an army musical revue written and produced by Peter Lind Hayes and Frank Loesser. The revue toured army bases throughout the United States and marked Lanza's return, of sorts, to the concert stage. The tenor reprised his

successful audition aria "E lucevan le stelle" in the production and was also heard in the group number "General Orders." Lanza's acting skills were put to the test in two comedy skits in which he portrayed the character Sylvia Storecheese.

20 November 1943
Winged Victory (S)

Lanza found continued solace from the rigors of army life by joining a fifty-man choral group in *Winged Victory*, a flag-waving extravaganza by playwright Moss Hart. The play-cum-musical eventually made it to Broadway, where it ran for 212 performances. Lanza later traveled to Hollywood where *Winged Victory* was filmed in 1944 by 20th Century Fox under the direction of George Cukor. Regrettably, Lanza was fired from the production due to tardy attendance on the Fox lot and is nowhere to be seen in the finished film.

Labor Day 1945
Association of Broadcasters' concert (S)
Atlantic City Convention Hall, New Jersey

A prestigious, one-off engagement for the young tenor and his first professional encounter with the NBC Symphony Orchestra conducted by Peter Herman Adler. The two men would later join forces on the musical score for *The Great Caruso*.

24 October 1945
The Celanese Hour: Great Moments in Music (R)*

Back in civilian life again, Lanza's career finally started to roll into high gear. Through the intervention of Metropolitan Opera baritone Robert Weede, Lanza signed on as a temporary replacement for tenor Jan Peerce on the popular weekly radio show *The Celanese Hour*. The program was broadcast live and provided invaluable experience for the young singer. For his first appearance he was featured in excerpts from Puccini's *Tosca* under the musical direction of Sylvan Levin. Lanza sang "E lucevan le stelle," "Recondita armonia," and the love duet (with Jean Tennyson, soprano). Roger Lyons was the narrator.

7 November 1945
The Celanese Hour: Great Moments in Music (R)*

For a program titled "Peace Must Be Won," Lanza's second appearance on *The Celanese Hour* featured his interpretation of Ernest Charles' "The House on the Hill," and "America the Beautiful" (with Robert Weede and Vivian Bauer, soprano). The "live" aspect of the show was especially evident when Lanza momentarily forgot the words to "America the Beautiful," though he recovered quickly. Burgess Meredith served as narrator.

14 November 1945
The Celanese Hour: Great Moments in Music (R)*

Lanza's youthful inexperience was put to the test on this, his third appearance on the series when he performed two selections from Verdi's *Otello*: the Act I "Brindisi," "Inaffia l'ugola" (with Robert Weede and chorus), and the love duet "Gia nella notte densa" (with Jean Tennyson, soprano). It was not a happy occasion, and he was clearly not up to the demands of the role at that point in his career. Roger Lyons again provided the narration, and the conductor this time was George Sebastian.

19 December 1945
Red Barber Review (R)*

The tenor's career on radio continued to move forward with a brief change of venue. This program featured sterling live performances from the singer of two of his favorite pieces: "Vesti la giubba" from *I Pagliacci* and the Victor Herbert evergreen "I'm Falling in Love with Someone."

26 December 1945
The Celanese Hour: Great Moments in Music (R)*

A return to *The Celanese Hour* and two especially memorable performances taken from Lehmann's *In a Persian Garden*: "A Jug of Wine" (with Frances Yeend, soprano) and "Ah, Moon of My Delight." George Sebastian conducted and Roger Lyons narrated.

23 January 1946
The Celanese Hour: Great Moments in Music (R)*

The Lanza voice was well suited to the music of the Great American Songbook and here he performed a number of standards written by Irving Berlin: "A Pretty Girl Is Like a Melody," "Blue Skies" (with Natalie Bodanya, soprano), and a medley comprising "All Alone" (Lanza) and "What'll I Do" (Bodanya) with Leonard Stokes, baritone, joining them for the finale. Sylvan Levin conducted.

20 February 1946

The Celanese Hour: Great Moments in Music (R)*

The selections from Sigmund Romberg's *The Student Prince* for *The Celanese Hour* marked Lanza's first recorded performances from a score he would eventually make his own. The immortal "Serenade" is given a youthful reading here, and the tenor is joined by soprano Winifred Smith for a charming "Deep in My Heart, Dear." Lanza would record "Golden Days" three times in his career but his performance for *The Celanese Hour* with Robert Weede was the only time he ever sang it correctly—as a duet. The conductor was Sylvan Levin. This was Lanza's final appearance on *The Celanese Hour*.

14 April 1947

State Teachers' College Auditorium, Shippensburg, Pennsylvania (S)

A recital that indeed proved to be a "great moment in music" in Mario Lanza's career. It was here that he first met Constantine Callinicos, a last-minute replacement for regular pianist Josef Blatt. Callinicos would go on to become Lanza's accompanist, conductor, and closest confidant in his musical life.

July 1947 to May 1948

The Bel Canto Trio Concerts (S)

Between 8 July 1947 and 27 May 1948, The Bel Canto Trio—a group comprised of Lanza, Frances Yeend, soprano, and George London, bass-baritone—made a total of eighty-six concert appearances at venues throughout the United States, Canada, and Mexico. Included on their itinerary were scheduled appearances at Milwaukee, Wisconsin; Ames, Iowa; Minot, North Dakota; La Porte, Indiana; Albion, Michigan; Middletown, New York; La Porte, Indiana; Albion, Michigan; Madison, Wisconsin; Wheeling, West Virginia; Middletown, New York; Sylcauga, Alabama; Wallingford, Connecticut; Oklahoma City; Halifax, Nova Scotia; St. John's, Newfoundland; and Chihuahua and Torreón, Mexico.

28 August 1947

Hollywood Bowl concert (S, R)*

The concert appearance that changed the course of Mario Lanza's career forever—a stunning performance that was capped off by an offer to audition for Louis B. Mayer, head of MGM film studios. With Eugene Ormandy conducting, Lanza was in magnificent voice on the night and his program of operatic arias and duets was particularly felicitous. Beginning with "Una furtiva lagrima" from Donizetti's *L'Elisir d'Amore*, Lanza delivered powerful renditions of the "Improviso" from Giordano's *Andrea Chenier*, and "E lucevan le stelle" from Puccini's *Tosca*. He was joined by Frances Yeend for three duets: "Parigi o cara" from *La Traviata*, the love duet from *Madama Butterfly* (thrillingly sung), and "O soave fanciulla" from *La Bohème*. The concert was recorded for NBC radio.

14 February 1948
Edgar Bergen/Charlie McCarthy Show (S)*
Fair Park Auditorium, Dallas, Texas
A lighthearted moment in the tenor's burgeoning concert career, where he mugged with the dummy and wowed the audience with a knockdown rendition of his favorite aria, "Vesti la giubba" from *I Pagliacci*. The orchestra was conducted by Ray Noble.

5 March 1948
Massey Hall, Toronto, Canada (S)*
Lanza was backed by the Toronto Symphony Orchestra conducted by Paul Scherman for the first half of this concert, three arias from which have survived on disc: "Lamento di Federico, "La donna e mobile," and "Vesti la giubba." Following the intermission, Lanza sang three songs accompanied by Leo Barkin on piano: "Softly, as in a Morning Sunrise," "Thine Alone," and "I'm Falling in Love with Someone." No recording of these three performances is known to exist.

8 and 10 April 1948
Madama Butterfly (S)
Municipal Auditorium, New Orleans
The occasion when all the "what might have beens" became, for two performances, what actually was. On the evening of 8 April 1948 Mario Lanza finally made his professional operatic debut as Pinkerton in a New Orleans Opera House Association production of *Madama Butterfly*. Cio-Cio-San was sung by the Japanese soprano Tomiko Kanazawa, with Jess Walters as Sharpless and Rosalind Nadell as Suzuki. Walter Herbert conducted the New Orleans Symphony Orchestra.

18 June 1948
The Bel Canto Trio, New York (R)*
Flush from his success in New Orleans, Lanza joined forces with Yeend and London one last time to record an excerpt in English from Act IV of Puccini's

La Bohème. The performance was part of a demo disc for a proposed NBC opera program and is the only recorded account of the trio known to have survived on record. The excerpt begins with Musetta's entrance with an ailing Mimi, and concludes just before the coat aria. Lanza, Yeend, and London are also joined on the recording by another soprano and a baritone, both of whom are unidentified.

24 July 1948

"MGM Night at the Hollywood Bowl" (S)*

This show featured Miklós Rózsa conducting the Hollywood Bowl Symphony Orchestra, with Roger Wagner and the Los Angeles Concert Chorale. Broadcast on NBC radio, this concert contained Lanza's only recorded performance of Bizet's "Agnus Dei." He followed it with a hair-raising delivery of "Nessun dorma," truly one of the great live performances of his career. Soprano Kathryn Grayson then joined Lanza, bass Lee Wintner, and actor Lionel Barrymore for Barrymore's decidedly offbeat "Halloween Suite." "O soave fanciulla" with Lanza and Grayson followed, and both singers concluded their set with a duet on Victor Herbert's "Thine Alone."

15 September 1948

"Salute to MGM" (R)*

Publicity appearance on live radio with Lanza singing "Vesti la giubba."

22 September 1948

"Salute to MGM" (R)*

Another appearance on the program, with Lanza singing Victor Herbert's "Thine Alone."

25 November 1948

"Elgin Watch Thanksgiving Special: Holiday Star Time" (R)*

Lanza joined host Dan Ameche, Edgar Bergen/Charlie McCarthy, and comedians Jack Benny, Red Skelton, and Dean Martin and Jerry Lewis for this Thanksgiving special. Broadcast live on NBC, the tenor sang "Cosi Cosa," "E lucevan le stelle" from *Tosca*, and the Thanksgiving hymn "All Ye Thankful People Come."

19 December 1948

Edgar Bergen/Charlie McCarthy Show (R)*

Lanza's second and final appearance on the popular comedy show, where, in an unusually solemn moment, he sang "The Lord's Prayer."

March to May 1949

First concert tour with Constantine Callinicos (S)

Lanza's promise to Callinicos after the Shippensburg recital that he would work with him again was not forgotten, as the two artists toured some of the smaller concert venues throughout the United States. Included on the itinerary were stops at Clinton, Iowa; Zanesville, Ohio; Athens, Ohio; Wilmington, Delaware; Troy, New York; Portland, Maine; Fort Wayne; Indiana; Duluth, Minnesota; Chicago; Minneapolis; New Orleans; Tulsa; Oklahoma; Sylcauga; Alabama; and Centralia, Illinois.

16 August 1949

"Salute to MGM" (S)*

Yet another MGM spectacular from the Hollywood Bowl. Under the baton of conductor Johnny Green, Lanza performed "E il sol dell'anima/Addio, addio" from *Rigoletto* with soprano Mary Jane Smith. Their spirited duet has survived on disc but not, seemingly, the tenor's solo aria "Celeste Aida."

29 August, 1949

Bellevue-Stratford Hotel Ballroom, Philadelphia

Citizen's Reception Committee luncheon in honor of Harry S. Truman, president of the United States, and Perry Brown, national commander of the American Legion. Tenor solo by Lanza. The selection was not listed. Truman was also scheduled to give a keynote speech at an another convention on that day and had to leave before Lanza sang.

29 September 1949

Screen Guild Theater program (R)*

Promotional radio tie-in with Lanza and Kathryn Grayson singing the praises of *That Midnight Kiss*. The program was broadcast on NBC and in between the sound bites the two duetted very nicely on "They Didn't Believe Me" and "Verranno a te sull'aure" from *Lucia di Lammermoor*. Lanza's solos were "Mamma Mia, Che Vo' Sapè?" and "I Know, I Know, I Know." Their conductor was Henry Russell.

Lanza and Grayson also promoted the film at a number of venues throughout the United States where they performed several numbers from the film. Their itinerary included stops at Philadelphia on 2 September; New Haven, Connecticut on 12 September; New York on 13 September; St. Louis on 15 September; and Kansas City on 18 September. They each sang one solo number then joined for a duet. Giacomo Spadoni accompanied the singers on piano.

29 November 1949
Life with Luigi (R)*

Lanza joined regulars J. Carrol Naish, Jim Backus, and Hans Conreid for a sketch on the popular weekly radio show. With the promotion of *That Midnight Kiss* still on the front burner, Lanza graced the program with a forceful live rendition of "Mamma Mia, Che Vo' Sapè?"

22, 24, and 27 March 1950
McKinley Auditorium in Honolulu, Hawaii (S)

Lanza and Callinicos flew to Hawaii for three concerts at McKinley Auditorium in Honolulu. A much photographed visit, with Tyrone Power and his wife, Linda Christian, joining the Lanzas for this working vacation.

22 April 1950
"Friar's Frolic Charity Show" (S)
Shrine Auditorium, Los Angeles

A gala charity affair with some of the top names in Hollywood at that time, including Al Jolson, Jack Benny, Harpo Marx, Dean Martin and Jerry Lewis, Burt Lancaster, Robert Mitchum, Red Skelton, Phil Silvers, Donald O'Connor, and Isaac Stern. Lanza appeared with maestro Giacomo Spadoni, who accompanied him on piano for two selections: "Vesti la giubba" and "O Sole Mio."

19 November 1950
Hedda Hopper's Hollywood (R)*

Two powerhouse performances by Lanza on the Hollywood gossip columnist's weekly variety show. Notable for his amazing breath control on "Vesti la giubba" and a "Be My Love" with a completely different orchestral arrangement to the classic version with Ray Sinatra. The announcer was Harlow Wilcox, and Frank Wirth conducted the orchestra.

16 February to 13 April 1951
The Great Caruso tour (S)

Lanza and Callinicos embarked on a nationwide concert tour to promote *The Great Caruso*. Cities included Scranton, Pennsylvania; Utica, New York;

Baltimore, Maryland; Richmond, Virginia; Pittsburgh; Columbus, Ohio; Philadelphia; Miami Beach, Orlando, Daytona Beach, and Tampa, Florida; New Orleans; Milwaukee; Chicago; St. Louis; Toledo; Cincinnati; Wichita; Kansas City, Missouri; Omaha; Ogden, Utah; and Fresno.

6 March 1951

Concert at Syria Mosque, Pittsburgh (S)

Callinicos was not on hand for this appearance, at which Lanza was backed by the Pittsburgh Symphony Orchestra under the baton of Vladimir Bakaleinikoff. Demand for tickets was so great that the promoters sold seats for the tenor's afternoon rehearsal. Lanza's program included "Lamento di Federico," "La donna e mobile," "Vesti la giubba," "'A Vuchella," and "Because," with "Be My Love" as an encore.

10 June 1951 to 5 September 1952

The Mario Lanza Show (R)*

No body of work in Lanza's career has produced more musical riches that the material recorded for his weekly radio series sponsored by the Coca-Cola Company. Sixty-six shows in all were broadcast over two years—the first seventeen with CBS and the remainder with NBC. For a complete listing of all the "Coke Show" songs, see the *Discography*.

30 September 1954

The Shower of Stars (TV)*

Sponsored by Chrysler Motors, this live broadcast of the *Shower of Stars* show marked the tenor's first appearance on television. However, while the show was live, the tenor's singing was not and he was roundly criticized for miming to old recordings: "Be My Love" (from *The Mario Lanza Show*), "Marechiare," and "Vesti la giubba." For once, his "lucky aria" did not live up to its reputation.

28 October 1954

The Shower of Stars (TV)*

Lanza returned to the Chrysler show a month later where this time the great voice rang out live to great acclaim. His performance that night was outstanding and his choice of music— "E lucevan le stelle" from *Tosca* and "Someday" from *The Vagabond King*—showcased the voice at its absolute best.

July 1957

Naples, Italy (S)

Lanza broke off filming *Seven Hills of Rome* to accept an award in Naples and was persuaded to sing one song at the charity event. This was the only time that Lanza performed in public before an audience in Italy.

31 October 1957

The Christopher Program (TV)*

Halloween at the Vatican as Mario and Betty Lanza talk about their life together with Father James Keller, founder of The Christophers, a New York–based Christian support organization. Recorded for broadcast in America, Lanza sang three songs on the show: "Because You're Mine," "Santa Lucia," and Schubert's "Ave Maria." Callinicos was not on hand at the time, and Lanza was accompanied by Paul Baron on piano.

16 November 1957

"The Royal Variety Performance" (S, R)*

London Palladium

Callinicos had returned to the podium when Lanza made an unforgettable appearance at the London Palladium before Queen Elizabeth and Prince Philip. Lanza sang three numbers: "Because You're Mine," "E lucevan le stelle," and "The Loveliest Night of the Year." Edited highlights from the show were broadcast three days later on radio.

24 November 1957

Sunday Night at the London Palladium (S, TV)*

Lanza's repeated his program to equal success the following week, and this time the show made it to ATV Television.

January to April 1958

The final tour (S)

In January 1958, with the ever-faithful Callinicos in tow, Lanza commenced a European concert tour with appearances at Sheffield City Hall, England (4 January); St Andrew's Hall, Glasgow, Scotland (7 January); City Hall, Newcastle, England (9 January); De Montford Hall, Leicester, England (12 January); Royal Albert Hall, London, England (16* and 19 January); Kongress-saal des Deutschen Museum, Munich, Germany (24 January); Liederhalle, Stuttgart, Germany (27 January); Colston Hall, Bristol, England (4 March);

King's Hall, Belle Vue, Manchester, England (6 March); City Hall, Newcastle, England (9 March); The Dome, Brighton, England (12 March); St. George's Hall, Bradford, England (13 March); Usher Hall, Edinburgh, Scotland (25 March); Croyd Hall, Dundee, Scotland (27 March); King's Hall, Belfast, Northern Ireland (29 March); De Montford Hall, Leicester, England (31 March); Olympia, Paris, France (2 April); Kursaal, Ostend, Belgium (5 April); Ahoy Hal, Rotterdam, Holland (7 April); Neidersachschalle, Hanover, Germany (11 April); Ostseehalle, Kiel, Germany (13 April). Lanza's first appearance at the Royal Albert Hall on 16 January 1958 was recorded and is available today on compact disc (see *Discography*).

18 January 1958

Saturday Night Spectacular (TV)*

Lanza's final appearance on television, a variety show introduced by David Jacobs and broadcast on ATV Television in London. With Callinicos at the piano, Lanza sang "Softly, as in a Morning Sunrise," "Marechiare," and "I'm Falling in Love with Someone."

13 April 1958

The last recital, Ostseehalle, Kiel, West Germany (S)

Mario Lanza's final, triumphant appearance on the concert stage, with Constantine Callinicos appropriately at his side.

RESOURCES

Mario Lanza Institute and Museum, Fan Clubs, and Websites

The Mario Lanza Institute and Museum
Mary Papola, president
c/o 712 Montrose Street
Philadelphia, PA 19147
USA
http://www.mario-lanza-institute.org

The Mario Lanza Educational Foundation
William Earl, chairman
20 Feversham Close
Shoreham-by-Sea
West Sussex BN43 5HD
England

The British Mario Lanza Society
c/o Ron and Wendy Stilwell
1 Kenton Gardens
Minster
Ramsgate
Kent CT12 4EN
England
http://www.bmls.co.uk

The Mario Lanza Society of New York
c/o Bill Ronayne
3315 Avenue J
Brooklyn, NY 11210
USA

Mario Lanza Fan Club of Germany

Susan and Helmut Klee
Isselberger Strasse 6
D-50733 Koln
Germany

The Mario Lanza Benelux Society

Cees Kouwenberg, secretary
Adriaan Dortsmanstraat 151
3067 NC Rotterdam
The Netherlands

The Belgian Mario Lanza Friends

Rudy Steuns, president
Kraanweg 39
2880 Bornem
Belgium

Mario Lanza Fan Club of Australia

c/o Barbara Simpson
Unit 71/289 Sydney Road
Wanneroo, Perth WA 6065
Australia

Websites

Mario Lanza: The Voice of the Century
Jeff Rense, host
http://www.mariolanza.net

The Australian Mario Lanza Society Webpage
Michael Davis, host
http://www.users.bigpond.net.au/marlan/mario.htm

NOTES

Chapter 1

1. Gatti-Casazza, *Memories of the Opera* (Charles Scribner's Sons, New York, 1941), 231.
2. Eddie Durso, as told to John Durso and Steve Vertlieb, *My Memories of Mario Lanza* (Philadelphia, 1992), 9.
3. Constantine Callinicos, radio interview, Columbus, Ohio, June 1974 (Courtesy British Mario Lanza Society).
4. Joseph Siciliano, interview with Richard Stevenson for the British Mario Lanza Society, 1992.
5. Mario Lanza speaking with host, Father James Keller, on *The Christophers* television program, 31 October 1957.
6. Phil Sciscione, interview with the author, 9 October 2000.
7. Ibid.
8. Program note, Easter Sunday Concert, Haddon Hall, Atlantic City, New Jersey, 5 April 1942, Leeds and Lippincott Company.
9. Humphrey Burton, *Leonard Bernstein* (Doubleday, New York, 1994), 73.
10. Mario Lanza, interview for Berlin radio, 1958.
11. Letter from William Judd, Columbia Concerts, Inc., New York, to Mario Lanza, 17 March 1942.

Chapter 2

1. Letter from the Reverend J. Herbert Owen, Church on the Hill, Lenox, Massachusetts, to Antonio and Maria Cocozza, 21 August 1942.
2. Noel Straus, *The New York Times*, 8 August 1942.
3. New York Post, 8 August 1942.
4. Letter from Maria Margelli to Michael De Pace, 10 November 1944 (Courtesy Vito Torelli).
5. Letter from Michael De Pace to Philadelphia Local Board, 16 December 1942 (Courtesy Vito Torelli).

6. Letter from the Countess (Lanza benefactress) to Uriah Doyle, Esq., 17 December 1942 (Courtesy Phil Sciscione).

7. Letter from Mario Lanza to Michael De Pace, 7 March 1943 (Courtesy Vito Torelli).

8. Ibid.

9. Letter from Jerry Adler to Stephen Pattinson, 17 May 1976.

10. As told to Alan Burns by Barney Greenwald.

11. Letter from Mario Lanza to Phil Sciscione, 4 April 1943 (Courtesy Phil Sciscione).

12. Bert Hicks, liner notes to *Mario Lanza: A Legendary Performer* LP, RCA Records, 1976.

13. Columbia Concerts, Inc., press release, 1946.

14. Letter from Maria Margelli to Michael De Pace, 10 November 1944 (Courtesy Vito Torelli).

Chapter 3

1. Betty Lanza, interview with Reba and Bonnie Churchill, 1953.

2. Letter from J. W. Murray, general manager, Record Division of RCA Victor, to Mario Lanza, 19 February 1945.

3. Letter from Maria Cocozza to Phil Sciscione, 28 June 1945 (Courtesy Phil Sciscione).

4. Mario Lanza interview with Hedda Hopper, 1948.

5. Constantine Callinicos, with Ray Robinson, *The Mario Lanza Story* (Coward-McCann, Inc., New York, 1960), 60.

6. Ibid., 63.

7. Ibid., 63.

8. Ibid., 65.

9. "My First Big Opportunity," Etude magazine, December 1949.

10. Dedication on a photograph by Mario Lanza to Enrico Rosati, 1947.

11. Claudia Cassidy, *Chicago Tribune,* 7 July 1946.

12. Reverend Mother Dolores Hart, O.S.B., recorded on tape to Colleen Lanza Davis, 1995. In 1963, after establishing herself in Hollywood as an accomplished young actress, Dolores Hart suddenly left the film industry and entered a convent. She is now the Reverend Mother Dolores Hart, O.S.B., at the Abbey of Regina Laudis in Bethlehem, Connecticut.

13. Postcard from Mario Lanza to Michael De Pace, 14 November 1946 (Courtesy Vito Torelli).

14. Lauretta Thistle, *Arts* review, 14 November 1946.

15. Letter from W. Kilpatrick, Coronet Concerts and Artists, Ontario, to Ada Cooper, Columbia Concerts, Inc., New York, 14 November 1946 (Courtesy British Mario Lanza Society).

Chapter 4

1. Callinicos, 25.
2. Ibid., 26.
3. Ibid., 26–27.
4. Constantine Callinicos, radio interview, Columbus, Ohio, June 1974 (Courtesy British Mario Lanza Society).
5. Edward Halline, *Milwaukee Sentinel*, 9 July 1947.
6. Richard Davis, *Milwaukee Journal*, 9 July 1947.
7. Claudia Cassidy, *Chicago Tribune*, 20 July 1947.
8. Callinicos, 73.
9. As told to Alan Burns by Leila Edwards, June 1987.
10. *Los Angeles Times*, 29 August 1947.
11. Lonsdale, *Los Angeles Examiner*, 30 August 1947.
12. *Los Angeles Daily News*, 29 August 1947.
13. Joe Pasternak, *The Mario Lanza Story*, BBC Radio, March 1974.
14. Gilles Mercier, *Quebec News Review*, 11 October 1947.
15. Notes made by a member of the audience at Tri-City Orchestra Concert, Masonic Temple Auditorium, Davenport, Iowa, 2 November 1947 (Courtesy Andrew Karzas, WFMT, Chicago).
16. William Judd, liner notes to *Mario Lanza: A Legendary Performer* LP, RCA Records, 1976.
17. Leila Edwards, interview with the author, 20 July 2004.
18. Dedication on a photograph by Mario Lanza to Leila Edwards, 1950 (Courtesy Alan Burns).
19. Laurence Oden, *St. Louis News*, 9 April 1948.

Chapter 5

1. Terry Robinson, interview with the author, 28 October 2000.
2. Ibid.
3. Callinicos, *The Mario Lanza Story*, 89.
4. *Daily Oklahoman*, 22 March 1949.
5. Richard Mohr, liner notes to *Mario Lanza: A Legendary Performer* LP, RCA Records, 1976.
6. Robinson, interview 28 October 2000.

7. *Variety*, September 1949.

8. Robinson, interview 28 October 2000.

9. Ibid.

Chapter 6

1. Sammy Cahn, *I Should Care: The Sammy Cahn Story* (W. H. Allen, 1975).

2. Joe Pasternak, *The Mario Lanza Story*, BBC Radio, March 1974.

3. Ann Helming, *Citizens-News*, 24 April 1950.

4. Peter Herman Adler, liner notes to *Mario Lanza: A Legendary Performer* LP, RCA Records, 1976.

5. Robinson, interview 28 October 2000.

Chapter 7

1. Spector, *The Pittsburgh Press*, March 1951.

2. Callinicos, 137.

3. Ward, *The Pittsburgh Press*, 7 March 1951.

4. Robinson, interview 28 October 2000.

5. Callinicos, 142.

6. Borowski, *Chicago Sun-Times*, 8 April 1951.

7. Robinson, interview 28 October 2000.

8. *Variety*, May 1951.

9. *New York Herald Tribune*, May 1951.

10. Crowther, *New York Times*, 11 May 1951.

11. Enrico Caruso Jr. and Andrew Farkas, *Enrico Caruso: My Father and My Family* (Amadeus Press, Portland, Oregon, 1990), 546.

12. Richard Leech, letter to the author, 17 November 2000.

13. Callinicos, interview with Lindsay Perigo for New Zealand radio, New York, 1982.

14. Joseph Di Fiore, interview with the author, 26 October 2000.

15. Robinson, interview 28 October 2000.

16. Ibid.

17. "Million Dollar Voice," *Time*, 6 August 1951.

18. Robinson, interview 28 October 2000.

19. Ibid.

20. Ibid.

21. *Variety*, September 1952.

22. Otis L. Guernsey Jr., *New York Herald Tribune*, September 1952.

Chapter 8

1. Robinson, interview 28 October 2000.
2. Ibid.
3. Ibid.
4. Ibid.
5. Edmund Purdom, *The Mario Lanza Story*, BBC Radio, March 1974.
6. Robinson, interview 28 October 2000.

Chapter 9

1. Hedda Hopper, *The Evening Bulletin*, 5 October 1954.
2. Robinson, interview 28 October 2000.
3. Al Teitelbaum as told to Jeff Rense, 2004.
4. Ibid.
5. Ibid.
6. Robinson, interview 28 October 2000.
7. Callinicos, 188.
8. Robinson, interview 28 October 2000.

Chapter 10

1. Licia Albanese, interview with the author, 12 March 1999.
2. Robinson, interview 28 October 2000.
3. *Newsweek*, 9 April 1956.
4. *New York Times*, 24 March 1956.
5. *Picturegoer*, 2 June 1956.
6. *Variety*, April 1956.
7. Robinson, interview 28 October 2000.
8. *Time*, 9 April 1956. *Time*'s peculiar dislike of the American tenor, evident throughout his career, manifested itself one last time in their brief and caustic obituary following his passing. To the writer, the Lanza career was an unfulfilled one, one that had produced little more than a handful of popular recordings and a number of easily forgettable films. The magazine stopped short of stating that he would be quickly forgotten, but the inference was clear. The decades that followed have proven just how monumentally wrong that assessment was.
9. Robinson, interview 28 October 2000.
10. Ibid.
11. Reverend Mother Dolores Hart, interview with the author, 16 July 2004.

Chapter 11

1. Memo from William Judd to John Coast, 20 May 1957.
2. Robinson, interview 28 October 2000.
3. Callinicos, 199.
4. Peter Prichard, interview with the author, 1992.
5. Callinicos, 15.
6. Cyril Ornadel, *The Mario Lanza Story,* BBC Radio, March 1974.
7. *Sporting Review and Show Business,* 22 November 1957.
8. Cyril Ornadel, The Mario Lanza Story, BBC Radio, March 1974.
9. Peter Prichard, interview with the author, 1992.
10. Ibid.
11. Constantine Callinicos, radio interview, Columbus, Ohio, June 1974 (Courtesy British Mario Lanza Society).

Chapter 12

1. Letter from John Coast to Callinicos, 20 December 1957.
2. Letter from Callinicos to John Coast, 23 December 1957.
3. *Sheffield News Review,* 5 January 1958.
4. James A. Drake, *Richard Tucker* (E. P. Dutton, Inc., New York, 1984), 169.
5. Richard Bonynge, interview with Armando Cesari, Auckland, New Zealand, 12 June 1976.
6. Dr. Karl Schumann, *Suddeutschland Zeitung,* 25 January 1958.
7. *Stuttgart-Zeitung,* 28 January 1958.
8. *Stuttgart Nachrichten,* 28 January 1958.
9. Callinicos, 209.
10. Peter Prichard, interview with the author, 1992.
11. Letter from John Coast to Mario Lanza, 29 January 1958.
12. Letter from William Judd to Mario Lanza, 5 February 1958.
13. Letter from John Coast to William Judd, 22 February 1958.
14. *Manchester Guardian,* 7 March 1958.
15. Christy Smith, interview with the author, 25 June 2000.
16. Letter from John Coast to William Judd, 3 April 1958.
17. Letter from John Coast to William Judd, 10 April 1958.
18. Cees Kouwenberg to author, 2004.
19. *Algemeen Dagblad,* 8 April 1958 (Translated by Cees Kouwenberg).
20. *Het Parool,* 8 April 1958 (Translated by Cees Kouwenberg).
21. Cees Kouwenberg to author, 2004.
22. *Hanoverische Algemein,* 12 April 1958.

23. Callinicos, 214.

24. Dr. Kurt Klukist, *Lubecher Nachricten*, 14 April 1958.

25. Callinicos, 219.

Chapter 13

1. Letter from John Coast to Mario Lanza, 22 April 1958.

2. Letter from John Coast to William Judd, Larry Kanaga, and Myrt Blum, 23 April 1958.

3. Callinicos, outtake interview for *Mario Lanza: The American Caruso*, 1983.

4. Zsa Zsa Gabor, interview for *Mario Lanza: The American Caruso*, 1983.

5. Hermann Hausner, *Tragodie Einer Stimmer* (Documenten-Verlag Books, Munich, 1962).

6. *New York Times*, 5 August 1959.

7. *New York Daily News*, 15 August 1959.

8. Telegram from Richard Mohr to Mario Lanza, 1958 (Courtesy Mario Lanza Museum, Philadelphia).

Chapter 14

1. Production information courtesy of Judith Earl.

2. Francis Robinson, liner notes from *Mario Lanza Sings Caruso Favorites*, RCA Records, 1960.

3. Callinicos, 241.

4. Ibid., 245.

5. Ibid., 248.

6. Constantine Callinicos, radio interview, Columbus, Ohio, June 1974 (Courtesy British Mario Lanza Society).

7. Robinson, interview 28 October 2000.

8. Peter Lind Hayes, radio interview, Rome, 29 September 1959.

9. Mario Lanza interview for RAI, 1959.

10. Hart, interview 16 July 2004.

11. Robinson, interview 28 October 2000.

12. Hart, interview 16 July 2004.

Chapter 15

1. Richard Leech, letter to the author, 17 November 2000.

2. Renée Fleming, letter to the author, 31 January 2000.

3. Notes from Peter Herman Adler's personal files, 27 April 1981 (Courtesy Maynard F. Bertolet).

Index